Phil Robinson

Under the Sun

Phil Robinson

Under the Sun

ISBN/EAN: 9783744744140

Printed in Europe, USA, Canada, Australia, Japan

Cover: Foto ©Thomas Meinert / pixelio.de

More available books at **www.hansebooks.com**

UNDER THE SUN.

BY

PHIL. ROBINSON,

LATE PROFESSOR OF LITERATURE AND LOGIC TO THE GOVERNMENT OF INDIA;
SPECIAL WAR CORRESPONDENT OF THE LONDON "DAILY TELEGRAPH"
IN AFGHANISTAN AND ZULULAND.

AUTHOR OF "IN MY INDIAN GARDEN," "UNDER THE PUNKAH,"
"NOAH'S ARK," &c., &c.

With a Preface

BY EDWIN ARNOLD,
AUTHOR OF "THE LIGHT OF ASIA."

BOSTON:
ROBERTS BROTHERS.
1882.

Copyright, 1882,
BY PHIL. ROBINSON.

UNIVERSITY PRESS:
JOHN WILSON AND SON, CAMBRIDGE.

DEDICATED

TO

𝕮𝖍𝖊 𝕾𝖆𝖛𝖆𝖌𝖊 𝖆𝖓𝖉 𝖙𝖍𝖊 𝕷𝖔𝖙𝖔𝖘 𝕮𝖑𝖚𝖇𝖘

OF LONDON AND NEW YORK,

BY

A SAVAGE OF THE LOTOS.

1882.

PREFACE TO LATEST EDITION.

AUTHOR'S EXPLANATORY NOTE.

I AM of opinion that no one living can be considered a greater authority upon the subject of Natural History and Unnatural History than my daughter Edith, for on the occasion of her second birthday (last Thursday) we gave her a Noah's Ark, and her life ever since has been devoted to original researches into the properties of its various inhabitants. Not only does she bathe and feed each individual of the menagerie every day, but she puts Noah and all his family, and as many of the Beasts as she can find, under her pillow every night. Moreover, she approaches her subject quite unprejudiced by previous information, and with a grasp that is both bold and comprehensive. This free, generous handling of the persons and animals that have come under her notice, convinces me, therefore, that

Note to Preface.

the contents of this volume will receive from her a fairer introduction to the Public than I could expect from a more precisely critical pen.

PHIL ROBINSON.

EDITH'S PREFACE.

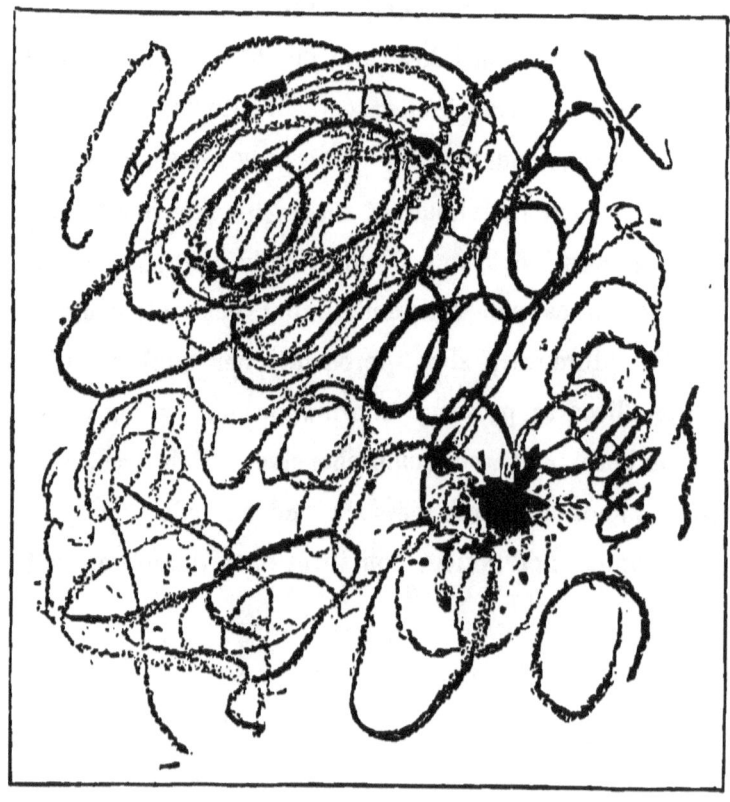

PREFACE TO THE FIRST EDITION.

I HAVE derived so much pleasure from reading the following sketches, humorous and pathetic, of Indian incidents, scenes, and objects, that I am glad to have the opportunity of recommending them to the two classes of readers who will, I think, be chiefly interested. One class consists of those who desire to know — what is not at present to be found in books — the out-of-door ordinary themes of observation in India; the other class, of those who — knowing India well, and all the familiar sights and sounds alluded to in this little volume — will easily fill up the slight and pleasant outline of the Author's sketches, and thus renew for themselves many and many a bygone happy hour and old association of their Eastern home. None but Anglo-Indians know what a treasure-mine of art, literature, and picturesque description lies unworked in the common experiences of our life in India. But some are unobservant; some are too soon familiarized and forget the charm of first impressions; some admire, or are amused, but lack the gift of expression; and nearly all official Indians have too much business to leave them time for the pursuit or record of natural history, and such light and laughing science as this little book contains. For here I think is one bright exception, — one Anglo-Indian who has not only felt the never-ceasing attraction of the "common objects" of India for a cultivated and observant fancy, but has found time and gifts to record them as they first struck him, in a style which, with all its lightness of manner and material, has great strength and value, like those fine webs of Dacca and Delhi with the embroidered beetle-wings and feathers. The Author writes of beetles, birds, frogs, squirrels, and the "small deer" of India, but always, as it seems to me, with so just a sense of the vivid vitality of these Indian scenes and creatures, and so much sympathy for the Asiatic side of our empire, down to its simplest every-day objects, that I should not know where to send an uninformed English reader for better hints of the out-of-door look and spirit of things in our Indian gardens.

They are only sketches, no doubt, which fill this little portfolio, but their outlines are often drawn with so true a hand, that nothing can be more suggestive to the memory of any one who has lived the same life. India may be hot, dusty, distant, and whatever else the weary exile alleges when his liver goes wrong, but she is never for one moment, or in any spot, as regards her people, her scenery, her cities, towns, villages, or country-places, vulgar. There is nothing in her not worth study and regard; for the stamp of a vast past is over all the land, and the very pariah-dogs are classic to those who know Indian fables and how to be entertained by them. Our Author is one of the happy few in whom familiarity with Indian sights and objects has not bred indifference, but rather suggested the beginnings of a new field of Anglo-Indian literature. If I am not wrong, the charm of looking at these utterly commonplace animals and people of India in this gay and pleased spirit is that we get that freshness of feeling which youth alone enjoys when all the world is new to it, interpreted by the adult and matured mind suddenly entering a practically new world, — for such India is to the English official on his first arrival. All we other Indians had of course noticed all those odd and tender points about the "syce's children," the "pea-boy," the "bheesty's mother," the "dâk-bungalow moorghees," the "mynas," crows, green parrots, squirrels, and the beetles that get into the mustard and the soup. Here, however, is one at last who writes down his observations, and opens, I think, thereby a rich and charming field of Indian literature, which ought hereafter to yield many other pages as agreeable as those which it gives me true satisfaction thus to commend to the public.

EDWIN ARNOLD.

CONTENTS.

	PAGE
A Preliminary Warning of the Contents of this Book	3

Part I. Indian Sketches.

I. IN MY INDIAN GARDEN 17

"When God set about creation, He first planted a garden."
Nugæ Oriclanæ.

THE BIRDS 17

"*Eucl.* — But of what sort, pray, is this life among the birds? for you know it accurately.
Hoopoe. — Not an unpleasant one to pass; where, in the first place, we must live without a purse.
Eucl. — You have removed much of life's base metal.
Hoopoe. — And we feed in gardens upon the white sesame and myrtle-berries and poppies and mint."
Aristophanes (Hickie's).

OF HENS 20

"Tame, villatic fowl." — *Milton.*
"The feathered tribe domestic." — *Cowper.*
"The careful hen." — *Thomson.*
"The dâk-bungalow fowls develop the bones of vultures and lay the eggs of finches." — *Nugæ Oriclanæ.*

II. VISITORS IN FEATHERS 26

CORVUS SPLENDENS.

"'Crows,' remarked the Ettrick Shepherd, 'are down in the devil's book in round-hand.'"— *Noctes Ambrosianæ.*

GREEN PARROTS 30

"The writer of the Mahabharata excluded green parrots from an ideal country. 'There are,' he writes, 'no parrots there to eat the grain.'"— *Nugæ Orielanæ.*

THE MYNAS (*Sturninæ*) 32

"To strange mysterious dulness still the friends." — *Byron.*
"Two starlings cannot sleep in one bed." — *Proverb.*

THE SEVEN SISTERS 36

"One for each of the wise men of Greece, one for each hill of Rome, each of the *divitis ostia Nili* and each hero of Thebes, one for each day of the week, one for each of the Pleiades, one for each cardinal sin." — *Nugæ Orielanæ.*

III. VISITORS IN FUR, AND OTHERS 39

THE MUNGOOSE 40

THE GRAY SQUIRREL 41

"The squirrel Adjidauno,
In and out among the branches,
Coughed and chattered in the oak tree,
Laughed, and said between his laughing,
'Do not shoot me, Hiawatha.'" — *Longfellow.*

THE ANTS 42

"To the emmet gives
Her foresight and the intelligence that makes
The tiny creatures strong by social league."
Wordsworth.
"The parsimonious emmet." — *Milton.*
"Us vagrant emmets." — *Young.*

Part II. The Indian Seasons.

I. IN HOT WEATHER 55
"A great length of deadly days."—*Atalanta in Calydon.*

II. THE RAINS 67
"For the rain it raineth every day." — *Twelfth Night.*

III. THE COLD WEATHER 90
"Ah! if to thee
It feels Elysian, how rich to me,
An exiled mortal, sounds its pleasant name!"
Endymion.

Part III. Unnatural History.

I. MONKEYS AND METAPHYSICS 105
Monkeys and Metaphysics. — How they found Seeta. — Yet they are not Proud. — Their Sad-Facedness. — Decayed Divinities. — As Gods in Egypt. — From Grave to Gay. — What do the Apes think of us? — The Etiquette of Scratching. — "The New Boy" of the Monkey-House. — They take Notes of us. — Man-Ape Puzzles. — The Soko. — Missing Links.

II. HUNTING OF THE SOKO 127
"My lords, a solemn hunting is in hand."
Titus Andronicus.

"It is no gentle chase." — *Venus and Adonis.*

"Whence and what art thou, execrable shape,
That darest, though grim and terrible, to advance
Thy miscreated front?" — *Paradise Lost.*

"You do it wrong, being so majestical,
To offer it the show of violence." — *Hamlet.*

"God made him, and therefore let him pass for a man."
Portia.

"With a groan that had something terribly human in it, and yet was full of brutishness, the man-ape fell forward on his face." — *Du Chaillu.*

		PAGE
III.	ELEPHANTS	152

> They are Square Animals with a Leg at each Corner and a Tail at both Ends. — "My Lord the Elephant." — That it picks up Pins. — The Mammoth as a Missionary in Africa. — An Elephant Hunt with the Prince. — Elephantine Potentialities. — A Mad Giant. — Bigness not of Necessity a Virtue. — A Digression on the Meekness of Giants.

IV.	THE ELEPHANTS' FELLOW-COUNTRYMEN . . .	170

> The Rhinoceros a Victim of Ill-Natured Personality. — In the Glacial Period. — The Hippopotamus. — Popular Sympathy with it. — Behemoth a Useless Person. — Extinct Monsters and the World they Lived in. — The Impossible Giraffe. — Its Intelligent use of its Head as a Hammer. — The Advantages and Disadvantages of so much Neck. — Its High Living. — The Zebra. — Nature's Parsimony in the matter of Paint on the Skins of Animals. — Some Suggestions towards more Gayety.

V.	CATS AND SPARROWS	186

> They are of Two Species, tame and otherwise. — The Artificial Lion. — Its Debt of Gratitude to Landseer and the Poets. — Unsuitable for Domestication. — Is the Natural Lion the King of Beasts? — The true Moral of all Lion Fables. — "Well roared, Lion!" — The Tiger not of a Festive Kind. — There is no Nonsense about the Big Cats. — The Tiger's Pleasures and Perils. — Its Terrible Voice. — The poor Old Man-Eater. — Caught by Baboos and Killed by Sheep. — The great Cat Princes. — Common or Garden Cats, approached sideways. — The Physical Impossibility of Taxing Cats. — The Evasive Habits of Grimalkin. — Its Instinct for Cooks. — On the Roof with a Burglar. — The Prey of Cats. — The Turpitude of the Sparrow. — As an Emblem of Conquest and an Article of Export. — The Street Boy among Birds.

VI. BEARS — WOLVES — DOGS — RATS 227
Bears are of three kinds, Big Bears, Middle-sized Bears, and Little Wee Bears. — Easily Provoked. — A Protest of Routine against Reform. — But Unreliable. — Unfairly Treated in Literature. — How Robbers went to steal the Widow's Pig, but found the Bear in the Sty. — The Delightful Triumph of Convictions in the Nursery. — The Wild Hunter of the Woods. — Its Splendid Heroism. — Wolf-men. — Wolf-dogs. — Dogs we have all met. — Are Men only Second-rate Dogs ? — Their Emotions and Passions the same as ours. — The Art of Getting Lost. — Man not inferior to Dogs in many ways. — The Rat Epidemic in India. — Endemic in England. — Western Prejudice and Eastern Tenderness. — Emblems of Successful Invasion. — Their Abuse of Intelligence. — Edax Rerum.

VII. SOME SEA-FOLK 262
Ocean-folk. — Mermaids and Manatees. — The Solemnity of Shapelessness. — Herds of the Sea-gods. — Sea-things. — The Octopus and its Kind. — Terrors of the Deep Sea. — Sea-serpents. — Credible and Incredible Varieties. — Delightful possibilities in Cuttle-fish. — Ancient and Fish-like Monsters. — Credulity as to Monsters, Disastrous. — Snakes in Legend and in Nature. — Mr. Ruskin on Snakes. — The Snake-folk. — Shesh, the Snake-god. — Primeval Turtles and their Contemporary Aldermen. — Impropriety of Flippancy about Turtles.

Part IV. Idle Hours under the Punkah.

I. THE MAN-EATING TREE 295
"But say, where grows this Tree, from hence how far ?"
Eve to Serpent.
"On the blasted heath
Fell Upas sits, the Hydra-tree of death." — *Darwin.*
"Here the foul harpies build their nests.
 . . . With rueful sound,
Perched in the dismal tree, they fill the air." — *Dante.*
"Not a tree to be found in the valley. Not a beast or bird, or any living thing, lives in its vicinity." — *Foersch.*

II. EASTERN SMELLS AND WESTERN NOSES 306

"We confess that beside the smell of species there may be individual odours ; . . ; but that an unsavoury odour is gentilitious or national, if rightly understood, we cannot well concede, nor will the information of reason or sense induce it." — *Sir Thos. Browne.*

"A nose stood in the middle of her face." — *Iago.*

"A good nose is requisite also, to smell out work for the other senses." — *Autolycus.*

"The literature of Noses is extensive. Sterne has a chapter on them in 'Tristram Shandy;' and other authors have contributed respectively 'A Sermon on Noses,' 'On the Dignity, Gravity, and Authority of Noses,' 'The Noses of Adam and Eve,' 'Pious Meditations on the Nose of the Virgin Mary,' 'Review of Noses.' Shakespeare was never tired of poking fun at the nose or drawing morals from it, but what is more remarkable it might easily be proved constructively, from what he has said, that he believed, with Professor Jäger, that 'the nose is the soul.'"
Orielana.

III. GAMINS 316

"They are not dirty by chance — or accident — say twice or thrice per diem, but they are always dirty."
Christopher North.

"Oh, for my sake do you with Fortune chide,
The guilty goddess of my harmful deeds,
That did not better for my life provide
Than public means, which public manners breeds."
Sonnet (Shakespeare).

IV. OF TAILORS 326

"Some foolish knave, I think, it first began
The slander that three tailors are one man." — *Taylor.*

"O monstrous arrogance ! Thou liest, thou thread,
Thou thimble ;
Thou yard, three quarters, half-yard, quarter, nail ;
Thou flea, thou nit, thou winter cricket, thou, —
Braved in mine own house with a skein of thread !
Away, thou rag, thou quantity, thou remnant !"
Taming of the Shrew.

"Give the gods a thankful sacrifice. When it pleaseth their deities to take the wife of a man from him, it shows to man the tailors of the earth." — *Antony and Cleopatra.*

"A tailor makes a man ?" "Aye, a tailor, sir." — *Lear.*

"Remember how Master Feeble, 'the forcible Feeble,' proved himself the best of Falstaff's recruits ; with what discretion Robin Starveling played the part of Thisby's mother before the Duke, and do not forget to their credit the public spirit of the tailors of Tooley Street."—*Orielana.*

"I have an honest lad to my taylor, who I never knew guilty of one truth — no, not when it had been to his advantage not to lye." — *Montaigne.*

V. THE HARA-KIRI 330

"Escape in death from obloquy I sought,
Though just to others, to myself unjust." — *Dante.*

"The pitiful, pitiless knife." — *Tennyson.*

"Oh ! happy dagger." — *Juliet.*

VI. MY WIFE'S BIRDS 341

VII. THE LEGEND OF THE BLAMELESS PRIEST . . . 359

UNDER THE SUN.

UNDER THE SUN.

Ridentem dicere verum, quid vetat?

I HAVE it not in my nature to look at the animal world merely as a congregation of beasts. Nor can I bring myself to believe that everything, whether in fur, feathers, or scales, was created for my own special benefit as a human being. Man was not created till the sixth day, and is therefore the junior among the animals. It took no better effort of creative will to produce him than to produce caterpillars. Moreover, earth was already populated before he came, and sufficiently complete without him. He was a noble afterthought. Indeed, rather than maintain that man was created "higher than the beasts," for the increase of his own self-importance, I would believe that he was created "a little lower than the angels," for the increase of his humility.

At any rate, I prefer to think of the things of "the speechless world" as races of fellow creatures that have a very great deal in common with ourselves, but whom the pitiless advance of human interests is perpetually dispossessing, and who are doomed to extinction under the Juggernath of civilization. Nature builds only upon ruins. The driving-wheel of Progress is Suffering.

Thus, so much the more should we feel tenderly towards the smaller lives about us, the things that the Creator has placed amongst us to enjoy the same earth as ourselves, but whom we compel to serve us so long as they can, and to die out when our end is served. Except in Holy Writ there is nothing so beautiful or so manful as the teaching of Buddha, the evangelist of universal tenderness; and approaching nature we ought to remember that it is the very Temple of temples, and that we may not minister there unless we have on the ephod of pity.

You will think, no doubt, that if I feel so seriously, I ought not to try to make fun out of these animals and birds and fishes and insects. But why not? *Ridentem dicere verum, quid vetat?* Besides, I know that if it were wrong to laugh over monkeys and cats and giraffes, I should feel that it was — and would n't do it. But, at any rate, if I say anything in this book that either the beasts or their friends think unkind or unjust, I am sorry for it. Attribute it, Reader, to want of knowledge, not to want of sympathy; and if you would be generous do not think me too much in earnest when I am serious, nor altogether in fun because I jest.

One of the very few positive facts we have about Adam is that he gave names to all the living things in Eden: not of course those by which even antiquity knew them, but names such as Primitive Man, wherever he still exists, distinguishes the creatures about him by. To him, for instance, the squirrel is "the thing that sits in the shadow of its tail," and in Akkadian nomenclature there is no lion, but only "the great-voiced one." We have only to see how the Red Indians individualize their fauna, to understand the nature of Adam's names.

But to be able to name the creatures, furred and feathered, with such picturesque appropriateness argues a knowledge of their habits founded upon personal observation, and the legend therefore that tells us how the Angels failed to execute the orders of the Creator is not at all an absurd one. Allah, it is said, told the Angels — who were sneering at man — to name the animals, and they tried to do so, but could not. So then he turned to Adam, and the Angels stood listening, ashamed, as the patriarch drew a picture of each creature in a word. The angelic host of course had no sympathy with them. Indeed, perhaps, they had no knowledge whatever of the earth and its things; for it is possible, as Milton supposes, that the Angels never left the upper sky except on special missions. With Adam it was different. In his habits of daily life he was in the closest sympathy with other animals, and virtually one of themselves. Each beast and bird therefore, as it passed before him, suggested to him at once some distinguishing epithet, and he found no difficulty in assigning to every individual an appropriate name, and appointing each his proper place in the system of creation. Now, Adam was probably nothing of an analogist, but he was certainly the father of naturalists.

It is generally supposed that this system has now developed into an unconstitutional monarchy, but there is much more to be said on the side of its being an oligarchy.

Thus in the beginning of days all power was in the hands of the Titans, the mammoths and the mastodons of antiquity; but in time a more vigorous race of beasts was gradually developed, and the Saturn and Tellus, Ops and Typhon, of the primeval earth were one by one unseated and dispossessed of power by the younger creatures, — the eagles of Jupiter and the tigers of Bacchus, the serpents of Athene and the wolves of Mars.

The elder rulers of the wild world accepted at their hands the dignity of extinction; and instead of a few behemoths, lording it over the vast commonwealth of the earth, there were developed many nations of lesser things, divided into their tribes and clans, and transacting, each within their own countries, all the duties of life, exercising the high functions of authority, and carrying on the work of an orderly world.

On land, the tiger and the lion, the python, the polar bear and the grizzly, gradually rose to the acknowledged dignity of crowned heads. In the air there was the royal condor and the eagle, with a peerage of falcons. In the mysterious empire of the sea there was but one supreme authority, the sea-serpent, with its terrible lieutenants, the octopus and the devil-fish.

Yet none of these are absolute autocrats beyond the immediate territory they reside in. They have all to pay in vexed boundaries the penalty of extended dominion. Thus, though the tiger may be supreme in the jungles of the Himalayan Terai, he finds upon his wild Naga frontier the irreconcilable rhinoceros, and in the fierce Guzerati country there is the maneless lion. Up among the hills are the fearless Ghoorkha leopards; and in the broken lowlands along the river that stout old Rohilla thakoor, the wild boar, resents all royal interference. The lion, again, they say, is king in Africa, yet the gorilla Zulus it over the forests within the lion's territory; the ostrich on the plain despises all his mandates, and in the earldom of the rivers the crocodile cares nothing for his favor or his wrath. The lion, indeed, claims to be king of the beasts; but, loud as his roar is, it does not quite reach across the Atlantic, and we find the puma not only asserting leonine authority, but actually usurping the royal title as "the American lion;" just as in Africa, under the lion's very nose, the leopard claims an equality of power by calling itself "the tiger." The polar bear can command no homage from the walrus, nor the grizzly bear levy taxes from the bison. The python, "the emperor" of Mexican folk-lore, has none to attack him, but on the other hand, he does not venture to treat the jaguar as a serf.

Among the birds of the air, though eagles are kings, the raven asserts a melancholy supremacy over the solitudes of wildernesses, and the albatross is monarch of the waves. No one will deny the aristocracy of the flamingo, the bustard, or the swan, or dispute the nobility of the ibis on the Nile, or of the birds of Paradise in their leafy Edens of the Eastern Seas. For pretenders to high place we have the peacock and the vulture; and as democrats, to incite the proletariat of fowldom to disaffection and even turbulence, we need not search further than the crows.

In the sea, the Kraken is king. It is the hierophant of the oceanic mysteries, secret as a Prince of the Assassins or Veiled Prophet, and sacred from its very secrecy, like the Lama of Thibet or the Unseen God of the Tartars. Yet there are those who dispute the weird majesty of the hidden potentate, for the whales, to north and south, enjoy a limited sovereignty, while all along the belt of the tropics the pirate sharks scourge the sea-folk as they will.

Even this, after all, is too narrow a view of the wild world. And I find myself, catholic as I am in my regard for the things in fur and feathers, offending very often against the dignity of beasts and birds. How easy it is, for instance, to misunderstand the animals; to think the worse of the bear for sulking, when it is only weary of seeking explanation for its captivity; to quarrel with the dulness of a caged fish-hawk that sits dreaming of spring-time among the crags that overlook Lake Erie. Remember the geese of Apfel, and take the moral of their story to heart. I have told it before, I know, but morals are never obsolete.

A farmer's wife had been making some cherry brandy; but as she found, during the process, that the fruit was unsound, she threw the whole mess out into the yard, and, without looking to see what followed, shut down the window.

Now, as it fell out, a party of geese, good fellows all of them, happened to be waddling by at the time, and, seeing the cherries trundling about, at once investigated them. The preliminary inquiry proving satisfactory, these misguided poultry set to and swallowed the whole lot. "No heeltaps" was the order of the carouse; and so they finished all the cherries off at one sitting, so to speak.

The effect of the spirituous fruit was soon apparent, for on trying to make the gate which led from the scene of the debauch to the horsepond, they found everything against them. Whether a high wind had got up, or what had happened, they could not tell, but it seemed to the geese as if there was an uncommonly high sea running, and the ground set in towards them with a strong steady swell that was most embarrassing to progress. To escape these difficulties some lashed their rudders and hove to, others tried to run before the wind, while the rest tacked for the pigsty. But there was no living in such weather, and one by one the craft lurched over and went down all standing.

Meanwhile the dame, the unconscious cause of this disaster, was attracted by the noise in the fowl-yard, and looking out saw all her ten geese behaving as if they were mad. The gander himself, usually so solemn and decorous, was balancing himself on his beak, and spinning round the while in a prodigious flurry of feathers and dust, while the old grey goose, remarkable even among her kind for the circumspection of her conduct, was lying stomach upwards in the gutter, feebly gesticulating with her legs. Others of the party were no less conspicuous for the extravagance of their attitudes and gestures, while the remainder were to be seen lying in a helpless confusion of feathers in the lee scuppers, that is to say, in the gutter by the pigsty.

Perplexed by the spectacle, the dame called in her neighbors, and after careful investigation it was decided in counsel that the birds *had died of poison*. Under these circumstances their carcasses were worth nothing for food, but, as the neighbors said, their feathers were not poisoned, and so, the next day being market day, they set to work then and there, and plucked the ten geese bare. Not a feather did they leave on the gander, not a tuft of down on the old grey goose; and, the job completed, they left the dame with her bag full of plumage and her ten plucked geese, not without assuring her, we may be certain, of their sympathy with her in her loss.

Next morning the good woman got up as usual and, remembering the feathers down stairs, dressed betimes, for she hoped, thrifty soul, to get them off her hands that very day at market. And then she bethought her of the ten plucked bodies lying out under the porch, and resolved that they should be buried before she went. But as she approached the door, on these decent rites intent, and was turning the key, there fell on her ears the sound of a familiar voice — and then another — and another — until at last the astonished dame heard in full chorus the well-known accents of all her plucked and poisoned geese! The throat of the old gander sounded, no doubt, a trifle husky, and the grey goose spoke in muffled tones suggestive of a chastening headache; but there was no mistaking those voices, and the dame, fumbling at the door, wondered what it all might mean.

Has a goose a ghost? Did any one ever read or hear of a spectre of a gander?

The key turned at last; the door opened, and there, quacking in subdued tones, suppliant and shivering, stood all her flock! There they stood, the ten miserable birds, with splitting headaches and parched tongues, contrite and dejected, asking to have their feathers back again. The situation was painful to both parties. The forlorn geese saw in each other's persons the humiliating reflection of their own condition, while the dame, guiltily conscious of that bag full of feathers, remembered how the one lapse of Noah, — in that "aged surprisal of six hundred years, and unexpected inebriation from the unknown effects of wine," — has been excused by religion and the unanimous voice of posterity. She, and her neighbors with her, however, had hastily misjudged the geese, and, finding them dead drunk, had stripped them, without remembering for a moment that if feathers are easy to get off they are very hard to put on. Here were the geese before her, bald, penitent, and shaking with the cold. There in the corner were their feathers, in a bag. But how could they be brought together? Even supposing each goose could recognize its own, how were they to be reclothed? Tarring and feathering were out of the question, for that would be to add insult to injury; and to try to stick all the feathers into their places again, one by one, was a labor such as only folk in fairy tales could ever hope to accomplish.

So she called in her neighbors again; but they proved only sorry comforters, for they reminded her that after all the fault was her own, that it was she and no one else who had thrown the brandied cherries to the geese. The poor fowls, brought up to confide in her, and repaying her care of them by trustful reliance, could never, her neighbors said, have been expected to guess that when she threw the vinous fruit in their path she, their own familiar mistress, at whose hands they looked for all that was good, could have intended to betray them into the shocking excesses of intoxication, and deceive them to their ruin. Yet so it had been. Accepting the feast spread out before them, the geese had partaken gladly, gratefully, freely, of the insidious cherry; and the result was this, that the geese were in one place and their feathers were in another! At last, weary of the reproaches of her friends, the widow gathered all her bald poultry about her round the kitchen fire, and sat down to make them flannel jackets,—registering a solemn vow, as she did so, never to jump hastily at conclusions about either bird or beast, lest she might again fall into the error of misconstruing their conduct.

The mischief, however, was done; for the geese, who had got drunk with brandied cherries, and been plucked by mistake in consequence, had good reason for withholding from human beings for ever afterwards that pleasing trustfulness which characterizes the domestic fowl. They would never again approach their food without suspicion, nor look upon a gathering of the neighbors except as a dark conspiracy against their feathers. The dame herself, whom hitherto they had been wont to greet with tumultuous acclaim, and whose footsteps to and fro they had been accustomed to follow so closely, would become to them an object of distrust. Instead of tumbling over each other in their glad hurry to meet her in the morning, or crowding round her full of gossip and small goose-confidences when she came to pen them up for the night, they would eye her askance from a distance, approach her only strategically, and accept her gifts with reproachful hesitation. And how keenly the dame would feel such estrangement I leave my readers to judge for themselves.

· · · · · · ·

This untoward inebriation of the geese points, however, another lesson; for I cannot but see in it one more of those deplorable instances of moral deterioration of the animal world which from time to time obtrude themselves, unwelcome, upon the notice of lovers of nature.

In Belgium and other places men try to make dogs believe they are donkeys or ponies by harnessing them to carts, but the attempt can never succeed; for a dog thus employed will always be a very indifferent donkey, and never a good dog. In Paris, again, the other day a man demoralized all his bees by bringing their hives into the city and putting them down next a sugar warehouse. The bees, hitherto as pure-minded and upright insects as one could have wished to meet in a summer's day, developed at once an unnatural aversion to labor, and a not less unnatural tendency to larceny. Instead of winging their industrious way to the distant clover-fields, and there gathering the innocent honey, they swarmed in disorderly mobs upon the sugar casks next door, and crawled about with their ill-gotten burdens upon the surrounding pavement. The owner of the hives benefited immensely by the proximity of the saccharine deposits, but it was at the sacrifice of all moral tone in the bees which he had tempted and which had fallen.

We never tire of protesting against the unnatural relations of lion and lion-tamer, and of reminding the keepers of menageries that instinct is irrepressible, untamable, and immortal; and every now and then a lion, tired of foolery, knocks a man into mummy. The narrative is always the same, whether it happens at San Francisco or at Birmingham. A lion's keeper goes into the beast's cage to clean it, and having, as he supposed, seen all the occupants safely out, sets to work. As it happens, however, the sliding door which divides the two compartments of the cage has not fallen securely into its place, and an old lion, seeing his opportunity, springs at the opening. The door gives way, and the next instant the beast has seized his keeper. A number of people, powerless of course to give assistance, are looking on; but fortunately there is also present some professional lion-tamer, belonging to the establishment, and this man, with great courage, rushes straight into the cage and confronts the lion. Discipline and a loaded stick triumph over instinct. The lion releases its prey and the unfortunate keeper is at once dragged out.

Now it is easy enough, after such an incident as this, to talk of lions as savage brutes, and then to moralize over the foolhardiness of men who have grown accustomed to lions, and think that lions have therefore grown accustomed to them. But surely it is much more just to the animals to remember that it is the most natural thing in the world for a flesh-eating animal to spring at meat when it sees it within its reach.

The marvel, indeed, in these narratives always is the lion's forbearance. In the end that staggering blow right between the eyes is accepted by him as a very forcible argument; but before the gallant lion-tamer comes to his friend's rescue, at such a terrible risk to himself, the lion has always had plenty of time to do what he liked with the keeper he had caught, or at any rate to gobble up a good luncheon. When a lion is in a hurry it does not as a rule take him long to make a meal; but in the accidents that occur in menageries it does not seem to occur to the beast that there is any necessity for haste. Long captivity has made his practices unnatural. He has forgotten his old habits of hurried feeding. He had caught a man sure enough, for there the man was, and it was quite early in the morning. But he had all the day before him, so he thought; and, though he remarked that there was a great deal of unusual excitement on the other side of his bars, and that the human beings who were generally so leisurely seemed strangely flurried about something on this particular occasion, he had the cage to himself, and there was no occasion that he saw for making a hurried meal. But he had misunderstood the facts of the case. He had no right to eat the keeper, for the man had only come in to clean his cage, and not to be eaten. The excitement outside was owing to the lion's own inconsiderate and greedy conduct. But if they did not want him to eat the keeper, why did they put him into the cage?

PART I.

INDIAN SKETCHES.

PART I.
INDIAN SKETCHES.

I.

IN MY INDIAN GARDEN.

A GARDEN everywhere is to the natural world beyond its walls very much what a good Review number is to the rest of literature. Shrubs and flowers, indigenous or of distant derivation, jumbled together, attract an equally miscellaneous congregation of birds and insects, and by their fresher leaves, brighter blossoms, or juicier fruit, detain for a time the capricious and fastidious visitors. An Indian Garden is *par excellence* Nature's museum — a gallery of curiosities for the indifferent to admire, the interested to study. It is a Travellers' Club, an Œcumenical Council, a Parliament of buzzing, humming, chirping, and chattering things.

The great unclouded sky is terraced out by flights of birds. Here, in the region of trees, church-spires, and house-tops, flutter and have their being the myriad tribes who plunder while they share the abodes of men; the diverse crew who jostle on the earth, the lowest level of creation, with mammals, and walk upon its surface plantigrade; the small birds whose names children learn, whom schoolboys snare, and who fill the shelves of museums as the Insessores, or birds that perch. They are the commonalty of birddom, who furnish forth the mobs which bewilder the drunken-flighted jay when he jerks, shrieking, in a series of blue hyphen-flashes through the air, — or which, when some owlet, as unfortunate as foolish, has let itself be jostled from its cosy hole beneath the thatch out into the glare of daylight, — crowd round the blinking stranger and unkindly jeer it from amongst them. These are the ground-floor tenants, our every-day walk acquaintances, who look up to crows as to Members of Congress, and think no mean thing of green parrots. And yet there are among them many of a notable plumage and song, more indeed than among the aristocracy of Volucres; just as, if the Indian proverb goes for aught, there are more pretty women among the lowest (the *mehter*) than any other caste. On the second floor, where nothing but clear ether checks their flight, swim the great eagles, the knightly falcons, and the vultures, — grand when on their wide, loose pinions they float and circle, — sordid only, like the gods of old, when they stoop to earth. These divide the peerage of the skies, and among them is universal a fine purity of color and form — a nobility of power. They are all princes among the feathered tribes, gentle and graceful as they wheel and recurve undisturbed in their own high domains, but fierce in battle and terribly swift when they shoot down to earth, their keen vision covering half a province, their cruel cry shrilling to the floors of heaven. See them now, with no quarry to pursue, no battle to fight, and mark the exceeding beauty of their motion. In tiers above each other the shrill-voiced kites, their sharp-cut wings bent into a bow, their tail, a third wing almost, spread out fanwise to the wind, — the vultures parallel, but wheeling in higher spheres on level pinions, — the hawk, with his strong bold flight, smiting his way up to the highest place; while far above him, where the sky-roof is cobwebbed with white clouds, float dim specks, which in the distance seem hardly moving — the sovereign eagles. They can stare at the sun without blinking; we cannot, so let us turn our eyes lower — to the garden level. Ah! pleasant indeed was my Indian Garden. Here in a green colonnade stand the mysterious, broad-leaved plantains with their strange spikes of fruit, — there the dark mango. In a grove together the spare-leaved peepul, that sacred yet treacherous tree that drags down the humble shrine which it was placed to sanctify; the shapely tamarind, with its clouds of foliage; the graceful neem; the patulous teak, with its great leathern leaves, and the bamboos the tree-cat loves. Below them grow a wealth of roses, the lavender-blossomed durantas, the cactus, grotesque in growth, the poyntzettia with its stars of scarlet, the spiky aloes, the sick-scented jessamine, and the quaint coral-trees; while over all shoots up the palm. The citron, lime, and orange-trees are beautiful alike when they load the air with the perfume of their waxen flowers, or when they are snowing their sweet petals about them, or when heavy-fruited they trail their burdened branches to rest their yellow treasure on the ground.

And how pleasant in the cool evening to sit and watch the garden's visitors. The crow-pheasant stalks past with his chestnut wings drooping by his side, the magpie with his curious dreamland note climbs the tree overhead, the woodpeckers flutter the creviced ants, the sprightly bulbul tunes his throat with crest erect, the glistening flower-pecker haunts the lilies, the oriole flashes in the splendor of his golden plumage from tree to tree, the bee-eater slides through the air, the doves call to each other from the shady guava grove, the poultry —

Poultry? Yes, they do not, it is true, strictly appertain to gardens, but rather to hen-houses and stable-yards, to the outskirts of populous places and the remoter corners of cultivated fields. Yet they are — and that not seldom — to be found and met with in gardens where, if ill-conditioned, they do not scruple to commit an infinity of damage by looking inquisitively, albeit without judgment, after food, at the roots of plants, and by making for themselves comfortable hollows in the conspicuous corners of flower-beds, wherein, with a notable assiduity, they sit to ruffle their feathers during the early hours of sunshine. These pastimes are not, however, without some hazard to the hens, for thereby they render themselves both obnoxious to mankind and noticeable by their other enemies. A cat who has two minds about attacking a fowl when in a decent posture and enjoying herself as a hen should do, does not hesitate to assault her when met with in a dust-hole, — her feathers all set the wrong way, and in an ecstasy of titillation. A kite will swoop from the blue to see what manner of eatable she may be; nor, when she is laying bare the roots of a rosebush, is the gardener reluctant to stone her, whereby the hen is caused some personal inconvenience and much mental perturbation, determining her to escape (always, let it be noticed, in the wrong direction) with the greatest possible precipitancy. These same hens are, I think, the most foolish of fowls; for on this point the popular proverb that makes a goose to be a fool is in error, as the goose is in reality one of the most cunning of birds, even in a domestic state, while in a wild state there are few birds to compare with it for vigilance. The hen, however, is an extraordinary fool, and in no circumstance of life does she behave with a seemly composure. Should a bird pass overhead she immediately concludes that it is about to fall upon her head; while if she hears any sound for which she cannot satisfactorily account to herself, she sets up a woeful clucking, in which, after a few rounds, she is certain to be joined by all the comrades of her sex, who foregather with her to cluck and croon, though they have not even her excuse of having heard the original noise. But their troubles are many.

Life is many-sided. Indeed, you may examine it from so many standpoints that had you even the hundred eyes of Argus, and each eye hundred-faceted like the orb of a dragon-fly, you could not be a master of the subject from all sides. And yet how often does the man who has surveyed his neighbors from two points only — the bottom of the ladder and the top — affect to have exhausted the experience of life! For Man to dogmatize wisely on this life is to argue simplicity in it.

For instance, have you ever looked at life from the standpoint of a staging-house fowl? Perhaps not; but it is instructive nevertheless as exemplifying the reciprocity of brain and body, and showing how one trait of character, by exaggerated development, may develop and exaggerate certain features physical as well as mental, obliterate others, and leave the owner as skeletonized in mind as in body. *Suspicion* is the fungus that, taking root in the mind of the dâk-bungalow fowl, strangles all its finer feelings (though fostering self-reliance), and makes the bird's daily life miserable. Think of the lives cursed by suspicion, and confer your pity on the hen, — Cromwell shifting from bedroom to bedroom, and the royal Louis refusing food. Adam Smith was stolen in infancy by gypsies, and his parents lived ever afterwards in terror for the rest of their children. But what was this compared to the life of the staging-house fowl? His whole life is spent in strategy. Every advance in his direction is a wile, each corner an ambuscade, and each conclave of servants a cabal. With every sun comes a Rye-House Plot for the wretched bird, and before evening he has had to run the gauntlet of a Vehm-gericht. His brother, suspicious yet all too confiding, would trust no one but the wife of the grain dealer who lived at the corner; and this single confidence cost him his life. So our bird trusts no one.

Indeed, now that I come myself to think seriously of the staging-house fowl, I would not hesitate to say that the washerman's donkey has the better life. The donkey can remember childhood's years as an interval of frivolity and light-heartedness; and even in maturer life it is free (with three of its legs), after the day's work is over, to disport itself with its kind. But the case is different with the bird. Pullets of the tenderest years are sought out for broth; adolescence is beset with peril in hardly a less degree than puberty; while alas! old age itself is not respected. Like Japanese youth it lives with sudden death ever in prospect; but the hara-kiri in the case of the fowl is not an honorable termination of life, while the lively apprehension of it unwholesomely sharpens its vigilance. It has, moreover, nothing to live on and plenty of it; and this diet affects its physique, inasmuch as it prevents the increase of flesh, while the constant evasion of death develops its muscles — the thigh-bones assuming vulturine dimensions. The feathers, by frequent escapings through small holes, become ragged and irregular; the tail is systematically discarded as being dangerous and a handle to ill-wishers. Death therefore must come upon some of them as a sharp cure for life — *il est mort guéri*.

But to others it is the bitter end of a life of perilous pleasure, — to such a one perhaps as the following. The bird I speak of was a fine young cock, a Nazarene in his unclipt wings, with the columnar legs of an athlete, snatching life by sheer pluck and dying without disgrace. His death happened in this wise. There came up the hill one day some travellers with whom the cook at the staging-house wished to stand well, and when they asked, "What is there to eat?" he replied with suavity, "Whatever your honors choose to order." So they ordered beef and then mutton, but there being neither, they desisted from "ordering" and left it to the cook to arrange their meal. And he gave them soup made of an infant poult, two side-dishes composed of two elder brothers, *a fine fowl roasted, by way of joint*, and the grandmother of the family furnished forth a curry. And one of the party watched the dinner being caught. With the soup there was little difficulty, for it succumbed to a most obvious fraud. The side-dishes fell victims to curiosity, for while they were craning their necks into the cook-room door, a hand came suddenly round the corner and closed upon them. The curry, poor old soul, was taken in her afternoon sleep. But the roast, the bird italicized above, showed sport, as well it might. For seven months it had daily evaded death, scorning alike the wiles of the cook and the artifices of his minions. Nothing would tempt it during the day within the enclosure in which so many of its family had lost their lives, and as it roosted high up in the walnut-tree behind the bungalow, night surprises were out of the question. Whenever travellers came in sight it would either fly on to the roof of the bungalow, and thence survey the preparations for dinner; or, slipping away quietly over the cliff, would enjoy healthful ease in some sequestered nook, whither was borne, tempered by distance and the comfortable sense of security, the last screech of the less wary. But its day had come. The fig-tree had drunk of the Neda. *The travellers had been expected.* An hour, therefore, before they came in sight preparations were made for the great capture; and, when on the appearance of the first horseman, the fowl turned as usual to escape, he found two boys on the roof of the bungalow, six more up the walnut-tree, and a cordon of men round the yard. There was nothing for it but to trust to its wings; so mounting on the wall he flew for his life. And his strong wings bore him bravely — up over the fowl-yard and the goat-house and the temple, over the upturned faces of the shouting men — up into the unbroken sky. Below him, far, far down he saw the silver thread of water that lay along the valley between the hills. But there was a worse enemy than man on the watch — a hungry eagle. And on a sudden our flier saw, between him and the red sunset, the king of birds in kingly flight towards him, and stopping himself in his course he came fluttering down — poor Icarus! — to the friendly covert of earth with outspread wings. But the eagle with closed pinions fell like a thunderbolt plumb from out the heavens, and striking him in mid-sky sent him twirling earthward; then, swooping down again, grasped him in his yellow talons before he touched the ground, and, rising with slow flight, winged his burdened way to the nearest resting-place — the roof of the staging-house. But his exploit had been watched, and hardly had his feet touched the welcome tiles before a shower of sticks and stones rained round him. One pebble struck him, and, rising hastily at the affront, his prey escaped his talons and, rolling over and over down the roof, fell into the arms of the exultant cook! But the scream of the baffled eagle drowned the death-cry of the fowl.

II.

VISITORS IN FEATHERS.

AMONG the common objects of my Indian Garden is the *Corvus splendens*. Such at any rate is the scientific name given by Vieillot to that "trebledated bird," the common crow of India, and although one naturalist yearned to change it to "shameless" (*impudicus*), and although another still declares that *splendens* is inappropriate and tends to bring scientific nomenclature into ridicule, that bird — as was only to be expected from a crow — has kept its mendacious adjective, and in spite of every one is still, in name, as fine a bird in India as it was time out of mind in Olympus. *Splendens* or not at present, the crow must have had recommendations either of mind or person to have been chosen, as Ovid tells us it was, as the messenger-bird of so artistic a deity as Apollo. But the crow lost paradise — and good looks with it — not for one impulsive act, but for a fortnight's hard sinning. Now punishment has a hardening influence on some people, and it has had a most dreadful effect on the corvine disposition. Heedless of all moral obligations, gluttonous, and a perverter of truth, Ovid tells us it was, even in its best days; but now it has developed into a whole legion of devilry. Lest a Baboo should think to trip me up by throwing Menu in my teeth and quoting from the great lawgiver, "A good wife should be like a crow," I would give it as my opinion that Menu, when he said this, referred to that doubtful virtue of the crow that forbids any exhibition of conjugal tenderness before the public eye, — an unnatural instinct and reserve, to my thinking. Crows cannot, like young sweeps, be called "innocent blacknesses," for their nigritude is the livery of sin, the badge of crime, like the scarlet V on the shoulder of the convict *voleur*, the dark brand on Cain's brow, the snow-white leprosy of Gehazi, or the yellow garb of Norfolk Islander; and yet they do not wear their color with humility or even common decency. They swagger in it, pretending they chose that exact shade for themselves. Did they not do this, perhaps Jerdon would not have begrudged them their flattering name, nor Hodgson have called them *impudicos*, but by their effrontery they have raised every man's hand against them; and were they anything but crows, they must have had to take, like Ishmael the son of Hagar, to the desert. Perhaps it is that they presume upon their past honors. If so, they should beware. Cole's dog was too proud to move out of the way of a cart of manure, and Southey has told us his fate. Again, their Greek and Latin glories have had a serious counterpoise in the writings of modern ancients, where the nature of crows is proven as swart as their Ethiop faces. Is it not written in the Singhalese Pratyasataka that nothing can improve a crow? Students of Burton will remember that in the *Anatomy of Melancholy* devils (including sprites and such like devilkins) are divided into nine classes; for though Bodine declared that all devils must of necessity be spherical in shape, perfect rounds, his theory we are expressly told was quashed by Zaminchus, who proved that they assume divers forms, " sometimes those of cats and crows." Zaminchus was doubtless right, and no one, therefore, should feel any tenderness for these shreds of Satan, these cinders from Tartarus. Zaminchus superfluously adds that in these forms they are "more knowing than any human being" (*quovis homine scientior*); and another old writer just as needlessly tells us that these "terrestrial devils" are in the habit of "flapping down platters" and "making strange noises." Some, however, may urge that because some crows are devils, it does not follow that all are. This is plausible but unworthy of the subject, which should be studied in a liberal spirit and without hair-splitting. When King John killed Jews, he did n't first finically investigate if they were usurers; he knew they were Jews, and that was enough. Besides, did any one ever see a crow that was not "*quovis homine scientior*"? If he did, he proved it by putting it to-death, and, as dead crows count for nothing, that individual bird cannot be cited as a case in point. Further, do not all crows "flap down platters" (when they get the chance) and "make strange noises"? Are not these unequivocal signs of bedevilment? Do not Zaminchus, Bustius, and Cardan agree on this point? Does not the old Chinese historian lay it down that in the south of Sweden is situate "the land of crows and demons"? Is there not in Norway a fearful hill called Huklebrig, whither and whence fiery chariots are commonly seen by the country people carrying to and fro the souls of bad men in the likeness of crows? Crows, then, are indubitably the connecting link between devils, Class 3, "inventors of all mischief," Prince Belial at their head, — and Class 4, "malicious devils," under Prince Asmodeus.[1] An

---

[1] I have here preferred to adopt Burton's classification. — P. R.

inkling of their fallen state seems to be floating in the cerebra of crows, for they sin naturally and never beg pardon. Did any one ever see a contrite and repentant crow? When taken *flagrante delicto* does this nobody's child provoke commiseration by craven and abject postures, deprecating anger by looks of penitence? Quite the contrary. These birds, if put to it, would deny that they stole Cicero's pillow when he was dying; or that they sat, the abomination of desolation, where they ought not — profaning the Teraphim of John de Montfort, insulting his household gods and desecrating his Penates, while in the next room that great soldier and statesman was receiving the last consolations of Extreme Unction? Yet it is known they did. They tread the earth as if they had been always of it. And yet it pleases me to remember how Indra, in wrath for their tale-bearing, — for had they not carried abroad the secrets of the Councils of the Gods? — hurled the brood down through all the hundred stages of his Heaven. Petruchio thought it hard to be braved in his own house by a tailor, and the tailor by an elephant; how keenly either would have felt the familiarity of Indian crows! In the verandahs they parade the reverend sable which they disgrace; they walk in the odor of sanctity through open doors, sleek as Chadband, wily as Pecksniff. Their step is grave, and they ever seem on the point of quoting Scripture, while their eyes are wandering on carnal matters. Like Stiggins, they keep a sharp lookout for tea-time. They hanker after fleshpots. They are as chary of their persons as the bamboo of its blossom, and distant to strangers. In England they pretend to be rooks (except during rookshooting), but in India they brazen it out upon their own infamous individuality — for there are no rooks.

Another prominent visitor of my garden is the green parrot. It is, I think, Cervantes who has recorded the fact that Theophrastus complained "of the long life given to crows." Now the argument of this complaint is not so superficial as at first it seems, and really contains internal evidence of a knowledge of bird-nature. Theophrastus, I take it, grumbled not simply because crows did in a long life get through more mischief than other birds can in a shorter one, but because, if Atropos were only more impartially nimble with her shears, crows would never be able to get through any mischief at all. And in this lies a great point of difference between the sombre crow and the dædal parrot.

The crow requires much time to develop and perfect his misdemeanors; the parrot brings his mischiefs to market in the green leaf. While a crow will spend a week with a view to the ultimate abstraction of a key, the parrot will have scrambled and screeched in a day through a cycle of larcenous gluttonies, and before the crow has finishing reconnoitring the gardener, the parrot has stripped the fruit-tree.

From these differences in the characters of the birds, I hold that Theophrastus chose "crows" advisedly, and made his complaint with judgment; but I wonder that, having thus headed a list of grievances, he did not continue it with a protest against the green color given to parrots. The probable explanation of the oversight is that he never saw a green parrot. But we who *do* see them have surely a reasonable cause for complaint, when nature creates thieves and then gives them a passport to impunity. For the green parrot has a large brain (some naturalists would like to see the Psittacid family on this account rank first among birds),

and he knows that he is green as well as we do, and,
knowing it, he makes the most of nature's injudicious
gift. He settles with a screech among your mangoes,
and as you approach, the phud! phud! of the falling
fruitlings assures you that he is not gone. But where
is he? Somewhere in the tree, you may be sure, probably with an unripe fruit in his claw, which is raised
half way to his beak, but certainly with a round black
eye fixed on you; for, while you are straining to distinguish green feathers from green leaves, he breaks with
a sudden rush through the foliage, on the other side of
the tree, and is off in an apotheosis of screech to his
watch-tower on a distant tree. To give the parrot his
due, however, we must remember that he did not choose
his own color, — it was thrust upon him; and we must
further allow that, snob as he is, he possesses certain
manly virtues. He is wanting in neither personal courage, assurance, nor promptitude, but he abuses these
virtues by using them in the service of vice. Moreover,
he is a glutton, and, unlike his neighbors, the needle of
his thoughts and endeavors always points towards his
stomach. The starlings, bigots to a claim which they
have forged to the exclusive ownership of the croquet
ground, divide their attention for a moment between
worms and intruders. The kite forbears to flutter the
dove-cotes while he squeals his love-song to his mate;
the hawk now and again affords healthy excitement to a
score of crows who keck at him as he flaps unconcerned
on his wide, ragged wings through the air. "Opeechee,
the robin," has found a bird smaller than himself, and is
accordingly pursuing it relentlessly through bush and
brier; the thinly feathered babblers are telling each
other the secret of a mungoose being at that moment

in the water-pipe; while the squirrels, sticking head downwards to their respective branches, are having a twopenny-half-penny argument across the garden path. Meanwhile, the green parrot is desolating the fruit-tree. Like the Ettrick Shepherd they never can eat *a few* of anything, and his luncheons are all heavy dinners. "That frugal bit of the old Britons of the bigness of a bean," which could satisfy the hunger and thirst of our ancestors for a whole day, would not suffice the green parrot for one meal, for not only is his appetite inordinate, but his wastefulness also, and what he cannot eat he destroys. He enters a tree of fruit as the Visigoths entered a building. His motto is, "What I cannot take I will not leave," and he pillages the branches, gutting them of even their unripest fruit. Dr. Jerdon, in his *Birds of India*, records the fact that "owls attack these birds by night," and there is, ill-feeling apart, certainly something very comfortable in the knowledge that while we are warm a-bed owls are most probably garrotting the green parrots.

I have spoken elsewhere, with some inadvertence, of "the Republic of Birds;" although by my own showing — for I write of sovereign eagles and knightly falcons — the constitution of the volucrine world is an unlimited monarchy, of which the despotism is only tempered by the strong social bonds that lend strength to the lower orders of birds. The tyrant kite is powerless before the corvine Vehm-gericht; and it is with hesitation that the hawk offers violence to a sparrows' club. But there are undoubtedly among the feathered race some to whom a republic would present itself as the more perfect form of government, and to none more certainly than the mynas.[1] The myna is, although a

---

[1] *Sturninæ*, the Starlings.

moderate, a very decided republican, for, sober in mind as in apparel, he sets his face against such vain frivolities as the tumbling of pigeons, the meretricious dancing of peafowl, and the gaudy bedizenment of the minivets; holding that life is real, life is earnest, and, while worms are to be found beneath the grass, to be spent in serious work. To quote " ane aunciente clerke," he " obtests against the chaunting of foolish litanies before the idols of one's own conceit"; would " chase away all bewildering humors and fancies"; and would say with the clerke " that, though the cautelous tregœtour, or, as the men of France do call him, the jongleur, doth make a very pretty play with two or three balls which seem to live in the air, and which do not depart from him, yet I would rather, after our old English fashion, have the ball tossed from hand to hand, or that one should propulse the ball aginst the little guichet, while another should repel it with the batting staff. This I hold to be the fuller exercise." The myna therefore views with some displeasure the dilettante hawking of bee-eaters and the leisurely deportment of the crow-pheasant, cannot be brought to see the utility of the luxurious hoopoe's crest, and loses all patience with the köel-cuckoo for his idle habit of spending his forenoons in tuning his voice. For the patient kingfisher he entertains a moderate respect, and he holds in esteem the industrious woodpecker; but the scapegrace parrot is an abomination to him; and had he the power, the myna would altogether exterminate the race of humming-birds for their persistent trifling over lilies. Life with him is all work, and he makes it, as Souvestre says, " a legal process." Of course he has a wife, and she celebrates each anniversary of spring by presenting him with a nestful of young mynas, but her company rather subdues and sobers him than makes him frivolous or giddy; for as the myna is, his wife is, — of one complexion of feather and mind. A pair of mynas (for these discreet birds are seldom seen except in pairs) remind one of a Dutch burgher and his frau. They are comfortably dressed, well fed, of a grave deportment, and so respectable that scandal hesitates to whisper their name. In the empty babble of the Seven Sisters, the fruitless controversies of finches, the bickerings of amatory sparrows (every sparrow is at heart a rake), or the turmoil of kites, they take no part, — holding aloof alike from the monarchical exclusiveness of the jealous Raptores and the democratic communism of crows. The gourd will not climb on the olive, and the olive-tree, it is said, will not grow near the oak. Between the grape of story and the cabbage there is a like antipathy, " and everlasting hate the vine to ivy bears." The apple detests the walnut, " whose malignant touch impairs all generous fruit." So with the myna. It shrinks from the neighborhood of the strong, and resents the companionship of the humble. But among vegetables, if there is antipathy there is also sympathy; for does not the Latin poet say that the elm loves the vine? Country folk declare that the fig grows best near rue; and the legend ballad of the Todas tells us how the cachew apple droops when the cinnamon dies. But among the mynas there is no such profligacy or tenderness, and over the annihilation of the whole world of birds they would be even such " pebble stones " as Launce's dog. At the same time they are not intrusive with their likes and dislikes. If the squirrel chooses to chirrup all day, they let him do so, and they offer no opposition to the ostentatious combats of robins. Nor do they trespass on their neighbors with idle curiosity. That butterflies should mysteriously migrate in great clouds, moving against the wind across wide waters, and even tempt the ocean itself with nothing more definite than the horizon before them as a resting-place, may set the inquisitive crow thinking, or furnish Humboldt with matter for long conjecturing; but the mynas would express no surprise at the phenomenon. They waste no time wondering with others why the wagtail so continuously wags its tail, nor would they vex the Syrian coney with idle questions as to its preference for rocky places. Such things have set others a-thinking, and would make the leaf-loving squirrel silly with surprise; but the Essene myna! — " Let the world revolve," he says; " we are here to work, and in the name of the Prophet — *worms.*" He comes of a race of poor antecedents, and has no lineage worth boasting of. The crow has Greek and Latin memories; and for the antiquity of the sparrow we have the testimony of Holy Writ. It is true that in the stories of India the myna has frequent and honorable mention; but the authors speak of the hill-bird — a notable fowl, with strange powers of mimicry, and always a favorite with the people, — and not of the homely Quaker bird who so diligently searches our grass-plots, and may be seen, from dawn to twilight, busy at his appointed work, the consumption of little grubs. The lust of the green parrot for orchard brigandage, or of the proud-stomached king-crow for battle with his kind, are as whimsical caprices, fancies of the moment, when compared to the steady assiduity with which this Puritan bird pursues the object of his creation. And the result is that the myna has no wit. Like the Germans, he is incomparable at hard, unshowy work, but they — as one, a wit himself, has said of them — are only moderately mirthful in their humor. Intelligence is his, of a high order, for, busy as he may be, the myna descries before all others the far-away speck in the sky which will grow into a hawk, and it is from the myna's cry of alarm that the garden becomes first aware of the danger that is approaching. But wit he has none. His only way of catching a worm is to lay hold of its tail and pull it out of its hole, — generally breaking it in the middle, and losing the bigger half. He does not tap the ground as the wryneck will tap the tree, to stimulate the insect to run out to be eaten entire; nor like the stork imitate a dead thing, till the frog, tired of waiting for him to move, puts his head above the green pond. "To strange mysterious dulness still the friend," he parades the croquet lawn, joins in grave converse with another by the roadside, or sits to exchange ignorance with an acquaintance on a rail. At night the mynas socially congregate together, and, with a clamor quite unbecoming their character, make their arrangements for the night, contending for an absolute equality even in sleep.

Has it ever struck you how fortunate it is for the world of birds that of the twenty-four hours some are passed in darkness? And yet without the protection of night the earth would be assuredly depopulated of small birds, and the despots, whom the mynas detest, would be left alone to contest in internecine conflict the dominion of the air.

As busy as the mynas, but less silent in their working, are those sad-colored birds hopping about in the dust and incessantly talking while they hop. They are

called by the natives the Seven Sisters,[1] and seem to
have always some little difference on hand to settle.
But if they gabble till the coming of the Coquecigrues
they will never settle it. Fighting? Not at all; do
not be misled by the tone of voice. That heptachord
clamor is not the expression of any strong feelings.
It is only a way they have. They always exchange
their commonplaces as if their next neighbor was out of
hearing. If they could but be quiet they might pass
for the bankers among the birds, — they look so very
respectable. But though they dress so soberly, their
behavior is unseemly. The Prince in Herodotus's history disappointed the expectations of his friends by
dancing head downwards on a table, "gesticulating
with his legs." If Coleridge's wise-looking friend had
preserved his silence through the whole meal, the poet
would have remembered him as one of the most intelligent men of his acquaintance; but the apple dumplings,
making him speak, burst the bubble of his reputation.
His speech bewrayed him, like the Shibboleth at the
ford of Jordan, "the bread and cheese" of the Fleming
persecution, or the Galilean twang of the impetuous
saint. Pythagoreans may, if they will, aver that these
birds are the original masons and hodmen of Babel, but
I would rather believe that in a former state they were old
Hindu women, garrulous[2] and addicted to raking about
amongst rubbish heaps, as all old native women seem
to be. The Seven Sisters pretend to feed on insects,
but that is only when they cannot get peas. Look at
them now, — the whole family, a septemvirate of sin,

[1] The Babbler-thrushes, *Malacocircus*.

[2] "Ten measures of garrulity," says the Talmud, "came down
from heaven, and the women took nine of them."

among your marrowfat peas, gobbling and gabbling as if they believed in Dr. Cumming. And it is of no use to expel them — for they will return, and

> " Often scared,
> As oft return: a pert, voracious kind."

When it is night they will go off with a great deal of preliminary talk to their respective boarding-houses; for these birds, though at times as quarrelsome as Sumatrans during the pepper harvest, are sociable and lodge together. The weak point of this arrangement is that often a bird — perhaps the middle one of a long row of closely packed snoozers — has a bad dream, or loses his balance, and instantly the shock flashes along the line. The whole dormitory blazes up at once with indignation, and much bad language is bandied about promiscuously in the dark. The abusive shower at length slackens, and querulous monosyllables and indistinct animal noises take the place of the septemfluous (Fuller has sanctified the word) vituperation, when some individual, tardily exasperated at the unseemly din, lifts up his voice in remonstrance, and rekindles the smouldering fire. Sometimes he suddenly breaks off, suggesting to a listener the idea that his next neighbor had silently kicked him; but more often the mischief is irreparable, and the din runs its course, again dwindles away, and is again relit, perhaps more than once before all heads are safely again under wing.

III.

VISITORS IN FUR, AND OTHERS.

AS a contrast to the fidgetty birds, glance your eye along the garden path and take note of that pink-nosed mungoose [1] gazing placidly out of the water-pipe. It looks as shy as Oliver Twist before the Board; but that is only because it sees no chance of being able to chase you about, catch you and eat you. If you were a snake or a lizard you would find it provokingly familiar, and as brisk as King Ferdinand at an *auto-da-fé*, for the scent of a lively snake is to the mungoose as pleasant as that of valerian to cats, attar to a Begum, aniseed to pigeons, or burning Jews to His Most Catholic Majesty aforementioned; and when upon the war-trail the mungoose is as different to the every-day animal as the Sunday gentleman in the Park, in green gloves and a blue necktie, is to the obsequious young man who served you across the counter on Saturday. Usually the mungoose is to be seen slinking timorously along the narrow watercourses, or, under cover of the turf edge, gliding along to some hunting-ground among the aloes; whence, if it unearths a quarry, it will emerge with its fur on end and its tail like a bottle-brush, its eyes dancing in its head, and all its body agog with excitement, — reckless of the dead leaves crackling as it scuttles after the flying reptile, flinging itself upon the

[1] The Ichneumon, *Viverrinæ*.

victim with a zest and single-mindedness wonderful to see. That pipe is its city of refuge, the asylum in all times of trouble, to which it betakes itself when annoyed by the cat who lives in the carrot-bed, or the bird-boy who by his inhuman cries greatly perplexes the robins in the peas, or when its nerves have been shaken by the sudden approach of the silent-footed gardener or by a *rencontre* with the long-tailed pariah dog that lives in the outer dust. The mungoose, although his own brothers in Nepaul have the same smell in a worse degree, is the sworn foe of musk-rats. "All is not mungoose that smells of musk," it reasons, as it follows up the trail of its chitt-chittering victim; but although it enjoys this *le sport* it sometimes essays the less creditable *battue*. Jerdon says, "It is very destructive to such birds as frequent the ground. Not unfrequently it gets access to tame pigeons, rabbits, or poultry, and commits great havoc, sucking the blood only of several." He adds that he has "often seen it make a dash into a verandah where caged birds were placed, and endeavor to tear them from their cages." The mungoose family, in fact, do duty for weasels, and if game were preserved in India would be vermin. Even at present some of the blame so lavishly showered on the tainted musk-rat might be transferred to the mungoose. A little more of that same blame might perhaps be made over to another popular favorite, the grey squirrel.

The palm squirrel, as it is more properly called, will come into a room and eat the fruit on your sideboard, or into a vinery and incontinently borrow your grapes. A rat-trap in such cases may do some good, but a complete cure is hopeless. Nothing but the Arminian doctrine of universal grace will save the squirrel from eternal damnation, for its presumption is unique. The plummet of reflection cannot sound it, nor the net of memory bring up a precedent. It is gratuitous, unprovoked, and aimless. It is all for love. There are no stakes such as the crow plays for, and in its shrill gamut there is no string of menace or of challenge. Its scrannel quips are pointless, — so let them pass. Any one, unless he be a Scotch piper, has a right to stone the Seven Sisters for their fulsome clatter, but the tongue of the squirrel is free as air. There is no embargo on it; it is out of bond, and wags when and where it lists. Let the craven kite (itself the butt of smaller birds) swoop at it, but give your sympathy to the squirrel. A woman who cannot kiss and a bird which cannot sing ought to be at any rate taught, but who would look for harmony from a squirrel? Was wisdom ever found in Gotham or truth in the compliments of beggars? Would you hook Leviathan by the nose, or hedge a cuckoo in? Again, besides its voice, people have been found to object to its tail. But Hiawatha liked it. There is no malice in the motion of a squirrel's tail. It does not resemble the cocked-up gesture of the robin's or the wren's. It does n't swing like the cat's, or dart like the scorpion's. It is never offensively straight on end like a cow's on a windy day, nor slinking like a pariah dog's. It has none of the odious mobility of the monkey's, nor the three-inch arrogance of the goat's. Neither is there in it the pendulous monotony of the wagtail's, nor the spasmodic wriggle of the sucking lamb's. Yet it is a speaking feature. That fluffy perkiness is an index of the squirrel mind. With an upward jerk it puts a question, with a downward one emphasizes an assertion; gives plausibility with a wave, and stings with sarcasm in a series of disconnected lilts; for the squirrel is as inquisitive as Empedocles, as tediously emphatic as the Ephesians, and in self-confidence a Crœsus. It would not have hesitated to suggest to Solomon solutions to the Queen of Sheba's conundrums, nor to volunteer likely answers to the riddle of the Sphinx. It is impervious to jibes. Scoffs and derision are thrown away upon it as much as solid argument. Hard names do it no hurt. It would not be visibly affected if you called it a parallelopiped, or the larva of a marine ascidian. Perhaps it is a philosopher, for, since squirrels dropped their nutshells on Primeval Man, no instance is on record of a melancholy squirrel. Its emotions (precipitate terror excepted) are shallow, and though it may be tamed, it will form no strong attachments; while its worldly wisdom is great. Like the frog in Æsop, it is "extreme wise." Given a three-inch post, the squirrel can always keep out of sight. You may go round and round, but it will always be "on the other side."

Squirrels excepted, the most prominent members of Indian garden life are ants, for they stamp their broad-arrow everywhere; their advertisements may be read on almost every tree-trunk, and samples of their work seen on all the paths. They have a head office in most verandahs, with branch establishments in the bathrooms; while their agents are ubiquitous, laying earth-heaps wherever they travel, — each heap the outward and visible sign of much inward tunnelling, which, towards the end of the rainy season, will fall in. Engineering seems to be their favorite profession, although some have a passion for plastering, and when other surfaces fail will lay a coat of mud on the level ground, for the after-pleasure of creeping under it. Others are bigots to geographical discovery, and are constantly wandering into dangerous places, whence they escape only by a series of miracles. Of some a pastoral life is all the joy, for they keep herds of green aphides — better known as "blight" — which they milk regularly for the sake of the sweet leaf-juice they secrete. Others, again, are hunters and live on the produce of the chase. They organize foraging parties and issue forth a host of Lilliputians to drag home a Brobdignag cricket; or, marshalled on the war-trail, file out to plunder the larders of their neighbors. The bulk, however, are omnivorous and jacks-of-all-trades, with a decided leaning towards vegetable food and excavation; and it is in this, the enormous consumption of seeds in the ant nurseries, that this family contributes its quota to the well-being of creation, a quota which after all scarcely raises it, in point of usefulness, to the level of butterflies and moths — popularly supposed to be the idlest and least useful of created insects. It ought, however, to be kept in mind that butterflies are only beautified caterpillars; and when we see them flying about, we should remember that their work is over and they are enjoying their vacation. They have been raised to the Upper House. From being laborious managers they have become the sleeping partners in a thriving business. While they were caterpillars they worked hard and well; so Nature, to reward them, dresses them up to look attractive, and sends them out as butterflies — to get married. The ants, on the other hand, did no work when they were grubs, so they have to do a good deal in their maturity. They have to provide food for successive broods of hungry youngsters, who, when grown up, will join them in feeding their younger brothers and sisters; or, if they are of the favored few, will enter ant life with wings, and be blown away by the wind a few hundred yards, to become the founders of new colonies. The actual balance of work done by caterpillars and ants respectively is indeed about equal; the only difference being that caterpillars check vegetation by feeding themselves, and ants by feeding their babies; while the balance of mischief done is very much against the ants. The commonest of all the Indian ants, or at any rate the most conspicuous, are the black ones, to be found marauding on every sideboard, and whose normal state seems to be one of criminal trespass. These from their size are perhaps also the most interesting, as it requires little exertion to distinguish between the classes of individuals that in the aggregate make up a nest of ants. There is the blustering soldier, or policeman ant, who goes about wagging his great head and snapping his jaws at nothing; furious exceedingly when insulted, but as a rule preferring to patrol in shady neighborhoods, the backwaters of life, where he can peer idly into cracks and holes. See him as he saunters up the path, pretending to be on the lookout for suspicious characters, stopping strangers with impertinent inquiries, leering at that modest wire-worm who is hurrying home. Watch him swaggering to meet a friend whose beat ends at the corner, and with whom he will loiter for the next hour. Suddenly a blossom falls from the orange-tree overhead. His display of energy is now terrific. He dashes about in all directions, jostles the foot-passengers, and then pretends that they had attacked him. He continually loses his own balance, and has to scramble out of worm-holes and dusty crevices; or he comes in collision with a blade of grass which he bravely turns upon and utterly discomfits, and then on a sudden, tail up, he whirls home to report at headquarters the recent violent volcanic disturbances, which, being at his post, he was fortunately able to suppress! Another and more numerous section of the community of ants are the loafers, who spend lives of the most laborious idleness. Instead of joining the long thread of honest worker ants, stretching from the nest to the next garden and busy importing food to the nurseries, they hang about the doors and eke out a day spent in sham industry by retiring at intervals to perform an elaborate toilet. Between whiles the loafer affects a violent energy. He makes a rush along the highroad, jostling all the laden returners, stops most of them to ask commonplace questions or to wonder idly at their burdens; and then, as if struck by a bright idea or the sudden remembrance of something he had forgotten, he turns sharp round and rushes home, — tumbling headlong into the nest with an avalanche of rubbish behind him which it will take the whole colony a long time to bring out again. The loafer, meanwhile, retires to clean his legs. Sometimes also, in order to be thought active and vigilant, he raises a false alarm of danger and skirmishes valiantly in the rear with an imaginary foe, a husk of corn-seed or a thistle-down. One such loafer came, under my own observation, to a miserable end. Thinking to be busy cheaply, he entered into combat with a very small fly. But the small fly was the unsuspected possessor of a powerful sting, whereupon the unhappy loafer, with his tail curled up to his mouth, rolled about in agony until a policeman catching sight of him, and seeing that he was either drunk, riotous, or incapable, nipped him into two pieces; and a "worker," happening to pass by, carried him off to the nest as food for the family! An honest ant, on the other hand, has no equal for fixedness of purpose, and an obstinate, unflagging industry. The day breaks, the front door is opened, and the honest ant ascends to daylight. He finds that a passer-by has effaced the track along which he ran so often yesterday, but his memory is good, and natural landmarks abound. He casts about like a pigeon when first thrown up in the air, and then he is off. Straight up the path to the little snag of stone that is sticking out — up one side of it and down the other — over the bank — through a forest of weeds — round a lake of dew, and then, with an extraordinary instinct, for a straight line, he goes whirling off across the cucumber-bed to some far spot, where he knows is lying a stem of maize heavily laden with grain. Then, with a fraction of a seed in his pincers, he hurries home, hands it over to the commissariat, and is off again for another. And so, if the grain holds out, he will go on until sunset, and when the pluffy, round-faced owls, sitting on the sentinel cypress-trees, are screeching an *ilicet* to the lingering day-birds, the honest ant is busy closing up his doors; and before the mynas passing overhead, and calling as they go to belated wanderers, have reached the bamboo clumps which sough by the river, he will be sleeping the sleep of the honest. With industry, however, the catalogue of the virtues of ants begins and ends. They have an instinct for hard work, and, useless or not, they do it — in the most laborious way they can; but except for the wisdom which industry argues, ants have no title whatever to the epithet of "wise." Until they learn that to run up one side of a post and down the other is not the quickest way of getting past the post, and that in throwing up mounds on garden-paths they are giving hostages to a ruthless gardener, they can scarcely be accused of even common sense.

* * * * * *

There has lately been discovered a species of ant which deserves to be at once introduced to the attention of all children, servants, and ladies keeping house. No vestry should be ignorant of the habits of so admirable a creature, and sanitary boards of all kinds should without loss of time be put in possession of the leading facts.

This excellent ant, it appears, abominates rubbish. If its house is made in a mess it gets disgusted, goes away, and never comes back. Dirt breaks its heart.

The insect in question is a native of Colombia, and hatches its eggs by artificial heat, procuring for this purpose quantities of foliage, which, in the course of natural fermentation, supply the necessary warmth. When the young brood is hatched the community carefully carry away the decomposed rubbish that has served its purpose as a hotbed, and stack it by itself at a distance from the nest. The damage which they inflict upon gardens and plantations when collecting the leaves required is so enormous that colonists have exhausted their ingenuity in devising means for their expulsion or extermination; but all in vain, for the ant, wherever it "squats," strikes very firm roots indeed, and neither plague, pestilence, nor famine, neither fire nor brimstone, nor yet holy water, can compel it to go away. It takes no notice whatever of writs of ejectment, and looks upon bell, book, and candle as mere idle mummeries. The nest may be dug up with a plough or blown up with gunpowder, soaked with hot water or swamped out with cold, smothered with smoke, or made abominable with chemical compounds, strewn with poison or scattered abroad with pitchforks, — the ants return all the same, and, apparently, with a gayety enhanced by their recent ordeals. The Inquisition would have had no chance with them, for all the tortures of the martyrs have been tried upon them in vain. Their heroic tenacity to their homesteads would have baffled the malignity of a Bonner or the persecuting zeal of an Alva. But where force may fail moral suasion often meets with success, and this has proved true with the ants in question. An observant negro, remarking that the creatures were impervious to the arguments of violence and knowing their cleanly habits, suggested that if the ants could not be hunted or blown or massacred off the premises, they might be disgusted with them. The experiment was made, and with complete success. The refuse foliage which the ants had so carefully stacked away in tidy heaps was scattered over the ground, and some other basketfuls of rubbish added, and the whole community fled on the instant!

They did not even go home to pack up their carpet-bags, but just as they were, in the clothes they stood in, so to speak, they fled from the disordered scene.

Ant habits have always furnished ample material for the moralist, but this, the latest recorded trait of their character, makes a delightful addition to the already interesting history of these "tiny creatures, strong by social league," the "parsimonious" emmet folk. It destroys, it is true, something of their traditional reputation for industry that they should thus abandon themselves to despair rather than set to work to clear away the rubbish strewn about their dwelling-places. It sets them in this respect below the bees, who never seem to weary of repairing damages, and far below the white ant of the East, which has an absolutely ferocious passion for mending breaches and circumventing accidents. Nothing beats them except utter annihilation.

The ants of Colombia, however, if they fail in that nobility of diligence which seems to be only whetted by disaster, rise infinitely superior to their congeners in the moral virtues of respect for sanitation and punctilious cleanliness. There is, however, even a more admirable psychological fact behind than this, for it appears that the rubbish which scatters them most promptly is not their own but their neighbors'. Their own rubbish, it is true, sends them off quickly enough, but the exodus is, if possible, accelerated by employing that from an adjoining nest. To have their own litter lying about makes home intolerable, but that their neighbors should "shoot" theirs also upon them is the very extremity of abomination. Life under such conditions is at once voted impossible, and rather than exist where the next-door people can empty their dust-bins and slop-pails over their walls, they go away headlong. A panic of disgust seizes upon the whole colony, and the bonds of society snap and shrivel up on the instant, like a spider's web above a candle-flame. Without a thought of wife or child, of household gods or household goods, they rush tumultuously from the polluted spot. No pious son stays to give the aged Anchises a lift; none loiters to spoil the Egyptians before he goes; none looks back upon the doomed city. Forward and anywhere is the motto of the pell-mell flight; all throw down their burdens that they may run the faster, and shamefully abandon their shields that their arms may not impede their course. Big and little, male and female, old and young, all scamper off alike over the untidy thresholds, and there is no distinction of caste under the common horror of a home that requires sweeping up.

Such a spectacle is truly sublime, for behind the ants there is no avenging Michael-arm, that they should thus precipitately fall into "hideous rout;" no Zulu *impi;* no hyena horde of Bashkirs, as there was after the flying Tartars; no remorseless pursuit of any kind. Indeed, persecution and fiery trials they confront unmoved, so there is no element of fear in their conduct.

It arises entirely from a generous impatience of neighbors' untidy habits, from a superb intolerance of dirt. When was such an example ever set, or when will it ever be followed, by human beings? No single city, not even a village, is ever recorded to have been abandoned on account of uncleanliness; and yet what a grand episode in national history it would be, if such had happened, — had the men of Cologne, for instance, ever gone out into the country-side and all encamped there, in dignified protest against the "six-and-seventy separate stinks" of their undrained city! No instance even is on record of a single householder rushing from his premises with all his family rather than endure cobwebs and dust; nor, indeed, of a single child refusing to stay in its nursery because it was untidy. We are still, therefore, far behind the Colombia ant in the matter of cleanliness.

In another aspect, perhaps, this impetuous detestation of dirt is not altogether admirable; for, as I have noticed, it argues a declension in industry from the true ant standard. Thus, the very creatures that urge so headlong a career, when the neatness of their surroundings is threatened, are marvels of diligence in collecting the very leaves which afterwards distress them so much. This assiduity has long been noted, In Cornwall the busy *murians*, as the people call the ants, are still supposed to be a race of "little people," disestablished from the world of men and women for their idle habits, and condemned to perpetual labor; while in Ceylon the natives say that the ants feed a serpent, who lives under ground, with the leaves which they pick off the trees, and that, as the reptile's appetite is never satisfied, the ants have to work on for ever. From West to East, therefore, the same trait of unresting diligence has been remarked; and, in one respect, it is no doubt a deplorable retrogression in the Colombia ants that the mere sight of rubbish should thus dishearten them. Yet, looked at from a higher standpoint, their consuming dislike of uncleanly surroundings is magnificent, for they do not hesitate to sacrifice all that is nearest and dearest, to risk even their public character, so long as sufficient effect can be given to their protest and sufficient emphasis laid upon their indignation. Anything short of flight, immediate and complete, without condition or reservation, would fail to meet the case or adequately represent their feelings. To them the degradation of submitting to a neighbor's cinders and egg-shells seems too despicable to be borne; and rather than live in a parish where the vestry neglects the drains and the dustbins, they abandon their hearths and homes for ever.

We human beings cannot all of us afford to show the same superb horror of defective sanitation, but we can admire the ants who do, and can hold them up as models to all slatterns and sluts, parochial or domestic.

PART II.

THE INDIAN SEASONS.

PART II.

THE INDIAN SEASONS.

I.

IN HOT WEATHER.

"And the day shall have a sun
That shall make thee wish it done."

IS Manfred speaking of the hot weather, of May-day in India? The hot weather is palpably here, and the heat of the sun makes the length of the twelve hours intolerable. The mango-bird glances through the groves, and in the early morning announces his beautiful but unwelcome presence with his merle-melody. The köel-cuckoo screams in a crescendo from some deep covert, and the crow-pheasant's note has changed to a sound which must rank among nature's strangest, — with the marsh-bittern's weird booming, the drumming of the capercailzie, or the bell-tolling note of the prairie campanile. Now, too, the hornets are hovering round our eaves, and wasps reconnoitre our verandahs. "Of all God's creatures," said Christopher North, "the wasp is the only one eternally out of temper." But he should have said this only of the British wasp. The *vespæ* of India, though, from their savage garniture of colors and their ghastly elegance, very formidable to look on, are but feeble folk compared with their banded congener of England, the ruffian in glossy velvet and deep yellow, who assails one at all hours of the summer's day, lurking in fallen fruit, making grocers' shops as dangerous as viper-pits, an empty sugar-keg a very cockatrice den, and spreading dismay at every picnic. But the wasp points this moral, — that it requires no brains to annoy. A wasp stings as well without its head as with it.

Flies, too, now assume a prominence to which they are in no way entitled by their merits. Luther hated flies *quia sunt imagines diaboli et hæreticorum;* and, with a fine enthusiasm worthy of the great Reformer, he smote Beelzebub in detail. "I am," he said one day, as he sat at his dinner, his Boswell (Lauterbach) taking notes under the table, "I am a great enemy unto flies, for when I have a good book they flock upon it, parade up and down upon it, and soil it." So Luther used to kill them with all the malignity of the early Christian. And indeed the fly deserves death. It has no delicacy, and hints are thrown away upon the importunate insect. With a persistent insolence it returns to your nose, perching irreverently upon the feature, until sudden death cuts short its ill-mannered career. In this matter my sympathies are rather with that Roman Emperor who impaled on pins all the flies he could catch, than with Uncle Toby who, when he had in his power a ruffianly bluebottle, let it go out of the window, — to fly into his neighbor's house and vex him. The only consolation is that the neighbor probably killed it.

The sun is hardly up yet, so the doors are open. From the garden come the sounds of chattering hot-weather birds. "While eating," said the Shepherd, "say little, but look friendly;" but the starlings (to give them their due and to speak more point-device, — the "rose-colored pastors") do not at all respect the advice of James Hogg, for while eating they say much, looking the while most unfriendly. They have only just arrived from Syria, — indeed, in their far-off breeding cliffs, there are still young birds waiting for their wings before leaving for the East, — and they lose no time in announcing their arrival. The unhappy owner of the mulberry-grove yonder wages a bitter conflict with them, and from their numbers his pellet-bow thins out many a rosy thief. The red semul-tree is all aflame with burning scarlet, each branch a chandelier lit up with clusters of fiery blossom; and to it in the early heat come flocking, "with tongues all loudness," a motley crowd of birds thirsting for the cool dew which has been all night collecting in the floral goblets and been sweetened by the semul's honey. Among them the pastors revel, drinking, fighting, and chattering from early dawn to blazing noon. But as the sun strengthens all nature begins to confess the heat, and even the crow caws sadly. On the water the sun dances with such a blinding sparkle that the panoplied crocodile, apprehensive of asphyxia, will hardly show his scales above the river, and the turtles shut up their telescope necks, shrewdly suspecting a sunstroke. On the shaded hillside the herded pigs lie dreamily grunting, and in the deep coverts the deer stretch themselves secure. The peasants in the fields have loosed their bullocks for a respite; and, while they make their way to the puddles, their masters creep under their grass huts to eat their meal, smoke their pipes, and doze.

But in the cities the heat of noon is worse. There is wanting even the relief of herbage and running water. The white sunlight lies upon the roads, so palpable a heat that it might be peeled off; the bare, blinding walls, surcharged with heat, refuse to soak in more, and reject upon the air the fervor beating down upon them. In the dusty hollows of the roadside the pariah dogs lie sweltering in dry heat; beneath the trees sit the crows, their beaks agape; the buffaloes are wallowing in the shrunken mud-holes, — but not a human being is abroad of his own will. At times a messenger, with his head swathed in cloths, trudges along through the white dust; or a camel, his cloven feet treading the hot, soft surface of the road as if it were again pressing the sand-plains of the Khanates, goes lounging by; but the world holds the mid-day to be intolerable, and has renounced it, seeking such respite as it may from the terrible breath of that hot wind which is shrivelling up the face of nature, making each tree as dry as the Oak of Mamre, suffocating out of it all that has life.

But the punkah-coolie is left outside. His lines have been cast to him on the wrong side of the *tattie*. The hot wind, whose curses the sweet kiss of the *kus-kus* turns to blessings, whose oven-breath passes into our houses with a borrowed fragrance, finds the punkah-coolie standing undefended in the verandah, and blows upon him; the sun sees him and, as long as he can, stares at him; until the punkah-coolie, in the stifling heat of May-day, almost longs for the flooded miseries of Michaelmas. But he has his revenge. In his hands he holds a rope — a punkah-rope — and beneath the punkah sits his master, writing. On either side and all round him, piled carefully, are arranged papers, — light, flimsy sheets, — and on each pile lies a paper-weight. And the punkah swings backward and forward with a measured flight, the papers' edges responsive, with a rustle, to each wave of air. And the writer, wary at first, grows careless. The monotony of the air has put him off his guard, and here and there a paper-weight has been removed. Now is the coolie's time. Sweet is revenge! and suddenly with a jerk the punkah wakes up, sweeping in a wider arc, and with a rustle of many wings the piled papers slide whispering to the floor. But why loiter to enumerate the coolie's small revenges, the mean tricks by which, when you rise, he flips you in the eye with the punkah fringe, disordering your hair and sweeping it this way and that,— the petty retaliation of finding out a hole in the tattie, and flinging water through it on to your matting, angering the dog that was lying in the cool, damp shade? These and such are the coolie's revenges, when the hot weather by which he lives embitters him against his kind. But at night he develops into a fiend, for whom a deep and bitter loathing possesses itself of the hearts of men. It is upon him that the strong man, furious at the sudden cessation of the breeze, makes armed sallies. It is on him that the mosquito-bitten subaltern, wakeful through the oil-lit watches of the night, empties the vial of his wrath and the contents of his wash-hand basin: who shares with the griff's dogs the uncompromising attentions of boot-jacks and riding-whips. For him ingenious youth devises rare traps, cunning pyramids of beer-boxes with a rope attached — curious penalties to make him suffer, — for the coolie, after the sun has set, becomes a demoralized machine that requires winding up once every twenty minutes, and is not to be kept going without torture. And thus for eight shillings a month he embitters your life, making the punkah an engine wherewith to oppress you.

It is Cardan, I think, who advises men to partake sometimes of unwholesome food if they have an extraordinary liking for it; it is not always well, he would tell us, to be of an even virtue. What a poor thing, for instance, were an oyster in constant health; ladies' caskets would then want their pearls. Who does not at times resent the appearance of a friend who is comfortably fat, come weal or woe? The uniform hilarity of Mark Tapley recommends itself to few. But to the punkah-coolie, how inexplicable our theorizing on the evil of monotonous good! To him anything good is so rare that he at once assimilates it, when he meets with it, to his ordinary evil. He cannot trust himself to believe the metal in his hand is gold. Given enough, he commits a surfeit, and tempted with a little he lusts after too much. Indulgence with the coolie means license, and a conditional promise a *carte blanche*. And thus he provokes ill-nature. Usually it depends upon the master whether service be humiliation; but the punkah-coolie is such "a thing of dark imaginings" that he too often defies sympathy.

I have three coolies, and I call them Shadrach, Meshach, and Abednego, for they have stood the test of fire. And Shadrach is an idiot. Upon him the wily Meshach foists his work; and at times even the crass Abednego can shuffle his periods of toil upon the broad shoulders of Shadrach. He is slate-colored when dry; in the rains he resembles a *bheesty's*[1] water-skin. In his youth he was neglected, and in his manhood his paunch hath attained an unseemly rotundity. Not that I would have it supposed he is portly. His dimensions have been induced by disease. His thin face knows it, and

[1] The water-carrier.

wears an expression of deprecating humility, to which his conscious legs respond in tremulous emotions. His life is a book without pictures. His existence is set to very sad music. The slightest noise within the house is sufficient to set Shadrach pulling like a bell-ringer on New Year's Eve; but a very few minutes suffice to plunge him into obese oblivion, and then the punkah waggles feebly until a shout again electrifies it into ferocity. It is always when Shadrach is pulling that the punkah-rope breaks; when more water than usual splashes through the tattie I make sure that the ladle is in Shadrach's hands. Meshach is of another sort. He is the oldest of the three and when he condescends to the rope, pulls the punkah well. But, as a rule, he allows Shadrach to do his work; for as often as I look out Meshach is lying curled up under a pink cloth asleep, and Shadrach is pulling. He has established a mastery over his fellows, and by virtue, so I believe, of that pink cloth which voluminously girds his wizened frame, exacts a respect to which his claim is forged. They are the Children of the Lotus, and he their wise Hermogene. In a grievance Meshach is spokesman, but in the case of a disagreement arising, the master's wrath falls always, somehow, on one of the others. When pay-day comes, Meshach sits familiarly in the verandah with the regular retainers of the household; while Shadrach and Abednego await their wages at a distance, standing foolishly in the sun. Abednego is a man of great physical power, and of something less than average intelligence. He is noisy at times, and may be heard quarrelling with the bheesty who comes to fill the tattie-pots, or grumbling when no one appears to relieve him at the right moment. But altogether he is a harmless animal, turning his hand cheerfully to other work than his own, and even rising to a joke with the gardener. But Meshach holds him in subjection.

But the hot day is passing. The sun is going down the hill, but yet not so fast as to explain the sudden gloom which relieves the sky. In the west has risen a brown cloud, and the far trees tell of a rising wind. It nears swiftly, driving before it a flock of birds. The wind must be high, for the kite cannot keep its balance, and attempts in vain to beat up against it. The crow yields to it without a struggle, and goes drifting eastward; the small birds shoot right and left for shelter. It is a dust-storm. The brown cloud has now risen well above the trees, and already the garden is aware of its approach. You can hear the storm gathering up its rustling skirts for a rush through the tree-tops. And on a sudden it sweeps up with a roar, embanked in fine clouds of dust, and strikes the house. At once every door bursts open or shuts to, the servants shout, the horses in the stables neigh, and while the brief hurricane is passing a pall lies upon the place. Out of windows the sight is limited to a few yards, beyond which may be only mistily made out the forms of strong trees bowing before the fierce blast, with their boughs all streaming in one direction. The darkness is like that mysterious murk which rested on the fabled land of Hannyson — "alle covered with darkness withouten any brightnesse or light: so that no man may see ne heren ne no man dar entren in to hem. And natheless thei of the Contree sey that some tyme men heren voys of Folk and Hors nyzenge and Cokkes crowynge. And men witen well that men dwellen there, but knowe not what men." Hark! there *are* voices of folk; from the stables comes the " nyzenge of hors," from the direction of the fowl-house a " voys of cokkes crowynge," and the murk of Hannyson is over all. As suddenly as it came the storm has gone. The verandahs are full of dead leaves, the tattie-door has fallen, and a few tiles are lying on the ground; but the dust-storm has passed on far ahead and is already on the river. Out upon the Ganges the sudden rippling of the water, the brown haze beyond the bank, have warned the native steersman to make for the land. Over his head sweep and circle the anxious river-fowl, the keen-winged terns and piping sand-birds, the egret and the ibis; and as his skiff nears the shore he sees a sudden hurrying on all the large vessel-decks, hears the cries of the boatmen as they hasten to haul down the clumsy sails, and in another minute his own boat is rocking about and bumping among the others. The dust-storm travels quickly. Between the banks is sweeping up the sand-laden wind, concealing from the huddled boats the temples and the *ghat* across the river, the bridge that spans it, and the sky itself. But only for a minute, for almost before the river has had time to ruffle into waves the storm has passed, and the Ganges is flowing as quietly as ever.

For a while the air is cooler, but the sun has not been blown out, and Parthian-like he shoots his keenest arrows in retreat. And as the shadows lengthen along the ground the heat changes from that of a bonfire to that of an oven. When the sun is in mid-heaven we recognize the justice of the heat, abhor it as we may. The sun is hot. But when he has gone, we resent the accursed legacy of stifling heat he leaves us. His posthumous calor is intolerable. It chokes the breath by its dead intensity, like the fell atmosphere that hung round the dragon-daughter of Ypocras in her bedevilled castle in the Isle of Colos.

A wind makes pretense of blowing, but while it borrows heat from the ground, it does not lend it coolness. The city, however, is abroad again. Children go by with their nurses; the shops are doing business. In the bazaars the every-day crowd is noisy, along the roads the red-aproned bheesties sprinkle their feeble handfuls, and the world is out to enjoy such pleasures as it may on May-day "in the plains." In the country the peasant is brisk again, and trudges away from his work cheerily; bands of women affect to make merry with discordant singing as they pass along the fields; the miry cattle are being herded in the villages. And in the garden the birds assemble to say good-night. They are all in the idlest of humors, and, their day's work over, are sauntering about in the air and from tree to tree, or congregating in vagrom do-nothing crowds — the elders idle, the younger mischievous. In birddom the crows take the place of gamins, and spend the *mauvais quart d'heure* in vexing their betters. An old kite, tired with his long flights and sulky under the grievance of a shabbily-filled stomach, crouches on the roof, his feathers ruffled about him. He is not looking for food; it is getting too late, and he knows that in half an hour his place will be taken by the owls, and that before long the jackals will be trying to worry a supper off the bones which he scraped for his breakfast. But the crow is in no humor for sentiment. He has stolen during the day, and eaten, enough to make memory a joy forever. On his full stomach he grows

pert, and in his vulgar street-boy fashion, affronts the
ill-fed bird of prey. With a wily step he approaches
him from behind and pulls at his longest tail-feather,
or, sidling alongside, pecks at an outstretched wing.
Even when inactive, his simple presence worries the
kite, for he cannot tell what his tormentor is devising.
But he has not long to wait, for the crow, which from a
foot off has been derisively studying the kite in silence,
suddenly opens his mouth, and utters a cry of warning.
The chattering garden is hushed, small birds escape to
shelter, the larger fly up into the air, or on to the highest coigns of vantage, and look round for the enemy.
The crow, encouraged by success, again warns the
world, and his brethren come flocking round, anxious to
pester something, but not quite certain as to the danger
that threatens. But the crow is equal to the occasion,
and by wheeling in a circle round the inoffensive kite,
and making a sudden swoop towards it, points out to
them the object of his feigned terror. At once his cue
is taken, and with a discord of cries, to which Pisani's
angry barbiton in the story of *Zanoni* was music, they
surround the sulking bird. It seems as if at every
swoop they would strike the crouching kite from his
perch, but they know too well to tempt the curved beak,
the curved talons, and though approaching near they
never touch him. The kite has only to make the motion
of flight, and his tormentors widen their circles. But
he cannot submit to the indignity long, and slowly unfolding his wide wings, the carrion-bird launches himself
upon the air. Meanwhile the sparrows are clubbing
under the roof, and their discussions are noisy. The
mynas pace the lawn, exchanging commonplaces with
their fellows by their side, or those who pass homeward

overhead. The little birds are slipping into the bushes, where they will pass the hours of sleep; while from everywhere come the voices of Nature making arrangements for the night.

One little bird closes the day with a song of thanks. He is a sweet little songster — do you know him? — a dapper bird, dressed, as a gentleman should be in the evening, in black and white, with a shapely figure, a neatly turned tail, and all the gestures of a bird of the world. Choosing a low bough, one well leafed, he screens himself from the world, and for an hour pours out upon the hot evening air a low, sweet, throbbing song. He appears to sing unconsciously: his notes run over of their own accord, without any effort. The bird rather thinks aloud in song than sings. I have seen him warbling in the wildest, poorest corner, the knuckle-end of the garden. At first I thought he was all alone. But soon I saw sitting above him, with every gesture of interested attention, two crested bulbuls, the nightingales of Hafiz. They were listening to the little solitary minstrel, recognizing in the pied songster a master of their song. And so he went on singing to his pretty audience until the moon began to rise. And with a sudden rush from behind the citrons' shade the night-jar tumbled out upon the evening air.

II.

THE RAINS.

"And the rain it raineth every day."
Twelfth Night.

FOR many weeks there had been nothing doing, — a piping time of heat, when the sun and the moon divided the twenty-four hours between them. But all that has been changed, and on Monday came the rain. At first only wind. But I had heard the jack-tree whispering of what was coming, and among the plantains I saw that there was a secret hatching — and then on a sudden came the strong gust, rain-heralding. The wind came sweeping up, clearing the way for the rain that was close behind, and then the rain, on the earth that was gasping for it, descended in great, round, solemn drops.

And how suddenly did all nature become aware of the change! The grateful earth sent up in quick response its thanks in a scent as fragrant to us in India as is the glorious bouquet of the hay-fields at home. The joyous birds flitted here and there, hymning the bursting of the monsoon, and all the dusty trees broke out into laughing green. The swallow came down from the clouds to hawk among the shrubs, for a strange insect world was abroad, the sudden rain having startled into uncustomary daylight the night-loving moth and the feeble swarm that peoples the crepuscule. The young parrots, insolent though tailless, revelled among the neem-trees' harsh berries, while from the softened earth, in spite of the falling rain, the mynas were busy pulling out the carelessly jocund worms. Even the wretched babblers, who had hoped to raise a second brood of young, and whose nest has in an hour become a dripping pulp, hopped, and not unmirthfully, about. The peacocks came out and danced. Even the crow was festive. But the rain that washed the aloes clean has also soaked out from their lair among them the ringed snakes, so the mungoose is holding high carnival. But hark! Already a frog?—yes, a shrivelled batrachian who, for many sun-plagued weeks had been lying by in a dusty waterpipe, feels suddenly the rush of warm rain-water, and his dusty, shrunken shell is carried out into the aqueduct. With reviving strength he stems the tide, and is soon safely on the bank. Can it be true? and he plunges into the living water again, his shrivelled body—like that curious Rose of Jericho—plumping out as it greedily absorbs the grateful liquid; and soon the lean and wretched frog, whom a week ago a hungry crow would have scorned to eat (though a stomach-denying crow is as rare as a Parsee beggar), becomes the same bloated monster in yellow and green that last year harassed us with his importunate demonstrations of pleasure. "And for als moche as" he has thus cheaply attained to respectability, he is inflated with pride. Mandeville thanked God with humility for the keeping of the good company of many lords, but the frog unasked thrusts himself and his amours upon our notice, holding with the Saracens that man is only the younger brother of swine. We welcome the rain, but could do well without the frogs.

"The croaking of frogs," said Martin Luther at his table, "edifies nothing at all; it is mere sophistry and fruitless;" and indeed I wish we were without these vile batrachians. It is not to me at all incredible that the Abderites should have gone into voluntary exile rather than share their country unequally with frogs.

In all "the majesty of mud" they crouch on the weedy bank, croaking proudly to their dames below, who, their speckled bodies concealed, rest their chins upon the puddle-top, croaking in soft reply. Was ever lady wooed with such damp, disheartening circumstance, — the night dark, the sky filled with drifting clouds, a thin rain falling? Round the puddle's sloppy edge — the puddle itself a two hours' creation — has sprouted up a rank fringe of squashy green-stuff, and in this the moist lover serenades the fair. She would listen flabbily to his beguilements all night long, but suddenly round the corner comes a dog-cart. His position might be heroic, certainly it is ridiculous. Shall he die at his post, be crushed by a whirling wheel for her he loves, or shall he — get out of the way? The earth shakes below the cavalier; this is no time to hesitate; shall he move? *Yes;* and plop! within an inch of his charmer's nose he has landed in the puddle. But such accidents are infrequent; the cavalier, we regret to know, generally serenades all night. By day he sleeps beneath a stone, fitting himself into a dry hole, — for frogs dare not go out in the daytime. Crows trifle with them, spit them on their black beaks, and perhaps eat them. Cats, too, will amuse themselves with frogs; even the more chivalrous dog will not disdain to bite a frog when he comes suddenly upon one round a corner. In the evening, however, he takes his hops abroad, makes his meal of ants, and starts off to the nearest place of pleasure. Shall it be the municipal tank, — the public assembly-rooms, — where the company, though numerous, is very mixed; or some private *soirée musicale*, where the company is select, and the risks of interruption fewer? His journey is not without its peculiar perils. What if, by mistake, he jumps down the well? the one in which live only those two old gentlemen, wretched bachelors, who, sallying forth one night — just such a night as this — to serenade a fair one, mistook their way, saw water glistening, thought they heard her voice, and plumped down twenty feet. They never got out again, and there they are to this day, old and childless; their croak is sullen and defiant, for they are down a deep well, and can't get out. "It *is* enough to sour one's temper," acknowledges our frog; and he goes forth delicately, looking before he leaps. "Living in such a world, I seem to be a frog abiding in a dried-up well." The Upanishad contains no happier illustration than this.

How the rain pours down! A wall, beneath which he has rested to croak awhile, cracks, gapes, and falls. By a miracle and a very long jump he escapes; but his jump has landed him in the lively rivulet which is now swirling down the middle of the road, and so, before he can draw his legs up or collect his thoughts, he is rolled along with sticks and gravel into a ditch, sucked into a water-pipe, squirted out at the other end, received by a rushing drain, and, ere he can extricate himself, is being whirled along towards the river, where live the barbarous paddy-bird and the ruthless adjutant-crane. Better, he thinks, that the wall had fallen on him. But if he does get safe to his friends, with what gusto is he hailed! At his first note the company becomes aware of a strange presence, and in silence they receive his second; and then they recognize his voice, and with redoubled volume the chorus recommences — for the night.

One of the twenty-one hells of Manu is filled with mud. I believe it to be for the accommodation of frogs.

The insect world, which during the hot weather was held in such small account, now holds itself supreme. Convinced themselves that entomology is the finest study in the world, the insects carry their doctrine at their tails' point to convince others. Every one must learn and be quite clear about the difference between a black mosquito with grey spots, and a grey mosquito with black spots. There must be no confusion between a fly which stings you if you touch it, and a fly which if it touches you stings. No one can pretend to ignore the insect invaders — the bullety beetles and maggoty ants. Nobody can profess to do so. It is impossible to appear unconscious of long-legged terrors that silently drop on your head, or shiny, nodular ones that rush at your face and neck with a buzz in the steamy evenings in the rains. A tarantula on the towel-horse, especially if it is standing on tiptoe, is too palpable, and no one can pretend not to see it there. Spiders weighing an ounce, however harmless, are too big and too puffy to be treated with complete indifference. Then there is a pestilent animal resembling a blackbeetle, with its head a good deal pulled off, having fishhooks at the ends of its legs, with which it grips you, and will not let go. Centipedes, enjoying a luxury of legs, (how strange that they are not proud!) think nothing, a mere trifle at most, of leaving all their toes sticking behind them when they run up your legs. It is an undecided point whether the toes do not grow new centipedes; at any rate the centipede grows new toes. Ridiculous round beetles tumble on their backs and scramble and slide about the dinner-table till they get a purchase on the cruet-stand, up which they climb in a deliberate and solemn manner, and having reached the top, go forthwith headlong into the mustard. Sometimes they get out again unperceived, but an irregular track of mustard on the cloth, with a drop wherever the beetle stopped to take breath, leads to the discovery of the wanderer sitting among the salad and pretending to be a caper. Then again there are oval beetles, which never tumble on their backs, but dart about so quickly that you are uncertain whether something did or did not go into the soup, until you find them at the bottom. Many other insects come to the festive board, unbidden guests; grasshoppers, with great muscular powers, but a deplorable lack of direction; minute money-spiders that drop from your eyebrows by a thread which they make fast to your nose; flimsy-winged flies that are always being singed, and forthwith proceed to spin round on their backs and hum in a high key; straw-colored crickets that sit and twiddle their long antennæ at you as if they never intended moving again, and then suddenly launch themselves with a jerk into your claret; fat, comfortable-bodied moths, with thick, slippery wings, which bang *phut-phut* against the ceiling, until they succeed in dropping themselves down the chimney of the lamp. All these, however, are the ruck, the rabble, the tag-rag and bob-tail that follow the leader — the white ant. The white ant! What an enormous power this insect wields, and how merciless it is in the exercise of it! Here the houses may not have gardens, there the builder must use no wood. In this place people have to do without carpets, and in that without a public park. Everything must be of metal, glass, or stone that rests on the ground even for a few hours, or when you return to it, it will be merely the shell of its former self. Ruthless, omnivorous, the white ant respects nothing. And when in the rains it invades the house, what horrors supervene! The lamps are seen through a yellow haze of fluttering things; the side-board is strewn with shed wings; the night-lights sputter in a paste of corpses, and the corners of the rooms are alive with creeping, fluttering ants, less destructive, it is true, than in the "infernal wriggle of maturity," but more noisome because more bulky and more obtrusive. The novelty of wings soon palls upon the white ants; they find they are a snare, and try to get rid of them as soon as possible. They have not forgotten the first few minutes of their winged existence, when they were drifting on the wind with birds all round them, when so many of their brothers and sisters disappeared with a snap of a beak, and when they themselves were only saved from the same fate by being blown into a bush. From this refuge they saw their comrades pouring out of the hole in the mud wall, spreading their weak, wide wings, giving themselves up to the wind, — which gave them up to the kites wheeling and recurving amongst the fluttering swarm, to the crows, noisy and coarse even at their food, to the quick-darting mynas, and the graceful, sliding king-crow. A mungoose on the bank made frequent raids upon the unwinged crowd that clustered at the mouth of the hole, keeping an eye the while on the kites, which ever and anon, with the easiest of curves, but the speed of a crossbow bolt, swooped at him as he vanished into his citadel. Overhead sat a vulture in the sulks, provoked at having been persuaded to come to catch ants ["Give me a good wholesome cat out of the river"], and wondering that the kites could take the trouble to swallow such small morsels. But the vulture is alone in his opinion if he thinks that white ants are not an important feature of the rains. The fields may blush green, and jungles grow, in a week, but unless the white ants and their allies — hard-bodied and soft-bodied — come with the new leaves, the rains would hardly be the rains.

RAINING! and apparently not going to stop. The trees are all standing in their places quiet as whipped children, not a leaf daring to stir while the thunder grumbles and scolds. Now and again comes up a blast of wet wind, driving the rain into fine spray before it and shaking all the garden. The bamboos are taken by surprise, and sway in confusion here and there; but, as the wind settles down to blow steadily, their plumed boughs sway in graceful unison. The tough teak-tree hardly condescends to acknowledge the stirring influence, and flaps its thick leaves lazily; the jamun is fluttered from crown to stem; the feathery tamarinds are shivering in consternation, and, panic-stricken, the acacias toss about their tasselled leaves. There is something almost piteous in the way the plantain receives the rude wind. It throws up its long leaves in an agony, now drops them down again in despair, now flings them helplessly about. But it is not often that there is high wind with the rain. Generally there is only rain, — very much. The birds knew what was coming when they saw the drifting clouds being huddled together, and the air has been filled this hour past with their warning cries. They have now gone clamorous home. The green parrots, birds of the world as they are, went over long ago, screaming and streaming by. The crows, too, after casting about for a nearer shelter, have flung themselves across the sky towards the hospitable city. But after a long interval come by the last birds, who have dawdled over that "one worm more" too long, calling out as they pass to their comrades far ahead to wait for them; and then, after another while, comes "the very last bird," — for when the storm is at its worst, there is always one more to pass, flying too busily to speak, and scudding heavily across the sloping rain. The young crow meant to have seen the storm out, and so he kept his seat on the roof, and in the insolence of his glossy youth rallied his old relatives escaping from the wet; but a little later, as he flapped his spongy wings ruefully homeward, he regretted that he had not listened to the voice of experience. For the rain is raining, — raining as if the water were tired of the world's existence, — raining as if the rain hated the earth with its flowers and fruits.

And now the paths begin to show how heavy the fall is. On either side runs down a fussy stream, all pitted with rain-spot dimples, from which the larger stones jut out like pigmy Teneriffes in a mimic Atlantic; but the rain still comes down, and the two fussy streams soon join into a shallow, smoothly flowing sheet, and there is nothing from bank to bank but water-bubbles hurrying down; yet, haste as they may, they get their crowns broken by the rain-drops before they reach the corner. And now you begin to suspect rain on the sunken lawn; but before long there is no room for mere suspicion, for the level water is showing white through the green grass, in which the shrubs stand ankle-deep. How patiently the flowers wait in their ditches, bending their poor heads to the ground, and turning up their green calices to be pelted! But besides the trees and flowers and washed-out insects, there are but few creatures out in the rain. Here comes a seal carrying a porpoise on his back. No! it is our friend the bheesty. Dripping like a seaweed, a thing of all weathers, he splashes by through the dreary waste of waters like one of the pre-Adamite creatures in the Period of Sludge. Who can want water at such a time as this? you feel inclined to ask, as the shiny bheesty, bending under his shiny water-skin, squelches past, his red apron, soaked to a deep maroon, clinging to his knees. A servant remembers something left out of doors, and with his master's wrath very present to him, detaches his mouth from the hookah bowl, and with his foolish skirts tucked round his waist, paddles out into the rain, showing behind his plaited umbrella like a toadstool on its travels. A young pariah dog goes by less dusty and less miserable than usual. The rain has taken much of the curl out of his tail, but he is, and he knows it, safer in the rain. There are no buggies passing now, from beneath whose hoods, as the vivid lightning leaps out of the black clouds, will leap sharp whip-lashes, curling themselves disagreeably round his thin loins, or tingling across his pink nose. There are no proud carriages with arrogant drivers to be rude to him. if he stands still for a minute in the middle of the road to think; no older dogs on the watch to dispute, and probably to ravish from him, his infrequent treasure trove. The worms, too, like the rain, for they can creep easily over the slab ground, opening and shutting up their bodies like telescopes. The dank frogs doat on it. They hop impatiently out, albeit in a stealthy way, from clammy corners, behind pillars, and under flower-pots, to see if their ditches are filling nicely, and hop back happy.

When it rains there are, to those inside the house, two sounds, a greater and a less, and it is curious, and very characteristic of our humanity, that the less always seems the greater. The one is the great dead sound of falling water — the out-of-doors being rained upon — almost too large to hear. The other is the splashing of our eaves. Outside, the heavens are falling in detail, but the sound comes to us only in its great expanse, more large than loud, heard only as a vast mutter. At our verandah's edge is a poor spout noisily spurting its contents upon the gravel-path, and yet it is only to our own poor spout that we give heed. If it gives a sudden spurt, we say, "How it is raining! just listen" — *to the spout.* The sullen roar of the earth submitting to the rain we hardly remark. We listen to the patch of plantains complaining of every drop that falls upon them, but take no note of the downward rush of water on the long-suffering, silent grass. But when it is raining be so good as to remark the ducks. They are being bred for your table, a private speculation of the cook's, but they are never fed, so they have to feed themselves. Dinner deferred maketh ducks mad, so they sally forth in a quackering series to look for worms. Nevertheless they loiter to wash. Was ever enjoyment more thorough than that of ducks accustomed to live in a cook-house (in the corner by the stove) who have been let out on a rainy day? They can hardly waddle for joy, and stagger past, jostling each other with ill-balanced and gawky gestures. And now they have reached the water. How they bob their heads and plume their feathers, turning their beaks over their backs and quackering in subdued tones! In their element they grow courageous, for the communist crow who has left his shelter to see "what on earth those ducks can have got," and who has settled near them, is promptly charged, beak lowered, by the drake, who waggles his curly tail in pride as the evil fowl goes flapping away.

But let the ducks quacker their short lives out in the garden puddles — the carrion crow is off to the river, for the great river is in flood, and many a choice morsel, it knows, is floating down to the sea. Videlicet the succulent kid; guinea-fowls surprised on their nests by the sudden water; young birds that had sat chirping for help on bush and stone as the flood rose up and up, the parent birds fluttering round, powerless to help and wild with protracted sorrow; snakes which hiding in their holes had hoped to tire out the water, but which, when the banks gave way, were swept struggling out into the current; the wild cat's litter, which the poor mother with painful toil had carried into the deepest cranny of the rock, drowned in a cluster, and floating down the river to the muggurs.[1]

The muggur is a gross pleb, and his features stamp him low-born. His manners are coarse. The wading heifer has hardly time to utter one terror-stricken groan ere she is below the crimson-bubbled water. Woe to the herdsman if he leads his kine across the ford. The water-fowl floating on the river, the patient ibis, the grave sarus-cranes, fare ill if they tempt the squalid

[1] Broad-snouted crocodile.

brute. The ghurial[1] is of a finer breed. Living in the water he seeks his food in it, and does not flaunt his Maker with improvidence by wandering on the dry earth in search of sustenance. But at times the coarse admixture of his blood shows out, and he imitates his vulgar cousin in lying by the water's edge, where the grazing kine may loiter, the weary peasant be trudging unobservant towards his home, his little son gathering drift-wood along the flood-line as he goes.

And the flood is out over the gardens and fields. Out on the broad lagoon, the gray-white kingfisher, with its shrill cry, is shooting to and fro where yesterday the feeble-winged thrush-babblers were wrangling over worms: the crocodile rests his chin on the grass-knoll where a few hours ago two rats were sporting. See the kingfisher, — how he darts from his watch-tower, checks suddenly his forward flight, starts upwards for a moment, hovering over the water with craning neck. And now his quick-beating wings close, and straight as a falling aërolite he drops, his keen, strong beak cleaving the way before him. And with what an exultant sweep he comes up, with the fish across his bill! The kingfisher is too proud to blunder: if he touches the water he strikes his prey; but rather than risk failure, he swerves when in his downward course to swerve had seemed impossible, and skimming the ruffled surface goes back to his watch-tower. He would not have his mate on the dead branch yonder see him miss his aim; rather than hazard discomfiture he simulates contempt, turning back with a cheery cry to her side, while the lucky fishlet darts deep among the weeds.

The great river is in flood. "Oh, Indra the Rain-

[1] Sharp-snouted crocodile.

giver, by all thy Vedic glories, we invoke thee, be merciful!" Miles down they will know it by the sudden rush, — the bridges of boats that will part asunder, and the clumsy, high-prowed native craft that will sink; but here, where the mischief has its source, where the heavy rain is falling and the deluge brewing, there is nothing to mark the change. But the river swells up secretly, as it were, from underneath. The flood is to be a surprise; and lo! suddenly, the water is spread out on either side, over crops and grass fields. Where are the islands gone on which the wiseacre adjutant-birds were yesterday promenading? Are those babool-trees or fishermen's platforms out yonder in the middle of the river? Surely there used to be a large field hereabouts with a buffalo's whitened skull lying in the corner, and a young mango-tree growing about the middle of it? Can that be the mango-tree yonder where the current takes a sudden swerve? Alas for the squirrels that had their nest in it! Alas for the vagrant guinea-fowl which far from home had hidden her speckled eggs in the tall tussock of sharp-edged grass which grew by the buffalo skull!

Those two villages yonder were yesterday separated only by a green valley streaked by a hundred footpaths; they now look at each other across a lake. The kine used to know their way home, but are puzzled. Here, they feel certain, is the tree at which yesterday they turned to the right, and this is the path which led them down a hill and up another, but it ends to-day in water! How cautiously they tread their way, sinking lower, lower — so gradually that we can hardly tell that they have begun to swim; but there is now a rod and more between the last cow and the shore where the herdsman stands watching. He sees them climb out on the other side, one behind the other, sees their broad backs sloped against the hill before him. Then they reach the top and lowing break into a trot, disappearing gladly behind the mud walls which contain their food; and the herdsman turns and trudges the circuit of the invading water.

One year the Ganges and the Jumna conspired together to flood the province, and suddenly swelling over their banks, desolated in a night half the busy city of Allahabad. We brought our boat up to the new lagoons, and for a whole day sailed about among nameless islands, great groves of bird-deserted trees, and the ruins of many villages, amid scenes as strange and as beautiful as we shall ever see again. The Máruts, armed with their hundred-jointed bolts, and the storm-god Peru, of the thunder-black hair and beard of lightning-gold, who goes rumbling over the midnight clouds astride a millstone — and all the little hearth-spirits quake at his going and fear falls upon the house — had been abroad for many days. And the river-gods were up at their bidding, and the clouds poured into the rivers, and the rivers drove down to the sea. And before the pitiless rush of the flood, what difference between man and beast? All of them rats alike, poor creeping folk, flooded out of their holes. The same wind and rain tore the crow's nest from the tree and the roof from the native's hut; the same flood carried the two away together. The tiger, the man, and the woodlouse were all on one platform, and that which crept highest was the best among them.

Starting in our boat from the spot where once four cross-roads had met, we crossed over towards the belt of trees that hides the city from sight as you look westward. Deep down beneath us, patient crops of millet were standing in their places, waiting for the water to pass away; acres of broad-leafed melons looked up at our boat as we wound in and out among the trees and little temples. With some thirty feet of water below us we floated over the brickfields and came to a village, and, skirting the ruins of the suburbs, passed out again through a tope of mango-trees into the open. A garden lay before us. The pillars of the gateway had strange animals upon the tops of them, rampant against shields; but in the flood they looked as if they were standing tiptoe upon their hind legs in the hope of keeping out of the water which lapped over their clawed feet. Over the wall and into the garden. Such a place for Naiads! The tops of plantain-trees instead of lotus-pads, for bulrushes bamboo spikes, and instead of water-tangle the fair green crowns of bushes, lit up with blossoms. Rustling through the guava-tops, half-ripened citrons knocking against our boat's keel, we pass out over the other wall of the garden, and found ourselves in a superb canal, avenued on either side with tamarinds, their lowest branches dipping in the flood, and closed in at the further end with a handsome pleasure-house that stood — the only building, except the stone-built temples, that had braved the rush of the escaping river — knee-deep in the water. The scene had all the charms of land and water, without the blemishes of either; for the water had no vulgar banks, no slimy slopes nor leprous sand-patches; while the houses had no lower stories, and the round crowns of foliage no unsightly trunks. And there was not a human being in sight! River terns swept in and out among the garden trees, furrowing the new water-fields with their orange bills, and resting, when tired, upon the painted balconies of the pleasure-house.

And we rowed past the dwarfed walls with the dreary, pleasant sound of the flood lapping against them, and passed down the stately reach of water till we came to the beautiful temple of Mahadeva, that lifts up its crown of maroon and gold high out of the solemn hush of the trees among which its foundations lie. A golden god glittered at the point — a star to the people. The gate was closed, but as we lay on our oars before it, there came, on the sudden from within, the clanging of the temple bell, that through all the year rings in every hour of night or day! Who was pulling the bell? A merman? Perhaps, forsaken by all his priests, the god himself! We shouted. A tern was startled by the shout, and an owl fell out of a hole in the wall; but there was no reply. Another shout, however, was answered — was it a human voice? — and then we heard the unseen bell-ringer swimming to the gate. It opened after much trouble and splashing, and we floated into the enclosure, came into the Lake of Silence, our guide swimming alongside. What a strangely sacred place it seemed, this temple to Mahadeva! Up to its terrace in water, the marble bulls *couchant* in the flood, on which floated here and there the last votive marigolds thrown before the god, the shrine was the very emblem of Faith, as it reared its glittering crown skyward up above the creeping, treacherous water, — in the hands of the Philistines perhaps, but the Samson nevertheless, — its feet in the toils, but head erect to heaven. We all talked in a more or less maudlin way, for sentiment made a fool of each in turn. But no one of us who saw it can forget that strange Indian scene. The gracious water sparkled from wall

to wall of the small enclosure, concealing all the dirt
of the common earth, and all that was impure or
unsightly round the foot of the temple. The flowering
bushes rested their blossoms on the water, and the shrubs
showed only their green crowns. The squalor and
clamor of an Indian temple were all gone, and in their
stead was the cleansing, mock-reverent water and the
silence of Dreamland. The glamour of the place was
strange beyond words. For sound there was only the
plash of the water-bird's wing, and the rhythmic lapping
of the flood against the balconades. For the view, it was
hemmed in by the tree-tops that overlooked the enclosure
on all four sides. But within the small area was all that
enchantment needed. It was Fairyland, with only a
bright summer's sun shining upon every thing to remind
us of the every-day earth. But suddenly the bell rang
again. Fairyland or not, the hours were passing. So
we floated out of the doorway again into the exquisite
water-road, and sailed away. Look where we would,
water, water, water, margined and broken by groves of
trees, with here and there a suspicion of ruined houses
from which now and again came wailing along the water
the cry of some deserted dog. But nothing of every-day
life! Where were the villages, with their cracked mud
walls? the loitering natives, the roads and their dusty
traffic? the creeping, creaking bullock-carts, and the
jingling ekkas, baboo-laden? There were no parrot-
ravaged crops, no muddy buffaloes, no limping, sneaking
pariah dogs to remind us of India. Even the kites, sailing in great circles above the broad sunlit water, did not
seem the same birds that a few days before wheeled in
hopes of offal round the village. The vulture on the
palm-top was a very Jatayus among vultures. Where

were we then but in Dreamland? A solitary palm — do you remember how Xerxes went out of his way with his army to do homage to the great plane-tree that queened it in the desert alone? — attracted us, and we sailed for it. All great trees grow alone. This one was standing between two round little islands bright with young grass, so close and clean that they looked like green velvet footstools for some giant's use. Their shores were fringed with drift-wood and strange jetsam, among which bobbed up and down some great round palm-fruit; and on the top of each island sat a solitary crow. They had come, no doubt, from Kurghalik, the capital (so Thibetan legends say) of crowdom. At any rate, they were Dreamland crows. They were less criminal in appearance than earth crows; they did not insult us by word or gesture, for they did not caw once; nor, when we approached, did they sidle or hop sideways. Some of my readers may not easily believe in such a revolution of crow nature, but those take high ground who maintain that no change of character, however violent, is impossible. Did not Alcibiades the volupt become a Spartan for the nonce! Remember Saul of Tarsus.

As we landed, one crow raised itself with all the dignity of a better bird, and with three solemn flaps passed over to the central top of the farther island; and when we went there to take possession of it also " in the Queen's name," both of them flapped with three strokes back to the first. And we christened one island Engedi, for we remembered Holy Writ, " exalted as the palm-tree in Engedi;" and the other we called the Loochoo Island, for Loochoo means in Japanese, " the Islet in a Waste of Waters " — a great deal for a word to mean, but true nevertheless. Humpty-

Dumpty would have called it a "portmanteau word." And we gave the crows commissions as Lieutenant-Governors from Her Majesty Queen Victoria, *quamdiu se bene gesserint*. And then we went on to another island, a long one with a tree in the middle. And under the tree stood a white calf, so we knew at once that this was a water-calf. For there was no land it could have come from within sight, and no human being but ourselves within a mile of it on either side. And at night when thieves bring their boats to steal what they consider quite an ordinary calf, deserted, they think, by its owner when the swift flood overtook him, the calf no doubt dives under the water, and thus evades them.

The rest of the islands were deserted. The ruins of houses and temples, waist-deep in water, showed that within recent times there had been inhabitants of this strange and beautiful archipelago. Icthyophagi no doubt. There was nothing else for them to eat. But just now the birds were alone. All round us the king-fishers (long may ye live before ye become poor men's barometers!) poised in the air, and, wild as the cry of the wild ass in the Bikanir deserts, came to us the scream of the fishing-hawk. But no — the birds were not alone. The flood had driven from the earth its multitude of creeping folk: snakes hung across the forks of trees, or basked on the branches; centipedes crawled upon floating rubbish; and many bushes were black to every tip with thronging ants. In one tree-hollow we surprised strange company — a pair of gorgeous dhaman snakes, three bran-new centipedes bright as copper, a most villainous-looking spider, and a gem of a frog, a little metallic creature that showed among the foul crew like the maiden among Comus's companions. We disturbed them rudely, and then went in pursuit of a bandicoot that was swimming to an unwonted roost — poor wretch! — in a citron tree. A little bird was sitting on a bush, scratching its head, its day's work over, and thinking of nothing in particular; but a hawk that had had no dinner came by, and gave it something to think about. A pariah dog had a litter upon a patch of tiles, all that remained of a house-roof, and we rescued the starveling brute. A rat floated by in a sieve: another was cruising more dryly in a gourd. Look at that squirrel! The imposture is out. So long as he had the firm earth to fall back upon, he lived bravely enough in the trees; but now that he has only the trees, he is starving. The "tree squirrel" forsooth! But was there no Isis or Osiris, no Apis of the "awful front," nor dog-headed Anubis to tell it that the floods were coming? In Egypt some one tells the crocodiles every year how high the Nile will rise; for let the sourceless river rise never so much, the great suarian's eggs are always found above the reach of the highest wave. But the squirrel without the ground is better off than a grasshopper without grass to hop in: it is then a poor thing indeed. One hopped into our boat — a desperate leap for life — such as egg-seekers take at the dangling rope on St. Kilda's face. I remember reading in Bacon that "the vigor of the grasshopper consists only in their voices." That they can make a noise out of all proportion to their size is true, but it seems to me that Bacon cast undeservedly a slur upon the "gaers toop." The particular grasshopper in point may have been a cripple, but, as a rule, the insect has a shrewd way of hopping that makes me think respectfully of his hind legs, and looking into the matter, I find I am borne out by Sir Thomas Browne, who says, " whereto [that is leaping] it is very well conformed, for therein the [grasshopper] the legs behind are longer than all the body, and make at the second joint acute angles at a considerable advancement above their bodies." Do not the French call the grasshopper *sauterelle*? A poor beetle with the shoulders of Atlas and the thighs of Hercules, which in dryer weather drove headlong through the solid earth, heaving great pebbles up as Enceladus heaves Etna, was sprawling helpless as a moth upon the water. We rescued Goliath and went on. A frog, great with rain-water and inordinately puffed up, sat pudgily on a stump. It narrowly escaped with life, for the sight of it enwrathed us. Had the floods then (a nation's history closing in a sudden stroke of picturesque fate) tragically closed an era, that a spotted frog might go comfortably? The Empire of Assyria expiring with the flames of Sardanapalus's pyre — Babylon poured out under the feet of the Mede with the wine along Belshazzar's palace floor — the Icthyophagi succumbing to the united wrath of a continent's mightiest rivers, and gone to feed the fish they fed on! All this that a gape-mouthed batrachian might give itself complacent airs! The earth submerged, the Caucasian a failure, and a frog happy! A deluge, whirling men and their houses away to the sea, to be a holiday and a Golden Age for a gross amphibian! The idea incensed us, and the frog was in a parlous state. But it escaped.

Meanwhile the sun is setting, and we turn homewards — home in the dusk. The terns are all gone, but in their place the flying-foxes flap heavily along the water, and the owls hail us from all the shadows. How appropriate to the owl are the words of the poet (to the nightingale) —

> " Sweet bird, that shunn'st the noise of folly,
> Most musical, most melancholy."

The very name too, *ooloo*, is a sweet symphony. The frogs jeered as we passed. One of us recalled the lines —

" You shall have most delightful melodies as soon as you lay to your oars.
" From whom?
" From swans — the frogs — wondrous ones."

And so through a chorus of exulting batrachians, home again to the solid earth, the noise of men, and the multitudinous chirping of birds.

III.

THE COLD WEATHER.

> "Ah! if to thee
> It feels Elysian, how rich to me,
> An exiled mortal, sounds its pleasant name!
> . . . .
> O let me cool me zephyr-boughs among!"
> *Endymion.*

CHRISTMAS EVE! Overhead is stretched the tent of heaven, and beneath the dome are ranged in full durbar the rajah-planets, attendant on them crowds of courtier-asteroids and stars. The durbar is assembled to welcome Christmas Day. The moon, the Viceroy of the day, presides, and all the feudatory luminaries of the empire are in their places, and the splendor of Hindoo Rájá or Mahomedan Nawáb is as nothing to that of Orion. How quiet all is! Not a whisper or a movement as the galaxy of night awaits the arrival of Christmas Day.

I was waiting for it too. The night seemed so still and calm that I felt as if somehow all the rest of the world had stolen away from their homes and gone somewhere, leaving me alone to represent Europe at this reception of Christmas. Not that there were no sounds near me. There was my pony munching gram very audibly, my servants' hookahs sounded more noisily than usual; the dogs under the tree were gnawing bones, and not far from me, crouching beside a fire of wood, three villagers were cleaning a leopard skin. On the jheel behind me the wild geese were settling with congratulatory clamor.

It is curious that those notes which, among birds, give expression to the unamiable feelings of anger and animosity, are more musical than the notes of love and pleasure. Among human beings no passion has evoked such sweet song as love. Among birds, however, the voice of love is more often wanting in sweetness. The bittern, when it calls to its mate, fills the dark reed-beds with the ghostliest sound that man has ever heard from the throat of a bird; the cluck of the wooing cock, that crows so grandly when aroused to wrath or jealousy, is ridiculous; the love-note of the bulbul is an inarticulate animal noise; the crow-pheasant, — who does not know the *whoo-whoo-whoo* with which this strange bird, hidden in the centre foliage of a tree, summons its brooding mate? The mynas, again, how curious and inappropriate are their love-notes! But show the bulbul another of his sex, and in a voice most musically sweet he challenges the intruder to battle. Look at that strident king-crow swinging on the bamboo's tip. A rival passes, and with a long-drawn whistle he slides through the air, and in melodious antiphony the strangers engage. Let the cock hear the lord of another seraglio emptying his lungs, and with what lusty harmony will he send him back the challenge!

Quite near me, too, the river was flowing over and among large stones, with a constant bubbling and occasional splash. But beyond the few yards lit by my camp-fires, in the great, pale, sleeping world, lit only by the cold stars, lying far and away beyond my tents, was a monochrome of silence.

And I sat at my tent-door smoking, smoking, thinking of the day I had passed, the days before that, and the days before them. Christmas Eve! In an hour all the bells in England will be ringing in the day; and, in one home at least, the little ones — an infrequent treat — will be sitting with firelit eyes and cheeks beside the fender, watching the chestnuts roast and the clock creep round to twelve. Yes; at home the children are sitting up, I know, to see Christmas Day in; and waiting, they grow tired. The moment arrives, the hand is at the hour, a chestnut is absorbing all attention; when on a sudden, with a clash from all the steeples, the mad bells fling out their music on the wild night. The great chestnut question is postponed, and, starting from the hearthrug, the little voices chime together, "A merry Christmas;" and then, with clamorous salutations, the kisses are exchanged, and, eager in conversation, the little ones climb upstairs to their cosy beds, the bells still clashing out on the keen winter air. And the old folks sit below, and, while the shivering Waits in the street are whining out their hideous thanksgiving, give one more thought to the year that is gone. And the last thought is always a sad one. For after all, on this planet of ours, Life, with its periods of hard work and its intervals of careless leisure, is happy enough. What though we do come into it with our miseries ready-made, and only the materials for our pleasures provided? Somehow I had fashioned my pleasures very much to my liking in the year that was gone, and as I looked back on it, there were few days, cold, hot, or rainy, that did not, now that they were dead, come back to me, as I sat there thinking, as pleasant memories.

Christmas Eve! no bells, no beef, no holly, no mistle-

toe nearer than the Himalayas! Christmas Eve without
a dance, without a single "merry Christmas" wish!
Christmas Eve and no chilblains, no miserable Waits,
no Christmas boxes or Christmas bills! well, well, —
the past is the past, a bitter sweet at best; let it pass.
Our Christmas Eve in India is a strange affair. Instead
of church-bells we have jackals, and instead of holly-
berries the weird moon-convolvulus. Look at the ghostly
creeper there, holding out its great dead-white moons of
blossom to beautify the owl's day. The natives in the
south of India have a legend, — the Legend of the Moon-
flower. There was once, they say, a maiden, exceedingly beautiful, and modest as she was beautiful. To
her the admiration of men was a sorrow from morning
to night, and her life was made weary with the impor-
tunities of her lovers. From her parents she could get
no help, for they only said, "Choose one of them for
your husband, and you will be left alone by the others."
From her friends she got less, for the men called her
heartless, and the woman said her coyness would be
abandoned before a suitor wealthier than her village
wooers. But how could they know that one evening,
soft and cool, as the maiden sat at her father's porch,
and there were no eyes near but the little owls' on the
roof and the fireflies' under the tamarinds, there had
come out from the guava-trees a stranger youth who
had wooed her and won her, and who, with a kiss on
her fair, upturned face, had sealed the covenant of their
love? But she knew it; and sitting, when the evenings
were soft and cool, at her father's porch, she waited for
the stranger's return. But he never came back; and
her life, sorely vexed by her lovers, became a burden
to her, and she prayed for help to the gods. And they,

in their pity for her, turned her into the great white moon-plant, which, clinging to her father's porch, still waits in the evenings with upturned face for the truant's kiss. For myself, I think they look like saucers. At all events, they are not, according to English tastes, the fit blossom of Christmas time. But then English tastes are not fit for Christmas time in India. The season of frost and ice and snow suggests to us fires, furs, and mulled port-wine; reminds us of skating on ice-covered ponds and dancing in holly-bright rooms. The Christmas bills are a skeleton to some; but even with the butcher, the baker, and the grocer dancing a cannibalic war-dance at the area-gate, there is hardly a home where Christmas is not "merry," and Hans Andersen's sexton, who struck the boy for laughing on Christmas Eve, is considered a prodigy of infamy. But "the cold weather," as we in India are pleased to call the months at the end and beginning of the year, does not suggest mirthfulness to our Aryan brother; it shrivels him up. Months ago, when the sun was killing the northern blood within us, the lizards lay happily basking on the hot stones, the coppery danais flitted at ease about the shrubs, above which the air of mid-day stood shimmering and tremulous with heat, and our Aryan brothers, stretched in the shade of tree and wall, were content with God's earth. But now that the crisp morning air lends vigor to English limbs, making home intolerable and a wild out-door life a necessity, the lizard has shrunk into a crack of the wall, the danais is hybernating, and our Aryan brother creeps about his daily avocations with the desiccated appearance of a frozen frog, or sits in dormouse torpidity with his knees about his ears. The revenge of the Briton is delicious to him, and in the cold weather he triumphs over the Aryan brother who in May and June was rustling comfortably in gauze and muslin. The morning ride or walk when the air is keen is to him (*pace* Charles Lamb!) as a passage of the Red Sea, every native an Egyptian; and he laughs, like King Olaf at the thin beggar, to see the wretched Hindoo, robbing his spare legs to protect his head, pass by silent with the misery of cold. At night he finds them curled into inconceivable spaces under their blankets, — and such blankets! a network of rough strings with hairs stretching across the interstices, the very ghosts of blankets, at which Witney would hold its woolly sides with laughter. And with many-folded cloths round his benumbed head, over all the blanket, the Hindoo walks deaf under your horse's nose, stands before your buggy-wheels like a frostbitten paddy-bird. The Tamils call the paddy-bird the "blind idiot." On a December morning the pompous chuprassie has no more self-respect than a sparrow or a hill sheep,[1] and a child may play with a constable as men handle a hybernating cobra. The fat bunyas are no more seen lolling beneath their shameeanas; the Hindoo, in short, is "occultated."

In the shop yonder, where earthen vessels are sold, — a shilling would buy the whole stock-in-trade, — with the walls festooned with chalky-surfaced chillums, the floor piled high with clay pots, sits the owner, frozen and voluminously swathed. He is not proud of his shop; there is none of the assumption of the thriving merchant

---

[1] A flock of hill sheep will meet at a corner of the zigzag path a burdened pony, and the leader of them will turn aside. Soon the woolly tribe are in headlong flight down the steep hillside, and the tattoo, astonished at his own importance, passes on in sole possession of the scanty way.

about him. He is too cold to concern himself about his wares, for when his neighbors want pots they will, he knows, come to him; if they do not want pots, advertisements and invitations are thrown away. Shouting is a mere waste of carbon. So he spends his mornings perched on the edge of his threshold, polishing his chattering teeth with a stick, and rinsing his mouth from the brass lotah beside him. In the next house there are no wares to sell, but in the centre, on a rag of carpet, sits a puffy man, painting, with much facial contortion, and frequent applications of his numbed fingers to the charcoal burning near him, the face of a mud monkey-god. By his side are ranged rows of similar monkey-gods awaiting their turn of the brush that shall tip their heads with scarlet and their tails with yellow. Before the door sits a careful mother, scouring her daughter's head with mud. Here two shivering baboos, shiny with patent leather as to their feet, with oil as to their heads, and with many folds of a gaudy comforter about their necks, are climbing cautiously into an ekka, a pariah dog half awake watching the operation with a dubious wagging of its tail. One and all are extinguished, suppressed, occultated, by the cold.

Christmas Day! Can this be really Yule-tide?

> "December came with mirth men needs must make
> E'en for the empty days' and leisure's sake."

So opens the Prologue of a modern poet's story of how, in those olden days when dolphins knew good music when they heard it, and love it was that made the world go round, — the Strong Man came down to the Tyrian merchant-vessel swinging in Mycenæ Bay, and, taking the helm himself when the great east wind began to blow its fiercest, steered straight for the island where the daughters of old Hesperus the Wise guarded the tree with the golden fruit. It is a December poem, and yet the scene of it is laid in a land where the boughs were blossomed and "unknown flowers bent down before their feet;" where there were the lilies of spring in the grass, the fruit of autumn on the trees, and, over all, the warm light of a summer sun. Well for the poet that his song was of olden times! The reader is content in his December tale to take him at his word, to see wade off from the shingle the man

> "Who had a lion's skin cast over him,
> So wrought with gold that the fell show'd but dim
> Betwixt the threads."

And afterwards to see him at the foot of the golden-fruited tree, in the land of roses and singing-birds, standing where

> "Three damsels stood naked, from head to feet,
> Save for the glory of their hair."

We see him pick the red-gleaming apples, note the branch spring back, and then watch him, with the round fruit in his hand, go down across the lawn, dappled with flowers and fallen fruit, to the Tyrian ship again.

> "His name is Hercules,
> And e'en ye Asian folk have heard of him."

We "Asian folk" have indeed heard of a land where, by some pantomime of nature, roses are winter flowers and fruit ripen in December, where there are singing-birds instead of old cock-robins and turkeys, and where the damsels of the land, instead of nestling in chinchilla or sable's fur, stand about in a rural manner, much as did the Hesperids. We know too that in that land there was once a magic tree with golden pagoda coin for fruit, which strong men, coming across the sea in ships of trade, shook at will. But vegetables are not auriferous now. The Golden Pippin is a species of apple unhappily extinct, and *Sir Epicure Mammon* was not far from the mark when he lumped Jason's Fleece, Jove's Shower, and the Hesperian Garden as "all abstract riddles of the philosopher's stone."

But though the tree is gone, the country is much what it was in the Genesis of Anglo-India — the antediluvian period that preceded the Mutiny of 1857. It is still a land of juggling seasons. December comes round as usual, and with it Christmas Day and its marigolds; and men, having no work to do, —.

> "Mirth needs must make
> E'en for the empty days' and leisure's sake."

I have spent Christmas in England, and there was honest merriment enough. And on the doorstep without, birds and beggars alike shared in the sudden flow of Christmas goodwill.

I have also spent Christmas Day in India, but not all the marigolds of Cathay will firk up Christmas spirits, or make me throw crumbs to a blue-jay. The blue-jay would not eat them in the first place, for there are plenty of flying things abroad for him to eat. But even if that unpleasant bird, with its very un-Christmas plumage of sunny blue, were to turn frugivorous for the nonce to humor me, since "Christmas comes but once a year," I would not feed him. I have no Yule-tide humor about me, for there is no Christmas around me. The jests of nature are too long in the telling to be mirthful. The crops have been yellow with mustard blossom this week past, the gardens in all their glory for many weeks; and how, all of a sudden, and simply because it is the 25th of December, can I feel more at peace with all men than I did last Thursday? If Nature would only meet me half way, or even the robins of the country wear red waistcoats instead of red seats to their trousers, I would try and squeeze some seasonable festivity into my thoughts. But it is out of the question. Why! there is at this moment a punkah-puller outside the tent talking about the affairs of the hot weather, and dunning my servant for four annas to which he prefers a forged claim. He was always interesting, that coolie. They are a feeble folk, the most of them, — the coneys amongst mankind, — and the intelligent are in a desperate minority. Look around at the crowds of coolies whose life is a long yarn of gray toil, crossed at intervals with tawdry threads of lazy, worthless self-indulgence. Of "remembrance fallen from heaven" they have none. When the high gods sat down to fashion them, they must — to turn the poet's words — have wrought with more weeping than laughter, more loathing than love. Swinburne has said that they gave them also life enough, perhaps, to make the bitterness of humanity keen to them; and that they gave them light enough to illustrate the deadliness of all life's pleasures, and to show them the way to their graves. They have limbs and a shadow, and yet I doubt if poor Peter Schlemil would have exchanged his bedevilled existence for theirs. The flight of time they congratulate themselves upon; and nobility of deed or speech in a finer race does not affect the level of their minds, for they cannot even think splendidly.

But this peculiar coolie of mine was an interesting study, for he owned a cow. How he got it I cannot guess, for he did not look like a person with rich relatives to remember him in a will; and with his own money he could not have bought it. Nor could he have stolen it, for his legal ownership was ostentatiously displayed at all hours. Yet it was not a cow to be very proud of. It was not a big cow, and gave no milk. Nor did it drag anything about it — a cart or vehicle of any kind. But it was very cheerful. It played bo-peep with my terrier between the pillars of the porch, and from pure light-heartedness used to scour about the compound, with its tail, from an ecstasy of mirthfulness, curled up into a knot on its back. It trotted about a good deal in the mornings; and when its owner was not pulling my punkah, he was generally running about slowly and indefinitely after it. The cow always went much faster than the coolie, for I never saw him catch it except when it was standing still; and when he came up with it he never seemed to know what he should do next. He used to pull it about in a possessive manner, and jerk its rope as if he wished it to move — first in the direction of the compound gate, and the cow would cheerfully trot alongside of him; but on a sudden there would be a violent jerk, and the cow would find the coolie pulling in the opposite direction, whither it would, without demur, follow him. Whatever the change of programme, the cow acquiesced in it with the utmost heartiness; and thus, after having blithely proceeded a little in each direction, it generally found itself pretty much where it started from. The coolie would then carefully tether his property to the largest weed that was near, the cow looking on at the elaborate process with a contemplative aspect; after which, the coolie having turned to go, it would eat the weed up, and gaily accompany its master towards the verandah. The cow was quite useless to the coolie, and he could not demonstrate his ownership by doing anything with it. So he would sometimes throw stones at it — just to show that the cow was his. It was all pride, the pride of ownership; and though the cow cost him at least threepence a week, for it was regularly impounded for frolicsome trespass, he never parted with it. But I was obliged to part with the coolie; for one day, the wind being high, — the Scythians said wind was the principle of life, — the cow was unusually lively, and, after a preliminary canter round the garden with the terrier, it proceeded, in spite of the gardener, to execute a fantastic but violent *pas seul* upon a croquet ground which was in course of construction. I felt, therefore, compelled to ask the coolie to take his cow away and not to bring it back again. Nor did he; for he never came back himself — not, at any rate, until the punkahs had been put away in the lumber-room, and the tatties were gone, wherever old tatties go. His cow, I think, must be dead now, for he seems to have nothing to do but to loaf about with my camp, waiting for me to pay him the four annas of wages which he tries to prove is due to him.

. . . .

Now, what a strange thing human nature is! Here I have been protesting for the last hour that I had no Christmas foolery left in me; and yet I have this moment paid that punkah-coolie the four annas he has no claim to — and which, on principle, as I have told my wife every day for the last month, I have refused for two months to pay him—*just because it was Christmas Day!* To increase the absurdity, I had to confess the reason to him! For having sworn solemnly on all the rules of arithmetic that I did not owe him one farthing, I was obliged to give a decent explanation for my sudden acknowledgment of the debt; and how could I, before my servants, better maintain my dignity, and at the same time get rid of an importunate coolie, than by making him a present of his extortionate demand in full, because it was a "Feast day with us Christians."

For yet another Christmas, then, have I kept alive a Yule spark!

I look up at the poem lying open before me, and with a fateful response, that may compare with the unhappy King's *Virgilii Sortes*, the book replies—

"Cast no least thing thou lovedst once away,
  Since yet perchance thine eyes shall see the day."

Perchance, indeed, we *shall* all see another Christmas Day "at home," and among romping children and welcoming friends rekindle the smouldering Yule spark into an honest English Christmas blaze.

PART III.

UNNATURAL HISTORY.

PART III.
UNNATURAL HISTORY.

I.

MONKEYS AND METAPHYSICS.

Monkeys are Metaphysics.— How they found Seeta.— Yet they are not Proud. — Their Sad-Facedness. — Decayed Divinities. — As Gods in Egypt. — From Grave to Gay. — What do the Apes think of us? — The Etiquette of Scratching. — "The New Boy" of the Monkey-House. — They take Notes of us. — Man-Ape Puzzles: — The Soko. — Missing Links.

MONKEYS are metaphysics, and it is no idle work meditating among them.

In the first place, there is an objective difficulty, for the monkeys themselves seem possessed by a demon of unrest, and are perpetually in kaleidoscopic motion. The individual that was here when you began to take a note is nowhere when you have finished. In the interval it has probably turned a dozen somersaults on as many different perches, taken a swing on the trapeze, pulled all the tails it found hanging about, and is now busy scratching a small friend up in the roof. In the next place, there is a subjective difficulty, for in thinking about monkeys the mind cannot relax itself as it would in thinking about cats or parrots, nor get into undress over it as it might over a more trifling subject.

A monkey suggests something more than matter. There is a suspicion of mind about the creature that prevents one thinking idly, and all its problems seem somehow or another to resolve themselves into human questions of psychology or ethics. Many of their actions require a rational explanation, and, though each one may be turned off with a laugh, the gravity of the monkey will tell in the long-run, and the looker-on will find himself at last speculating as to whether and if, and hesitating as to the neuter genders of pronouns being proper to be used when speaking of monkeys. Fortunately for us the monkey is not proud. He has no reserve whatever, and betrays by his candor much that, if he were more reticent, would puzzle human beings beyond endurance. But the monkey makes us free of the whole of him, and conceals nothing. Yet, in spite of all this, the monkey remains a conundrum to human beings; and the more one thinks about him the less one feels sure of understanding.

If pedigree and lofty traditions could make any creatures proud, surely the monkeys should be proud, for their history runs back without a fault to the heroic times when their ancestors, living in the very hills which the monkey-folk still haunt, were the allies of the gods, and their chiefs were actually gods themselves.

The story goes — it is one of the oldest stories ever told — that when Seeta, the lady of the lotus eyes, the wife of Rama, had been carried away to Ceylon by Ravana, the black Raja of the Demons, her husband went out from the jungles of Dandaka to ask help of the Vulture King. This was Jatayus, the son of that Garuda the quills of whose feathers were like palm-tree trunks, and the shadow of his flying overhead like the passing

of a thunder-cloud in the month of the rains. But the
Demons had already killed the princely bird because
Jatayus had tried to stop them from carrying Seeta away ;
so Rama, having lit the funeral pyre for his friend, went
on farther, to ask the help of one who was even more
powerful than the Vulture King. This was Hanuman,
the son of Vargu, the chief of all the monkey nations,
who held his court upon the mountain peaks by the
Pampas Lake. And the sentinel apes, sitting on the
topmost rocks, saw Rama approaching, and recognized
him, and Hanuman himself came down towards him
reverently, stepping from ridge to ridge, and led the hero
up to the council-peaks, and called all the princes of the
four-handed folk together to give him their advice.
Hanuman himself sat apart upon a peak alone, for there
was not room enough on one mountain top for both him
and the rest, for to the council had come all the greatest
monkey warriors. Varana, the white ape, was there,
resting at full length upon a ridge, and looking like a
snow-drift that rests upon the Himalayas ; and there too
was Arundha of the portentous tail, with the strength
of a whole herd of elephants in each of his hairy arms ;
and there too Darvindha, that matchless baboon. And
after long council it was decided that the monkey nation
should be divided into four armies, and that each army
should search a quarter of the universe. The southern
quarter fell to Hanuman, and he linked his warriors
together in long lines and they searched the whole south
before them, examining the ravines among the mountains
and the creeks along the seashores as narrowly as the
ants search the crevices of the bark in the neem-trees ;
but night came on and they had not found Seeta. So
she must be beyond the Black Water, the monkeys said,

as they stood at the end of the land, looking about them across the sea for other countries. And when the day broke they saw a cloud lying upon the sea, and told Hanuman, but as soon as he saw it the sagacious son of Vargu said, "It is an island," and, stepping back a few paces, he ran and jumped, right away from India and across the straits into the Island of Ceylon. There he found Seeta shut up in a garden, and went back and told Rama. And then the old story goes on to say how Nala, the monkey-wizard, made stones float upon the sea for a bridge; and how Jambuvat, the king of the shaggy bears, led his people down from the hills to help the monkeys; and how the whole host crossed over to Ceylon and fought for many days with the Demons, and were always beaten till Sushena, the wisest of all the apes, sent Hanuman back to the Himalayas for the mystical Herb of Life, and with it called back all the souls of the dead monkey warriors; and how even then they could not conquer Indrajit, the mighty son of Ravana. At last the gods took part with Rama against the Demons. Vishnu lent him his chariot and Brahma gave him his quiver, and then, after a terrible fight, the steed of Indrajit went back riderless into the city, and Ravana, seeing his son was dead, came out himself to lead his hosts, bursting from the city gates as fire bursts from the peaks of the islands in the Eastern Sea, and slew one by one all the monkey chiefs, and last of them all slew Hanuman himself. Then Rama, the husband of Seeta, stood up in his chariot before Ravana, and would neither die nor move, and the Demon King at last grew faint with fighting, and turned towards the city, but the monkeys had set it on fire; and when he saw the smoke ascending, Ravana turned again in his despair, and sent his chariot forward with the crash of a thunderbolt against Rama. But Rama was immovable, and, standing upright among the dead, he loosed a great bolt, and Ravana's soul fled to Yama, where it floats in the River of the Dead. Then the monkeys destroyed the city of the Demons, and escorted Rama back to India; and Sushena, the magician ape, made the stone bridge sink again; and Rama went back again with his wife to Ayodhya, and the monkey people back to their merry hills by the Pampas Lake.

This is surely a splendid episode in the history of a people; and the monkeys of to-day are the lineal descendants of those very monkeys that fought for Rama. There is no gap in the long descent, and to-day the inheritors of Hanuman's fame inherit also his sanctity, sharing in the East the abodes and property of men, and possessing besides many temples of their own.

Yet the monkeys are not proud. They will condescend quite cheerfully to eat the Hindoo's humble stores of grain and fruit put out for sale on the village stall; and when these fail, in consequence perhaps of the grain-dealer's miserly interference, they will fall to with an appetite upon the wild berries and green shoots of the jungle, or even pick a light luncheon off an ant-hill. No, there is no pride about them, but much gravity and sadness of face, induced, perhaps, by the recollection of their classical glories and a consciousness of the present decadence of their race.

The ape in Æsop wept copiously on passing through a cemetery. "What ails you, my friend?" asked the fox, affected by this display of grief. "Oh, nothing," was the reply of the sensitive creature, "but I always weep like this when I am reminded of my poor dead ancestors!"

Such susceptibility to grief is honorable, but in the monkeys, by constant indulgence, it has stereotyped a tearful expression of countenance, which even when at play is never altogether lost. Take them, for instance, when, in fun, they have tied themselves into a knot, and pretend that they cannot undo themselves. But look at the faces that peep out of the bundle of tails and paws! They might belong to orphans of an hour's standing, so wistful and disconsolate are their eyes. Another one, peeling an orange, gazes on it with a look of such immeasurable grief as the Douglas's features might have showed when holding the Bruce's heart in his hand; and next to him sits an ape, sorrowfully cuffing a youngster; while overhead, surveying all the heedless throng, sits an old baboon, with a profound expression of melancholy pity on his reverend countenance, that recalls to my mind a Sunday picture-book of my early youth, and, as depicted therein, the aspect of Moses, when, from a mountain top, he sadly overlooked the Hebrews dancing round the golden calves.

Hanuman himself, saddest of monkeys, may himself be here, for his species is a common one; and so too others of high renown. Here, looking wofully among the straw for a fallen nut, sits the very god of "mad Egypt," the green monkey of Ethiopia, which was held in such reverence in old Memphis as the type of the God of Letters, or as Thoth himself, the emblem of the moon, symbol of the Bacchus of the Nile, and dignifying the obelisks of Luxor and the central sanctity of a hundred shrines. Yonder, musing pensively over a paper bag, still redolent of the gingerbread it once contained, sits Pthah, the pigmy baboon, the God of Learning, without whom Hermopolis would have been desolate, at once the genius of life and the holder of the dreadful scales after death, more potent than the ibis, and guardian of all the approaches to hundred-gated Thebes. A reverend pair, truly, and sadly come down in the world.

Do they know it? It is hard to say. They inherited their sad faces, no doubt, from some sad-faced progenitor; but how came he — the primitive ape — by so mournful a countenance? Did some tremendous catastrophe in the beginning of time overtake the four-handed folk, — so terrible in its ruin, that the sorrow of the survivors was impressed forever upon their features and transmitted by them to their kind? Everything, we are told, is inherited. The farmyard goats, when doing nothing else, still perch themselves on the highest point of the bank they can find, or on the wall, because their wild ancestors used once upon a time to stand on the hill peaks, as sentinels for the herd, to watch for the hunter and the eagle and the lynx. The dog still turns himself round before going to sleep, because in the old wolf days his progenitors, before they lay down, cautiously took one last look all round them. Is there, then, any reason in the far past for the melancholy demeanor of the monkeys of the present?

Perhaps they still remember the Flood with personal regret.

It is impossible to speak with disrespect of animals having such antecedents; and, besides, this monkey before you knows perhaps a secret that science cannot find out — the secret of the Sources of the Nile. As he passes by, a tail hanging down from the perch above him attracts his notice, and pulling it, he brings down upon himself a monkey smaller than itself, which had thought itself concealed, but had forgotten its dependent tail. The tiny creature is to-day "the new boy" of the school, and, as yet, has found his comrades rude and unsympathetic.

They ask his sisters' names, and where he came from, how old he is, and what he can do; and whatever his answer may be, the rejoinder is much the same, either a pinch or a push, a tug at his tail, or a box on the ear. So, as the keeper says, "whenever he sees one coming towards him he just sits down and hollers; but he'll get used to it. They all hollers a bit at first."

But the grivet after all is only going to scratch the capuchin, in a sociable sort of way, for they are most of them sociable, and a pleasing community of fur obtains among them.

But you must not watch a monkey too long at a time, or it will be certain to abuse your curiosity by flippant conduct, and the illusion of respectability will be at once destroyed. Turn for a moment to any family of monkeys, and for a time nothing can be more becoming than their behavior. The young ones romp, while the old one, discountenancing such frivolity, sits severely on a perch, turning every now and then to look out wistfully over the spectators' heads at the bright sun shining out of doors. But on a sudden a change comes over the scene. A young one, grovelling under the straw, forgets that it has left its tail protruding, and the temptation is greater than the old one can resist. In a twinkling the challenge to a romp is accepted; and lo! while the senior makes a fool of himself among the straw with one of the children, the other child is on his perch, looking just as grave as he did, and gazing at intervals in the same wistful way out into the open air. The old monkey, lately so solemn, so respectable, so care-worn, has suddenly resolved itself into an irresponsible fool, committing itself to every possible absurdity, and subjected to the irreverent liberties of its juniors. Those who do not respect themselves cannot, of course, look for respect from others; but, from the elder monkey's attitude when we first approached it, such a complete abandonment to buffoonery was hardly to be expected.

Or, take again some austere-looking monkey in solitary confinement. She has apparently no temptations to romp, for she has no comrades; but here again the same deplorable disregard of appearances occurs. Her cage is lined with straw, and in the centre of the straw she sits, as composed as a mummy, and with a face like an old Mussulman moulvie. Surely, the crack of doom itself could not disturb such serene equanimity. The thought, however, is hardly past before the monkey, with a velocity that suggests an explosion from below, springs to the roof, carrying with her as much of the bed as her four hands can hold, and in the next instant is down again and spinning round and round on the bare floor in pursuit of her own tail, while the straw comes straggling down upon her silly old head from the perch above. The creature has suddenly, to all appearance, become a hopeless idiot!

It is just the same in the next cage, and the next, and the next. Intervals of profound contemplation and admirable gravity alternate with fits of irrelevant frivolity; and it is just these extraordinary alternations of conduct and demeanor that make monkeys metaphysics. There is no arguing from probabilities with them, or concluding from premises. It is always the unforeseen that occurs.

Perhaps they may have a *lingua franca* among themselves, but against man they conspire together to be dumb; provoking him to speculation by imitating human manners, and then frustrating all his conclusions by suddenly lapsing — into monkeys.

It is difficult enough to catch a monkey's eye, but to catch one of its ideas is impossible. Neither in look nor in mind will it positively confront man, but just as it lets its eye pass over his, yet never rest upon it full, so its " mind " glances to one side or the other of the human intelligence, but never coincides with it.[1] It may be that they were once all human, that the link still exists, and that in time all will be human again; but meanwhile it is quite certain that race after race is becoming extinct, and that as yet no single individual in all the " wilderness of monkeys " is quite a man.

* * * * *

Stanley the traveller has told us that sometimes when he entered an African *boma*, intending to take notes of the strange beings who lived in it, and their odd appearance and eccentric ways, he was greatly disconcerted to find that he himself, and not the natives, was considered singular in that part of the world. They, the savages, were ordinary, every-day folk; but he, their discoverer, was a curious novelty, that deserved, in their opinion, to be better known than he was. So the majority turned the tables on the explorer; for while they were all of one orthodoxy, in looks, habits, and language, the stranger appeared to them a ridiculous exception. He had not a single precedent to cite, or example to appeal to, in

[1] For an admirably sympathetic sketch of monkey character — and much more besides — read Miss Frances Power Cobbe's delightful book, "False Beasts and True."

justification of the preposterous color of his skin, the ludicrous clothing he wore, or his queer ways. In the middle of Africa he found himself a natural solecism, a " sport," as botanists say, from the normal type, — a *lusus naturæ*, an interesting monstrosity.

The savages, therefore, would solemnly proceed to discover Stanley, and after deliberate examination pronounce him, in Brobdingnagian phrase, to be simply a *relplum salcath* — something, in fact, which they could not understand, but which they considered very absurd. Meanwhile, what with taking his clothes off and putting them on again to please his explorers, and beating up the various articles of property, socks and so forth, which different households had appropriated as curiosities, the traveller found his time so fully occupied that his notes of the other manners and customs of the natives were often of the briefest description, and he had to go on his way, considerably out of countenance at finding that, while he thought he was discovering Central Africa, the Central Africans were really discovering him.

Something of the same feeling grows upon the observer after a morning with monkeys. We, on the one hand, remark the pensive demeanor of the four-handed folk, and sympathize with the unknown causes of their melancholy, — are amused by their irrational outbreaks of frivolity, and scandalized by their sudden relapses from an almost superhuman gravity and self-respect into monkey indecorum and candor. But while we are watching one of them it suddenly occurs to us that we ourselves are being watched by the rest, and that as we take notes of the monkeys so they take notes of us.

They, no doubt, remark that our faces are usually

characterized by a senseless smile, and, full of lofty pity for us, wonder at creatures that can thus pass their days in causeless mirth, and differ so much in their fur and feathers that it is nothing short of a marvel that they ever distinguish each other's species. While we, the spectators, are moralizing over the divine honors of the ape in the Past, and his fallen state, the ape of the Present sits puzzling over the man of the Future. Some of the types which he sees round his cage are so like his own that he seems to make an involuntary gesture of recognition, but his relative has gone by before he has been able to explain himself; so he retires again into contemplation, regretting his lost opportunity, but content to wait patiently till, as he says, "some more of my sort happen to come round."

While we outside are noting the unformed heel, the leg without a calf, the lines of the skeleton that prevent an erect attitude, they within have observed that human beings cannot run up the wire netting, or swing by their tails on the railings; that they have no flea-hunting to relieve the tedium of life, and that when a child wishes to look over any obstacle its parents have to hold it aloft to do so, as the poor little thing cannot scamper up a pole. While we are commiserating the monkeys on their narrow escape from human intelligence, the monkeys are wondering how long it will be before men grow wise enough to use their tails instead of hiding them, and see the folly of keeping two of their hands in boots.

We surmise enough about their antecedents to feel misgivings as to relationship, but do you really suppose that these creatures with the thoughtful eyes think nothing? They look at you quite as keenly as you at them, whenever you happen to turn your head aside; and if you suddenly surprise them in their scrutiny they shift their glance at once with affected indifference but extraordinary rapidity, and subside into a studied carelessness, — the perfection of acting, it is true, but nevertheless so palpably assumed that it fills you with uncanny suspicions. Again and again the experiment may be tried, and every time with the same result — the swift withdrawal of that furtive searching gaze, and the utter collapse into vacuous but sinister complacency. By perseverance you can pursue the monkey, so it seems, through a regular series of human thoughts, stare it out of countenance, make it ashamed of its stealthy scrutiny, and feel uncomfortable and conscious; you can even make it get up and go away, further and further and further, drive it from one untenable subterfuge to another, till at last it loses its temper at your relentless pursuit of its inner thoughts, and, jumping on to a perch, tries to shake the cage about your ears, chattering furiously and showing all its teeth. Does such a creature as this never retaliate in its meditations upon men and women, or find amusement in our proceedings?

In time the smaller one is soothed, and lies down so flat that it looks at last like a monkey-skin stretched out on the straw, while the larger, with an elaborate affectation of studious interest, searches each tuft of fur.

This possession of each other is, by the way, a curious feature of monkey life, for they seem to hold their fur in common. No one individual may take himself off to the top of the cage, and say, " You shan't scratch me," for his skin belongs to all his neighbors alike, and if a larger monkey than himself expresses a wish to scratch him, the smaller must at once turn over on his back and submit to the process. Nor is it etiquette to refuse one's self to be scratched by another of equal size; and indeed, without derogation of dignity, a larger may abandon the surface of his stomach to a smaller. At times, it is true, scratching degenerates into sycophancy, for several tiny monkeys may be seen tickling one large, lazy ape-personage. They hold up his arms for him while they tickle his ribs, and watch obsequiously the motions of his head, as the luxurious magnate turns first one cheek and then the other to be attended to. But this is a mere accident in habits, and does not affect that singular commonwealth of fur which seems to obtain among the monkey-folk, and which prevents any single member of it selfishly retiring into solitude with his own fleas.

. . . . . .

Have the monkeys, again, nothing to say about the man-ape problems that have puzzled humanity from the first?

Beginning with the dog-faced men of Tartary and Libya, whom Herodotus and Pliny handed down to Marco Polo and to Mandeville, or "the men of the Hen Yeung kingdom,"— those Chinese pygmy-men who had short tails and always walked arm in arm, lest the birds should think they were insects,— and ending, at present, with the Soko of the Uregga forests, and the Susumete of Honduras, the list of man-apes is both long and varied. For want of absolute contradiction or confirmation we human beings have to hold our decision in abeyance, but why should the monkeys have any doubt about the connecting link?

What a work might be written, both horrible and grotesque, about all the ape-men or man-apes that have been introduced by travellers to the notice of the world! Science, it is true, ignores them all, but Fancy, I think, gets along better without Science. Classification and microscopic investigation are no doubt excellent things in their way, but they interfere very awkwardly with the hearty conception of a good-all-round monster; and, as a matter of fact, if travellers had been mere hair-splitting, "finicking" professors, we should never have had that substantial Fauna of Mystery which we now possess. Fortunately, however, they have, as a rule, been courageous, open-handed fellows, who would as soon think of sticking at an extra horn or hoof, or shirking a mane or a tail, as of deserting a comrade in danger.

The result of their generous labors has been the collection of as wholesome a set of monsters as could have been wished; gravitating, moreover, as it is right they should, towards mankind, until, indeed, they actually merge in humanity. Professor Owen, who wages desperate war, and very properly, against the existence of all things of which he has not seen a bit, refuses, of course, to admit the last gradation altogether. But Professor Huxley, who, I believe, is really in his heart of hearts pining secretly for a tailed man to be found, laughs to scorn the dry theory of the hippocampus minor; and if he were only to travel to-morrow into an unknown land, I am not at all sure that he would not ultimately emerge from some primeval forest hand in hand with the "missing link." In the meantime he could not do better than accept the Soko. For the establishment of the Soko's individuality there are teeth, skin, and skulls in existence, and the last have been declared by Professor Huxley to be human. They were brought from Africa by Mr. H. M. Stanley, as being the fragments of a great ape which certain natives had eaten, and which they themselves called " meat of the forest." Nevertheless, the Professor declares that they are the remains of defunct humanity, male and female.

After this the Soko must rank as one of the most interesting mysteries of Nature. Is it human or not? Is it the chief of monkeys or the lowest of men? Dr. Livingstone was not quite certain, and Mr. Stanley told me he was himself only half convinced.[1] In reviewing the work of the latter explorer for a London journal I drew special attention to the Soko, for, though actually known only by report, the repeated references to it make this ape-man one of the features of the book. On one occasion Mr. Stanley actually startled to its feet a great monkey-person that was asleep on the river-bank; but his boat was shooting down the stream so swiftly that he could not tell whether it was beast or man. Circumstantial evidence of the existence of a half-human creature, however, thrust itself upon the explorer day after day. In Manyema, in the Uregga forests, at Wane Kirumbu, at Mwana Ntaba, the Soko was heard after nightfall or during broad daylight roaring and chattering. At more than one place its nest was seen in the fork of a tall bombax; and, both at Kampunzu and a village on the Ariwimi, its teeth, skin, and skulls

---

[1] When editing Mr. Stanley's "Through the Dark Continent," I heard from the explorer and read in his notes much that was not published. His Soko lore was considerable; but in a few words his man-ape problem is this. The natives gave Stanley skulls, teeth, and skins of a creature *they* called an ape. Professor Huxley says the skulls are human. The teeth and skin are not.

were obtained from the people, who never differed in their description of the creature they called the Soko, and insisted that it was only a monkey. The skulls, at any rate, have been proved to be human, and the teeth are some of them human, too; but if the tough skin, thickly set with close gray hair came off the body of a man or a woman, he or she must have been of a species hitherto unknown to science. For as yet no family of our race has confessed to a soft gray fur, nearly an inch long in parts and inclining to white at the tips. Yet such is the skin of the Soko, the creature whose skull Professor Huxley says is human.

Two fascinating theories at once suggest themselves to help us out of the Soko mystery; for, premising that Mr. Stanley and Professor Huxley are both right, — and it is very difficult to see how either can be wrong, — it may happen that under either theory the thing described by the tribes along the Livingstone River as "a fruit-stealing ape, five feet in height, and walking erect with a staff in its left hand, may prove to be human. The first is that the tribes who eat the Soko are really cannibals, and that they know it, but feeling that curious shame on this point which is common to nearly all cannibals, they will not confess to the horrid practice, and prefer, when on their company manners with uneatable strangers, to pass off their human victims as apes. The other is that there actually does exist in the centre of the Dark Continent a race of forest men so degraded and brute-like that even the cannibals living on the outskirts of their jungles really think them to be something less than human, and as such hunt them and eat them. Either theory suffices to supply the missing link, for if it be true that the skulls of the Soko are human skulls — and that the Soko skin belongs to the Soko-skulls—then the tribes of the Livingstone have among them a furry-skinned race of men that feed by night and have no articulate speech. If, on the other hand, these furred creatures are so like monkeys that even savages cannot recognize their humanity, and yet so like men that even Professor Huxley cannot recognize any trace of monkey in their skulls, the person called the Soko must be a very satisfactory missing link indeed; for it is essential in such a person that he should so nearly resemble both his next of kin as to be exactly assignable to neither.

Man himself would, I believe, be glad, in his present advanced state of sympathetic civilization, to admit the monkey's claim to alliance with himself; for it is a fact that our race finds a pleasure in referring loftily to the obscurity of its own origin, and feels a natural pride in having raised itself above its fortunes.

In India, where the monkeys live among men, and are the playmates of their children, the Hindoos have grown so fond of them that the four-handed folk participate in all their simple household rites. In the early morning, when the peasant goes out to yoke his plough, and the crow wakes up, and the dog stretches himself and shakes off the dust in which he has slept all night, the old monkey creeps down from the peepul-tree, only half awake, and yawns, and looks about him, puts a straw in his mouth, and scratches himself contemplatively.

Then one by one the whole family come slipping down the tree-trunk, and they all yawn and look about and scratch. But they are sleepy and peevish, and the youngsters get cuffed for nothing, and begin to think life dull. Yet the toilet has to be performed; and, whether they like it or not, the young ones are sternly pulled up, one by one, to their mother to undergo the process. The scene, though regularly repeated every morning, loses nothing of its delightful comicality, and the monkey-brats never tire of the joke of taking in mamma. But mamma was young herself not so very long ago, and treats each ludicrous affectation of suffering with profoundest unconcern, and, as she dismisses one cleaned youngster with a cuff, stretches out her hand for the next one's tail or leg in the most businesslike and serious manner possible. The youngsters know their turns quite well, and as each one sees the moment arriving it throws itself on its stomach, as if overwhelmed with apprehension, the others meanwhile stifling their laughter at the capital way so-and-so is doing it, and the instant the maternal paw is extended to grasp its tail the subject of the next experiment utters a dolorous wail, and, throwing its arms forward in the dust, allows itself to be dragged along, a limp and helpless carcass, winking all the time, no doubt, at its brothers and sisters, at the way it is imposing on the old lady. But the old lady will stand no nonsense, and turning the child right side up proceeds to put it to rights; takes the kinks out of its tail and the knots out of its fur; pokes her fingers into its ears and looks at each of its toes, the inexpressible brat all the time wearing on its face an absurd expression of hopeless and incurable grief. Those who have been already cleaned look on with delight at the screaming farce, while those who are waiting wear a becoming aspect of enormous gravity. The old lady, however, has her joke, too, which is to cuff every youngster before she lets it go; and nimble as her offspring are, she generally, to her credit be it said, manages to give each of them a box on the ears before it is out of reach. The father, meanwhile, sits gravely with his back to all these domestic matters, waiting for breakfast.

Presently the mats before the hut-doors are pushed down, and women with brass vessels in their hands come out; and, while they scour the pots and pans with dust, exchange between yawns the compliments of the morning.

The monkeys by this time have come closer to the preparations for food, and sit solemnly, household by household, watching every movement. Hindoos do not hurry themselves in anything they do, but the monkey has lots of time to spare and plenty of patience, and in the end, after the crow has stolen a little, and the dog has had its morsel, and the children are all satisfied, the poor fragments of the meal are thrown out on the ground for the *bhunder-logue*, the monkey-people; and it is soon discussed — the mother feeding the baby before she eats herself. When every house has thus, in turn, been visited, and no chance of further "out-door relief" remains, the monkeys go off to the well. The women are all here again, drawing the water for the day, and the monkeys sit and wait, the old ones in the front, sententious and serious, and the youngsters rolling about in the dust behind them, till at last some girl sees the creatures waiting, and "in the name of Ram" spills a lotah full of water in a hollow of the ground, and the monkeys come round it in a circle and stoop down and drink, with their tails all curled up over their backs like notes of interrogation. There is no contention or jostling. A forward child gets a box on the ear, perhaps, but each one, as it has satisfied its thirst, steps quietly out of the circle and wipes its mouth. The day thus fairly commenced, they go off to see what luck may bring them.

The grain-dealer's shop tempts them to loiter, but the experience of previous attempts makes theft hopeless; for the bunnya, with all his years, is very nimble on his legs, and an astonishing good shot with a pipkin. So the monkeys merely make their salaams to him and pass on to the fields. If the corn is ripe they can soon eat enough for the day; but, if not, they go wandering about picking up morsels, here an insect and there a berry, till the sun gets too hot, and then they creep up into the dark shade of the mango tops and snooze through the afternoon. In the evening they are back in the village again to share in its comforts and entertainments.

They assist at the convocation of the elders and the romps of the children, looking on when the faquir comes up to collect his little dues of salt and corn and oil, and from him in their turn exacting a pious toll. They listen gravely to the village musician till they get sleepy, and then, one by one, they clamber up into the peepul.

And the men sitting round the fire with their pipes can see, if they look up, the whole colony of the bhunderlogue asleep in rows in the tree above them.

. . . .

But outside of Asia the monkey has never become a friend, even though we have adopted him as a relative. Literature has nothing to his credit, and Art ignores him. In olden times they never took augury from a monkey, and nowadays no one even takes it for armorial bearings.

Yet the tailed ones are already considerably advanced

towards civilization. As Darwin tells us, they catch colds and die of consumption, suffer from apoplexy and from cholera, inflammation, cataracts, and so forth, can pass on a contagious affection to men, or take the sickness from them, eat and drink all that human beings do, and suffer from surfeits precisely as men and women do; for if drunk over-night they have headaches next morning, scorn solid food, and are exasperated by the mere smell of strong liquors, but turn with relish to the juice of lemons and effervescing draughts.

II.

HUNTING OF THE SOKO.

LYING on my back one terribly hot day under the great tamarind that shades the temple of Saravan, in Borneo, I began to think naturally of iced drinks, and from them my mind wandered to icebergs, and from icebergs to Polar bears.

Polar bears! At the recollection of these animals I sat bolt upright, for though I had shot over nearly all the world, and accumulated a perfect museum of trophies, I had never till this moment thought of Greenland, nor of Polar bears! Before this I had begun to think I had exhausted Nature. From the false elk of Ceylon to the true one of Canada, the rhinoceros of Assam to the coyote of Patagonia, the panther of Central India to the jaguars of the Amazon, I had seen everything in its own home, and shot it there. And for birds, I had hunted a so-called *moa* at Little Farm in New Zealand, the bustard in the Mahratta country, dropped geese into nearly every river of America, Europe, and Asia, and flushed almost all the glorious tribe of game birds, from the capercailzie of Norway to the quail of Sicily. My museum, however, wanted yet another skin — the Polar bear! I cannot say the prospect pleased me. I would much rather have sent my compliments to the Polar bear and asked it to come comfortably into some warm climate to be shot; but regretting was useless, so I gave the order of the day — the North Pole.

In London, however, I heard of Stanley's successful search for Livingstone, and then it was that the sense of my utter nothingness came over me. All Africa was unshot! It is true I had once gone from Bombay to Zanzibar, Dr. Kirke helping me on my way, and, thanks to Mackinnon's agents (who were busy prospecting a road into the interior) had bagged my hippopotamus, and enjoyed many a pleasant stalk after the fine antelope of the Bagomoyo plains. But the Dark Continent itself, with its cloud-like herds of hartebest and springbok, its droves of wind-footed gnu, its zebras, ostriches and lions, was still a virgin ground for me. But more than all these — more than ostrich, gnu, or zebra, more than hippopotamus or lion — was that mystery of the primeval forest, the Soko. What was the Soko? Certainly not the gorilla, nor the chimpanzee, nor yet the ourang-outang. Was it a new beast altogether, this man-like thing, that shakes the forest at the sources of the Congo with its awful voice — that desolates the villages of the jungle tribes of Uregga, carries off the women captive, and meets their cannibal lords in fair fight? With Soko on the brain it may be easily imagined that the Polar bear was forgotten, and I lost no time in altering my arrangements to suit my altered plans. My snow-shoes were countermanded and solar helmets laid in: fur gloves and socks were exchanged for leather gaiters and canvas suits.

In a month I was ready, and in another two months had started from Zanzibar with a following of eighteen men. During my voyage I had carefully read the travels of Grant, Speke, Burton, Livingstone, Cameron, Schweinfurth, and Stanley, and in all had been struck by the losses suffered from fatigue on the march. With large expeditions it was of course necessary for most to go on foot, but with my pygmy *cortège* I could afford to let them ride. Good strong donkeys were cheap at Zanzibar, and I bought a baker's dozen of them, reserving three of the best for myself, and allotting ten among my men, to relieve them either of their burdens or the fatigue of walking, according to any fair arrangements — fair to the donkeys and to themselves — they chose to make among themselves. The result was no sickness, little fatigue, and constant good spirits. My goods consisted of my own personal effects, all on one donkey; my medicine-chest, etc., on another; fifteen men-loads of beads, wire, and cloth, for making friends with the natives and purchasing provisions; and three loads of ammunition. I was lucky in the time of my start, for Mirambo, "the terror of Africa," who had been scouring the centre of the continent for the past year, had just concluded peace with the Arabs, his enemies, and had moreover ordered every one also to keep the peace. The result to me was that each village was as harmless as the next.

Gaily enough, then, we strolled along, enjoying occasionally excellent sport, and wondering as we went where all the horrors and perils of African travel had gone. We had, it is true, our experience of them afterwards; but the ground has now become so stale, that I will pass over the interval of our journey from Zanzibar to Ujiji and thence to the river, and ask you to imagine us setting out for the forests that lie about the sources of the Livingstone in the district of Uregga, the Soko's home.

Nearly every traveller before me had spoken of the Soko, the man-beast of these primeval forests. Livingstone had a large store of legends and anecdotes about them, their intelligent cruelty and their fierce, though frugivorous, habits. Stanley constantly heard them. In one place he saw a Soko's platform in a tree, and in several villages found the skin, the teeth, and the skulls in possession of the people.

Wherever we went I was eager in my inquiries, but day after day slipped by, and still I neither heard the Soko alive nor saw any portion of one dead. But even without encountering the great simia, our journey in these nightshade forests was sufficiently eventful, for great panther-like creatures, very pale-skinned, prowled about in the glimmering shades; and from the trees we sometimes saw hanging pythons of tremendous girth. But the reptile and insect world was chiefly in the ascendant here, and it was against such small persecutors as puff-adders, centipedes, poisonous spiders, and ants, that we had to guard ourselves. Travelling, however, owing to the dense shade, was not the misery that we had found it in the sun-smitten plains of Uturu, or the hideous ocean of scrub-jungle that stretches from Suna to Mgongo-Zembo. The trees, nearly all of three or four species of bombax, mvule, and aldrendon, were of stupendous size and impossible altitude, but growing so close together their crowns were tightly interwoven overhead, and sometimes not a hundred yards in a whole day's march was open to the sky. Moreover, in the hot-house air under this canopy had sprung up with incredible luxuriance every species of tree-fern, rattan and creeping palm known, I should think, to the tropics, and amongst themselves in a stratum, often thirty feet below the upper roof of tree-foliage, had closely intermeshed their fronds and tendrils, so that we marched often in an oven atmosphere, but protected alike from the killing sun and flooding rain by double awnings of impenetrable leafage. The ground itself was bare of vegetation, except where, here and there, monster fungi clustered, like a condemned invoice of umbrellas and parasols, round some fallen giant of the forest, or where, in a screen of blossom, wonderful air-plants filled up great spaces from tree-trunk to tree-trunk.

At intervals we crossed rivulets of crystal water, icy cold, finding their way as best they might from hollow to hollow over the centuries' layers of fallen leaves, and along their courses grew in rich profusion masses of a broad-leafed sedge, that afforded the panther safe covert and easy couch; and sometimes, on approaching one of these rills, we would see a ghostly herd of deer flit away through the twilight shade. And thus it happened that one evening I was lying on my rug half asleep, with the pleasant deep-sea gloom about me and a deathly stillness reigning over this world of trees, and wondering whether that was or was not a monkey perched high up among the palm fronds, when out from the sedges by a runnel there paced before me a panther of unusual size. From his gait I saw that it had a victim in view, and turning my head was horrified to see that it was one of my own men, who was busy about something at the foot of a tree.

I jumped up with a shout, and the panther, startled by the sudden sound, plunged back in three great leaps into the sedges from which it had emerged. All my men jumped to their feet, and one of them, in his terror at the proximity of the beast of prey, turned and fled away into the depth of the forest. I watched his retreating figure as far as the eye could follow it in that light, and laughing at his panic, went over to where my ass was tied, intending to stroll down for a shot at the panther. And while I was idly getting ready, the sound of excited conversation among my men attracted me, and I asked them what was the matter. There was a laugh, and then one of them, the most sensible, *English*-minded African I ever met, stepped forward.

"We do not know, master," said he, "which of us it was that ran away just now. *We are all here.*"

The full significance of his words did not strike me at first, and I laughed too. "Oh, count yourselves," I said, "and you will soon find out."

"But we *have* counted, master," replied the man, "and all eighteen are here."

His meaning began to dawn on me. I felt a queer feeling creep over me.

"*All* here!" I ejaculated. "Muster the men."

And mustered they were — and to my astonishment, and even horror, I found the man was speaking the truth. Every man of my force was in his place.

Then who was the man that had run away, when all the party started up from their sleep? *A ghost?* I looked round into the deepening gloom. All my men were standing together, looking rather frightened. Around us stretched the eternal forest. *A ghost!* And then on a sudden the thought flashed across me — I had seen the Soko.

I had seen the Soko! and seeing it had mistaken it for a human being! And while I was still loading my cartridge-belt, Shumari, my gun-boy, had crept up to my side, with my express in one hand and heavy elephant rifle in the other; but on his face there was a strange, concerned expression, and in the tone of his voice an uneasy tremor, with which something in my own feelings sympathized.

"Is the master going to hunt the wild man?" asked the lad.

"The Soko? Yes, I want its skin," I replied.

"But the wild man cried out, '*Ai! ma-ma*' ['Oh! mother, mother'] as it ran away, and —"

"Here is the wild man's stick," broke in Mabruki, the Zanzibari; and as he spoke he held out towards me a long staff, seven feet in length. All the blood in my body ran cold at the sight of it. It was a mere length of rattan, without ferule or knot, but at the upper end the bark had been torn down from joint to joint in parallel strips, *to give the holder a firmer grip* than one could have had on smooth cane, and just below the second joint the stumps of the corresponding shoots on two sides had been left sticking out *for the hand to rest on*.

How can I describe the throng of hideous thoughts that whirled through my brain on the instant that I recognized these efforts of reason in the animal that I was now going to hunt to the death? But swift as were my thoughts, Mabruki had thought them out before me, and had come to a conclusion. "The *mshenshi mtato* [pagan ape] had stolen this stick from some village," said he; "see," and he pointed to the smoothed offshoots, "they have stained them with the mvule juice."

The instant relief I felt at this happy solution of the dreadful mystery was expressed by me in a shout of joy; so sudden and so real that, without knowing why, my men shouted too, and with such a will that the monkeys that had been gravely pondering over our preparations for the evening meal were startled out of their self-respect and off their perches, and plunged precipitately into a tangle of lianes. My spirits had returned, and with as light a heart as ever I had, I ambled off in the direction the Soko had taken.

But soon the voices of the camp had died away behind me, and there had grown up between me and it the wall of mist that in this sunless forest region makes every mile as secret from the next as if you were in the highest ether — surely the most secret of all places — or in the lowest sea. And over the soft, rich vegetable mould the ass's feet went noiseless as an owl's wing upon the air; and, except for the rhythmical jingling of his ass's harness, Shumari's presence might never have been suspected. And then in this cathedral solitude — with cloistered tree-trunks reaching away at every point of view into long vistas closed in gray mist; overhead, hanging like tattered tapestry, great lengths and rags of moss-growths, strange textures of fungus and parasite, hanging plumb down in endless points, all as motionless as possible; without a breath of life stirring about me — bird, beast, or insect — the same horrid thoughts took possession of me again, and I began to recall the gestures of the wild thing which, when I startled the panther, had fled away into the forest depths.

It had stood upright amongst the upright men, and turning to run had stooped, but only so much as a man might do when running with all his speed. In the gait there was a one-sided swing, just as some great man-ape — gorilla or chimpanzee — might have when, as travellers tell us, they help themselves along on the knuckles of the long fore-arm, the body swaying down to the side on which the hand touches the ground at each stride. In one hand was a small branch of some leafy shrub, for I distinctly remembered having seen it as it began to run. The speed must have been great, for it was very soon out of sight; but there was no *appearance* of rapidity in the movement, — like the wolf's slow-looking gallop, that no horse can overtake, and that soon tires out the fleetest hound. As it began to run it had made a jabbering sound, — an inarticulate expression of simple human fear I had thought it to be; but now, pondering over it, I began to wonder that I could have mistaken that swiftly retreating figure for human.

It is true that I did not want to think of it as human, and perhaps my wishes may have colored my retrospect; at any rate, whatever the process, I found myself, after a while, laughing at myself for having turned sick at heart when the suspicion came across me that perhaps the Soko of the forests of Uregga, the feast-day dish of the jungle tribes, might be a human being. The long, lolloping gait, the jabbering, should alone have dispelled the terror. It is true that my men heard it say, "Oh, ma-ma!" as it started up to run by them. But in half the languages of the world, *mama* is a synonym for "mother," and it follows, therefore, that it is not a word at all, but simply the phonetic rendering of the first bleating, babbling articulation of babyhood, — an animal noise uttered as articulately by young sheep and young goats as by young men and women. The staff, too, was of the common type in these districts, and had been picked up, no doubt, by the Soko in some twilight prowling round a grain store, or perhaps gained in fair fight from some villager whom it had surprised, solitary and defenceless. And then my thoughts ran on to all I had read or heard of the Soko, of its societies for mutual defence or food-supply, and the comparative amiability of such communities, — of the solitary outlawed Soko, the vindictive, lawless bandit of the trees, who wanders about round the habitations of men, lying in wait for the women and the children, robbing the granaries and orchards, and stealing, for the simple larceny's sake, household chattels, of the use of which it is ignorant. Shumari, a hunter born and bred, was full of Soko lore; the skin, he said, was covered, except on the throat, hands, and feet, with a short, harsh hair of a dark color, and tipped in the older individuals with gray; these also had long growths of hair on the head, their cheeks and lips. It had no tail.

"Standing up," said he, "it is as tall as I am [he was only five feet one inch], and its eyes are together in the front of its face, so that it looks at you straight. It eats sitting up, and when tired leans its back against a tree, putting its hands behind its head. Three men of my village came upon one asleep in this way one day, and so quietly that before it awoke two of them had speared it. It started up and threw back its head to give a loud cry of pain, and then leaning its elbow against the tree, it bent its head down upon its arms, and so died, — leaning against the tree, with one arm supporting the head and the other pressed to its heart. There was a Soko village there, for they saw all their platforms in the trees, and the ground was heaped up in places with snail-shells and fruit-skins. But they did not see any more Sokos. . . . Another day I myself was out hunting with a party, and we found a dead Soko. I had thrown my spear at a tree-cat, and going to pick it up, saw close by a large heap of myombo leaves. I turned some up with my spear, and found a dead Soko underneath. . . . When a Soko catches a man it holds him, and makes faces at him, and jabbers; sometimes it lets him go without doing him any harm, but generally it bites off all his fingers one by one, spitting them out as it bites them off, and his nose and ears and toes as well, and ends up by strangling him with its fingers or beating him to death with a branch. Women and children are never seen again, so I suppose the Sokos eat them. They have no spears or knives, and they do not use anything that men use, except that they walk with sticks, knocking down fruit with them, and that they drink water out of their hands. Their front teeth are very sharp, and at each side is one longer and sharper than the rest."

And so he went on chattering to me as we ambled through the dim shade in a stupid pursuit of an invisible thing. The stupidity of it dawned upon me at last, and I stopped, and without explaining the change to my companion, turned and rode homewards.

The twilight shadows of the day were now deepening into night, and we hurried on. The fireflies began to flicker along the sedge-grown rills and, high up among the leaf coronets of the elais palm, were clustering in a mazy dance. Passing a tangle of lianes, I heard an owl or some night bird hoot gently from the foliage, and as we went along the fowl seemed to keep pace with us, for the ventriloquist sound was always with us, fast though we rode; and first from one side and then from the other we heard the low-voiced complaining following. And the "eeriness" of the company grew upon me. There was no sound of wings or rustling of leaves;

but for mile after mile the low *hoot, hoot,* of the thing that was following, sounded so close at hand that I kept on looking round. Shumari, like all savages — they approach animals very nearly in this — was intensely susceptible to the superstitious and uncanny, and long before the ghostliness of the persistent voice occurred to me, I had noticed that Shumari was keeping as close to me as possible. But at last, whether it was from constantly turning my head over my shoulder to see what was coming after us, or whether I was unconsciously infected by his nervousness, I got as fidgety as he, and, for the sake of human company, opened conversation.

"What bird makes that noise?" I asked.

Shumari did not reply, and I repeated the question.

And then in a voice, so absurd from its assumption of boldness that I laughed outright, he said, —

"No bird, master. It is a *muzimu* [spirit] that is following us. Let us go quicker."

Here was a position! We had all the evening been hunting nothing, and now we were being hunted by nothing! The memory of Shumari's voice made me laugh again, and just then catching sight of the twinkling camp fires in the far distance, I laughed at myself too. And, on a sudden, just as my laugh ceased, there came from the rattan brake past which we were riding a sound that was, and yet was not, the echo of my laugh. It sounded something like my laugh, but it was repeated twice, and the creature I rode, ass though it was, turned its head towards the brake. Shumari meanwhile had seen the camp fires, and his terror overpowering discipline, he gave one howl of horror and fled, his ass, seeing the fires too, falling into the humor with all his will, and carrying off his rider at full speed. My ass wanted to follow, but I pulled him up, and to make further trial of the hidden jester, shouted out in Swahili, "Who is there?"

The answer was as sudden as horrifying. For an instant the brake swayed to and fro, and then there came a crashing of branches as of some great beast forcing his way through them, and on a sudden, close behind me, burst out — the Soko!

Shumari had carried off my guns, and, except for the short knife in my belt, I was defenceless. And there before me in the flesh stood the creature I had gone out to hunt, but which for ever so many miles must have been hunting us. I had no leisure for moralizing or even for examination of the creature before me. It seemed about Shumari's height, but was immensely broad at the shoulders, and in one hand it carried a fragment of a bough. Had it been simply man against man, I would have stood my ground — but *was* it? The dim light prevented my noting any details, and I had no inclination or time to scrutinize the features of the thing that now approached me. I saw the white teeth flashing, heard a deep-chested stuttering, inarticulate with rage, and flinging myself from the ass, which was trembling and rooted to the spot with fear, I ran as I had never run before in the direction of the camp.

The Soko must have stopped to attack the ass, for I heard a scuffle behind me as I started, but very soon the ass came tearing past me, and looking round I saw the Soko in pursuit. The heavy branch fortunately encumbered its progress, but it gained upon me. Close behind me I heard the thing jabbering and panting, and for an instant thought of standing at bay. I was running my hardest, but it seemed, just as in a nightmare, as if horror had partly paralyzed my limbs, and I were only creeping along. The horror of such pursuit was, I felt, culminating in sickness, and I thought I should swoon and fall. But just then I became aware of approaching lights, the camp fires seemed to be running to me. The Soko, however, was fast overtaking me, and I struggled on, but it was of no use, and my feet tripping against the projecting root of an old mvule, I fell on my knees; but, rising again, I staggered against the tree, drew my knife, and waited for the attack. In an instant the Soko was up with me, and, dropping its bough, reached out its arms to seize me. I lunged at it with my knife, but the length of its arms baffled me, for before the point of my knife could find its body, the Soko's hands had grasped my shoulders, and with such astonishing force that it seemed as if my arms were being displaced in their sockets. The next moment a third hand seized hold of my leg below the knee, and I was instantly jerked on to the ground. The fall partially stunned me, and then I felt a rough-haired body fall heavily upon me, and, groping their way to my throat, long fingers feeling about me. I struggled with the creature, but against its strength my hands were nerveless. The fingers had now found my throat; I felt the grasp tightening, and gave myself up to death. But on a sudden there was a confusion of voices — a flashing of bright lights before my eyes, and the weight was all at once raised from off me. In another minute I had recovered my consciousness, and found that my men, the gallant Mabruki at their head, had charged to my rescue with burning brands, and arrived only just in time to save my life.

And the Soko?

As I lay there, my faithful followers round me with their brands still flickering, the voice of the Soko came to us, but from which direction it was impossible to say, soft and mysterious as before, the same *hoot, hoot*, that had puzzled us on our homeward route.

My narrow escape from a horrible though somewhat absurd death was celebrated by my men with extravagant demonstrations of indignation against the Soko that had hunted me, and many respectful reproaches for my temerity. For myself, I was more eager than ever to capture or kill the formidable thing that had outwitted and outmatched me; and so having had my arms well rubbed with oil, I gave the order for a general muster next morning for a grand Soko hunt.

Now, close by our camp grew a great tree, from which hung down liane strands of every rope-thickness, and all round its roots had grown up a dense hedge of strong-spined cane. One of my men, sent up the tree to cut us off some of these natural ropes, reported that all round the tree, that is, between its trunk and the cane-hedge, there was a clear space, so that though, looking at it from the outside, it seemed as if the canes grew right up to the tree trunk, looking at it from above, there was seen to be really an open pathway, so to speak, surrounding the tree, broad enough for three men to walk abreast. I had often heard of similar cases of vegetable aversions, where, from some secret cause of plant prejudice, two shrubs, though growing together, exercise this mutual repulsion, and never actually combine in growth. Meanwhile, however, the phenomenon was interesting to me for other reasons, for I saw at once what a convenient receptacle this natural well would make for the baggage we had to leave behind.

Leaving our effects therefore inside this brake, which we did by slinging the bales one after the other over an overhanging bough, and so dropping them into the open pathway, and removing from the neighborhood every trace of our recent encampment, we started westward with four days' provisions, ready cooked, on our backs. The method of march was in line, each man about a hundred yards from the next, and every second man on an ass, the riders carrying the usual ivory horns, without which no travellers in the Uregga forests ever move from home, and the notes of which, exactly like the cry of the American wood-marmot, keep the party in line. By this means we covered a mile, and being unencumbered, marched fast, scouring the wood before us at the rate of four miles an hour for three hours.

And what a wild, weird time it was, those three hours, marching with noiseless footfalls, looking constantly right and left and overhead. I could see the line of shadowy figures advancing on either side, not a sound along the whole line, except when the horns carried down in response to one another their thin, wailing notes, or when some palm fruit, over-ripe, dropped rustling down through the canopy of foliage above us. And yet the whole forest was instinct with life. If you set yourself to listen, there came to your ears, all day and night, a great monotone of sound humming through the misty shade, the aggregate voices of millions of insect things that had their being among the foliage or in the daylight that reigned in the outer world above those green clouds which made perpetual twilight for us who were passing underneath. Along the tree-roof streamed also troops of monkeys, and flocks of parrots and other birds; but in their passage overhead, we could not, through the dense vault of foliage, branch, and blossom, hear their voices, except as merged in the one great sound that filled all space, too large almost to be heard at all. In the midst, then, of this vast murmur of confused nature, we seemed to walk in absolute silence. The ear had grown so accustomed to it, that a sneeze was heard with a start, and the occasional knocking together of asses' hoofs made every head turn suddenly, and every rifle move to the shoulder.

At the end of the three hours' marching we came to a river, — perhaps that which Stanley, in his "Dark Continent," names the Asna, — flowing northwest, with a width here of only one hundred yards, — a deep, slow stream, crystal clear, flowing without a ripple or a murmur through the perpetual gloaming, between banks of soft, rich, black leaf-mould. We halted, and, after a rapid meal, re-formed in line, and marching for two miles easterly up the river, made a left wheel; and in the same order, and at the same pace as we had advanced, we continued nearly two hours rather in a northerly direction; and then making a left wheel again, started off due west, crossing the tracks of our morning's march in our fourth mile, and reaching the Asna again in our tenth mile, — a total march of nearly thirty-two miles, of which, of course, each man had traversed only one half on foot. No cooking was allowed, and our collation was therefore soon despatched, and before I had lighted my pipe and curled myself up I saw that all the party were snug under their mosquito nets.

I had noticed, when reading travellers' books, that they always suffered severely from mosquitoes and other insects. I determined that *I* would not; so, before leaving Zanzibar, served out to every man twenty yards of net. These, in the daytime, were worn round the head as turbans, and at night spread upon sticks, and furnished each man a protection against these Macbeths of the sedge and brake. The men thoroughly understood their value, and before turning in for the night, always carefully examined their nets for stray holes, which they caught together with fibres. But somehow I could not go to sleep for a long while; the pain in my arm where the Soko seized me was very great at times; besides, I felt haunted; and indeed, when I awoke and found it already four o'clock, it did not seem that I had been asleep at all. But the time for sleep was now over; so, awakening the expedition, we ate a silent meal, and noiselessly remounting, were again on the war-trail. On this, the second day, we marched some three miles down the river, northwest, and then taking a half right wheel, started off northeast, passing to the north of our camp at about the eleventh mile. Here the first sign of life we had seen since we started broke the tedium of our ghost-like progress.

Between myself and the next man on the line was running a little stream, fed probably by the dews that here rained down upon us from the mvule-trees. These, more than all others, seem to condense the heated upper air, their leaves being thick in texture, and curiously cool, — for which reason the natives prefer them for butter and oil dishes. Along the stream, as usual, crowded a thick fringe of white-starred sedge. On a sudden there was a swaying of the herbage, and out bounced a splendidly spotted creature of the cat kind. Immediately behind him crept out his mate; and there they stood: the male, his crest and all the hair along the spine erect with anger at our intrusion, his tail swinging and curling with excitement; beside him, and half behind him, the female crouching low on the ground, her ears laid back along the head, and motionless as a carved stone. My ass saw the pair, and instinct warning it that the beautiful beasts were dangerous to it, with that want of judgment and consideration so characteristic of asses, it must needs bray. And such a bray! At every *hee* it pumped up enough air from its lungs to have contented an organ, and at every *haw* it vented a shattering blast to which all the slogans of all the clans were mere puling. It brayed its very soul out in the suddenness of the terror. The effect on the leopards was instant and complete. There was just one lightning flash of color, — a yellow streak across the space before me, and plump! the splendid pair soused into a murderous tangle of creeping palms. That they could ever have got out of the awful trap, with its millions of strong spines barbed like fish-hooks and as strong as steel, is probably impossible; but the magnificent promptitude of the suicide, its picturesque completeness, was undeniable.

The ass, however, was by no means soothed by the meteor-like disappearance of the beasts of prey, and the gruesome dronings that, in spite of hard whacks, it indulged in for many minutes, betrayed the depth of its emotions and the cavernous nature of its interior organization. The ass, like the savage, has no perception of the picturesque.

After the morning meal I allowed a three hours' rest, and in knots of twos and threes along the line, the party sat down, talking in subdued tones (for silence was the order of the march), or comfortably snoozing. I slept myself as well as my aching arm would let me. The march resumed, I wheeled the line with its front due west, and after another two hours' rapid advance we found ourselves again at the river, some seven miles farther down its course than the point from which we had started in the morning; and after a hurried meal, I gave the order for home. Striking southeasterly, we crossed in our fifth mile the track of the morning, and in the thirteenth reached our camp. By this means it will be seen we had effectually triangulated a third of a circle of eleven miles radius from our camp — and with absolutely no result. During the next two days I determined to scour, if possible, the remaining semicircle. Meanwhile, we were at the point we had started from, and though it was nearly certain that at any rate one Soko was in the neighborhood, we had fatigued ourselves with nearly seventy miles of marching without finding a trace of it.

As nothing was required from our concealed store, we had only to eat and go to sleep; and so the men, after laughing together for a while over the snug arrangements I had made for the safety of our goods, and pretending to have doubts as to this being the real site of the hidden property of the expedition, were soon asleep in a batch. I went to sleep too; not a sound sleep, for I could not drive from my memory the hideous recollection of that evening, only two days before, when, nearly in the same spot I was lying in the Soko's power. And thinking about it, I got so restless that, under the irresistible impression that some supernatural presence was about me, I unpegged my mosquito net, and getting up, began to pace about. I wore at nights a long Cashmere dressing-gown, in lieu of the tighter canvas coat. I had been leaning against a tree; but feeling that the moisture that trickled down the trunk was soaking my back, I was moving off, when my ears were nearly split by a shout from behind me — "Soko! Soko!" and the next instant I found myself flung violently to the ground, and struggling with — Mabruki! The pain caused by the sudden fall at first made me furious at the mistake that had been made; but the next instant, when the whole absurdity of the position came upon me, I roared with laughter.

The savage is very quickly infected by mirth, and in a minute, as soon as the story got round how Mabruki had jumped upon the master for a Soko, the whole camp was in fits of laughter. Sleep was out of the question with my aching back and aching sides; and so, mixing myself some grog and lighting my pipe, I made Mabruki shampoo my limbs with oil. While he did so he began to talk,—

"Does the master ever see devils?"

"Devils? No."

"Mabruki does, and all the Wanyamwazi of his village do, for his village elders are the keepers of the charm against evil spirits of the whole land of Unyamwazi, and they often see them. I saw a devil to-night."

"Was the devil like a Soko?" I asked, laughing.

"Yes, master," he replied, "like a Soko; but I was always asleep, and never saw it, but whenever it came to me it said, 'I am here,' and then at last I got frightened and got up, and then I saw you, master, and " —

But we were both laughing again, and Mabruki stopped.

It was strange that he, too, should have felt the same uncanny presence that had afflicted me. But under Mabruki's manipulation I soon fell asleep. I awoke with a start. Mabruki had gone. But much the same inexplicable, restless feeling that men say they have felt under ghostly visitations, impelled me to get up, and this time, lighting a pipe to prevent mistakes, I resumed my sauntering, and tired at last of being alone, I awoke my men for the start, although day was not yet breaking. Half-asleep a meal was soon discussed, and in an hour we were again on the move. Shumari had lagged behind, as usual, and on his coming up I reproved him for being the last.

"I am not the last," he said; "Zaidi, the Wangwana, is not here yet. I saw him climbing up for a liane" (the men got their ropes from these useful plants) "just as I was coming away, and I called out to him that you would be angry."

"Peace!" said Baraka, the man next to me; "is not that Zaidi the Wangwana there, riding on the ass? It was not he. It was that good-for-nothing Tarya. He is always the last to stand up and the first to sit down."

"No doubt, then," said Shumari, "it was Tarya; shame on him. He is no bigger than Zaidi, and has hair like his. Besides, it was in the mist I saw him."

But I had heard enough — the nervousness of the night still afflicted me.

"Sound the halt!" I cried; "call the men together."

In three minutes all were grouped round me — not one was missing! Tarya was far ahead, riding on an ass, and had therefore been one of the first to start.

"Who was the last to leave camp?" I asked, and by the unanimous voice it was agreed to be Shumari himself.

Shumari, then, had seen the Soko! and our storehouse was the Soko's home!

The rest of the men had not heard the preceding

conversation, so, putting them in possession of the facts, I gave the order for returning to our camp. We approached. I halted the whole party, and binding up the asses' mouths with cloths, we tied them to a stout liane, and then dividing the party into two, led one myself round to the south side of the camp by a *détour*, leaving the other about half a mile to the north of it, with orders to rush towards the canebrake and surround it at a hundred yards' distance as soon as they heard my bugle. Passing swiftly round, we were soon in our places, and then, deploying my men on either side so as to cover a semicircle, I sounded the bugle. The response came on the instant, and in a few minutes there was a cordon round the brake at one hundred yards radius, each man about twenty yards or so from the next. But all was silent as the grave. As yet nothing had got through our line, I felt sure; and if therefore Shumari had indeed seen the Soko, the Soko was still within the circle of our guns. A few tufts of young rattan grew between the line and the brake in the centre of which were our goods, and unless it was up above us, hidden in the impervious canopy overhead, where *was* the Soko? A shot was fired into each tuft, and in breathless excitement the circle began to close in upon the brake.

"Let us fire!" cried Mabruki.

"No, no!" I shouted, for the bullets would perhaps have whistled through the lianes amongst ourselves. "Catch the Soko alive if you can."

But first we had to sight the Soko, and this, in an absolutely impenetrable clump of rope-thick creepers, was impossible, except from above.

Shumari, as agile as a monkey, was called, and

ordered to climb up the tree, the branches of which had served us to sling our goods into the brake, and to see if he could espy the intruder. The lad did not like the job; but with the pluck of his race obeyed, and was soon slung up over the bough, and creeping along it, overhung the centre of the brake. All faces were upturned towards him as he peered down within the wall of vegetation. For many minutes there was silence, and then came Shumari's voice, —

"No, master, I cannot see the Soko."

"Climb on to the big liane," called out Mabruki. The lad obeyed, and made his way from knot to knot of the swinging strand. One end of it was rooted into the ground at the foot of the tree inside the canebrake, the other, in cable thickness, hanging down loose within the circle. We, watching, saw him look down, and on the instant heard him cry, —

"Ai! ma-ma! the Soko, the Soko!" and while the lad spoke we saw the hanging creeper violently jerked, and then swung to and fro, as if some creature of huge strength had hold of the loose end of it and was trying to shake Shumari from his hold.

"Help! help, master!" cried Shumari. "I am falling;" and then he lost his hold, and fell with a crash down into the brake, and for an instant we held our breath to listen — but all was quiet as death. The next instant, at a dozen different points, axes were at work clearing the lianes. For a few minutes nothing was to be heard but the deep breathing of the straining men and the crashing of the branches; and then on a sudden, at the side farthest from me, came a shout and a shot, a confused rush of frantic animal noises, and the sounds of a fierce struggle.

In an instant I was round the brake, and there lay Shumari, apparently unhurt, and the Soko — dying!

"Untie his hands," I said. This was done, and the wounded thing made an effort to stagger to its feet.

A dozen arms thrust it to the ground again. "Let him rise," I said; "help him to rise;" and Mabruki helped the Soko on to its feet.

Powers above! If this were an ape, what else were half my expedition? The wounded wood-thing passed its right arm round Mabruki's neck, and taking one of his hands, pressed it to its own heart. A deep sob shook its frame, and then it lifted back its head and looked in turn into all the faces round it, with the death-glaze settling fast in its eyes. I came nearer, and took its hand as it hung on Mabruki's shoulder. The muscles, gradually contracting in death, made it seem as if there was a gentle pressure of my palm, and then — the thing died.

Life left it so suddenly that we could not believe that all was over. But the Soko was really dead, and close to where he lay I had him buried.

"Master said he wanted the Soko's skin," said Shumari, in a weak voice, reminding me of my words of a few days before.

"No, no," I said; "bury the wild man quickly. We shall march at once."

III.

ELEPHANTS.

They are Square Animals with a Leg at each Corner and a Tail at both Ends. — " My Lord the Elephant." — That it picks up Pins. — The Mammoth as a Missionary in Africa. — An Elephant Hunt with the Prince. — Elephantine Potentialities. — A Mad Giant. — Bigness not of Necessity a Virtue. — A Digression on the Meekness of Giants.

ELEPHANTS are square animals with a leg at each corner and a tail at both ends. This may be said to be the popular description of the Titan among mammals.

Nor is its moral character more accurately summed up by the crowd. It has, indeed, come to be a time-honored custom when looking at Jumbo, the elephant which Barnum has bought from " the Zoo " in London, to applaud first its sagacity, as evidenced, they say, in that old story of the tailor who pricked an elephant's trunk with his imprudent needle; next, its docility, as shown (so the crowd would have us believe) by its carrying children about on its back; in the third place the great sensitiveness of its trunk, inasmuch as it can pick up a pin with it; and, finally, its great size. After this, nothing apparently remains but to congratulate ourselves, in. a lofty way, upon having thus comprehensively traversed all the elephant's claims to respect, and to pass on to the next beast in the show.

But, as a matter of fact, nothing could well be more offensive, more unsympathetic, more unworthy of the elephant, than this stereotyped formula of admiration. That an elephant did once so unbecomingly demean himself as to squirt the contents of a puddle over a tailor and his shop is infinitely discreditable to the gigantic pachyderm; and every compliment of sagacity paid to it on account of that dirty street-boy trick is an affront to the lordly beast which ranks to-day, in the Belgian expedition to Africa, as one of the noblest pioneers of modern commerce and the greatest of living missionaries, and in the Afghan war as one of the most devoted and valued of her Majesty's servants in the East.

His docility, again, is an easy cry, for was not Jumbo to be seen, every day of the week, carrying children up and down a path, and round and round a clump of bushes, backwards and forwards, forwards and backwards, without doing the children any harm, or even needing the keeper's voice to tell him when a fair pennyworth of ride had been enjoyed? But upon such docility as this it is an insult to found respect, for surprise at such results argues a prior suspicion that the elephant would eat the children or run amuck among the visitors to the Zoölogical Gardens. Of its splendid docility there are abundant anecdotes, and among them are some which are really worthy of the sole living representative of the family of the mastodon and the mammoth.

Such a one is the old Mahratta story of the standard-bearing elephant that by its docility won a great victory for its master the Peishwa. The huge embattled beast was carrying on its back the royal ensign, the rallying-point of the Poona host, and at the very commencement of the engagement the elephant's mahout, just as he ordered it to halt, received his death wound and fell off its back. The elephant, in obedience to his order, stood its ground. The shock of battle closed round it and the standard it carried, and the uproar of contending armies filled the scene with unusual terrors. But the elephant never moved a yard, refusing to advance or to retire the standard entrusted to it by so much as a step; and the Mahrattas, seeing the flag still flying in its place, would not believe that the day was going against them, and rallied again and again round their immovable standard-bearer. Meanwhile the elephant stood there in the very heart of the conflict, straining its ears all the while to catch above the din of battle the sound of the voice which would never speak again.

And soon the wave of war passed on, leaving the field deserted; and though the Mahrattas swept by in victorious pursuit of the now routed foe, still as a rock standing out from the ebbing flood was the elephant in its place, with the slain heaped round it, and the standard still floating above its castled back! For three days and nights it remained where it had been told to remain, and neither bribe nor threat would move it, till they sent to the village on the Nerbudda, a hundred miles away, and fetched the mahout's little son, a round-eyed, lisping child; and then at last the hero of that victorious day, remembering how its dead master had often in brief absence delegated authority to the child, confessed its allegiance, and with the shattered battle harness clanging at each stately stride, swung slowly along the road behind the boy.

Such splendid docility as this — the docility which in our human veterans we call discipline — is worthy of our recollection when we look at our great captives. But why should we offend against the majesty of the elephant by applauding him for carrying children to and fro unhurt? A bullock could not do less.

Then, again, the marvel that the elephant should pick up a pin! It can do so, of course, but it is a pity that it should; for elephants that go about picking up pins derogate something from their dignity, just as much as those others who, to amuse the guests of Germanicus, carried a comrade on a litter along tight ropes, and executed thereafter a Pyrrhic dance. It is surely preferable, recalling the elephants of history, to forget these unseemly saltations and the mocking records of Ælian and of Pliny, and to remember rather that one single elephant alone sufficed to frighten the whole nation of Britons into fits; that as the leaders of armies they played a splendid part in nearly every old-world invasion, from that of Bacchus to that of Hannibal; and that their classic glories and the traditions of their intelligent co-operation with men have invested them with special sanctity for millions of men and women in the East. How magnificently they loom out from the military records of Pyrrhus and Mithridates, Semiramis and Alexander and Cæsar; and what a world of tender reverence gathers round their name when we think of them to-day as the objects of gentle worship in India, — "My Lord the Elephant!" To look at an elephant through the wrong end of a telescope is to put an affront upon the animal to whom Asia and Africa now appeal for an assistance, otherwise impossible, in war and in commerce.

It was they who dragged to Candahar and Cabul the guns that shook Shere Ali from his Afghan throne and avenged the British Envoy's murder; and now they are swinging across Africa from the East to meet the steamers coming up the Livingstone from the West, and thus clasp the girdle of commerce round the Dark Continent.

But the narrative of this expedition is so full, as it seems to me, of picturesque interest, that I think it may find a place in these discursive pages.

The animals, then, were supplied by the Poona stud — at the expense of the King of the Belgians — and in marching them along the high road to Bombay, elephants being common objects of the country in that presidency, no exceptional difficulties presented themselves.

Arrived, however, at the seashore, where elephants do not abound, it was discovered that no one knew what to do with the bulky pachyderms, or how to get them off the wharf into the ship. A crowd collected round the strangers, and, while everybody was offering advice, the elephants took fright and charged the council, who precipitately fled. To a practical person, who, it would appear, had remained out of the way while the charging was going on, it then suggested itself, that, as elephants had been slung on board ship during the Abyssinian war, they might be slung again, provided the gear was of elephantine calibre. The weight of an elephant, however, was an unknown quantity, but a general average of twenty tons being mooted was accepted by the company as a safe estimate — an elephant as a rule being something less than three tons. The gear was therefore adapted to a weight of twenty tons, and the mammoths, being got into position, were safely slung on board, and the steamer sailed.

During the voyage the elephants would persist in standing up all day and night, and the swaying of their huge bodies with the motion of the ship nearly dislocated even their columnar legs, — nearly fractured also the timbers of the deck. But at last they were urged into kneeling down, while a judicious addition of props kept the deck in its place: and thus the elephants got safely across the seas to Zanzibar. Then came another difficulty: how were the creatures to be landed? The ship could not go nearer to the shore than two miles, and there was neither raft, nor lighter, nor any other appliance for transporting them to land. Could they swim? No one knew.

There was nothing for it but to try. So one of the monsters — its name was the Budding Lily and it stood ten feet high — was gravely dropped overboard, with a man on its back. The elephant solemnly sank until the man was under water, and then as solemnly reappeared. One look round sufficed to explain the position to the poor beast, which, hopeless of ever reaching the distant shore, turned round and made frantic efforts to get on board again! In vain the mahout belabored it. The elephant kept its head against the ship's side. In vain they tried to tow it behind a boat, for though, when exhausted with strugling, the huge bulk was dragged a short distance, returning strength soon enabled it to drag the boat back to the ship.

And so for an hour, rain pelting hard all the time, the wretched monster floundered about in the sea, and scrambled against the ship's timbers, now floating alongside without any sign of life, now plunging madly round with the ridiculous boat in tow. That it would have drowned ultimately seemed beyond doubt, but on a sudden the great thing's intelligence supplemented that of the human beings who were with it, and making up its mind that life was worth another effort, and that the ship was unscalable, the elephant began to swim. Again and again, before it reached the first sandbank, its strength or pluck failed; but the boat was always at hand to encourage or irritate it to renewed exertions, and so at last, after nearly four hours' immersion, the first Behemoth got on shore. Away in the distance those watching from the ship could make out the great black bulk creeping up the sward. Under a tree close by stood its attendant, and in the enjoyment of the monstrous cakes of sugar, rum, flour, and spices which had been prepared for it, and the luxury of a careful rubbing down with warm blankets, the Captain Webb of the elephant world recovered its equanimity and spirits.

Her companions, the Flower Garland, Beauty, and the Wonder-Inspirer, emboldened by Budding Lily's performance, soon joined her on African soil.

The object of their deportation was twofold, for they had in the first place to prove, in their own persons, the adaptability of their kind to be the carriers of merchandise across the Central African solitudes, and in the next to tame and civilize to the service of man the great herds of their wild congeners, the African elephants, roaming in the forests through which the highways of Arab trade now pass.

There is very little difference between the two species, the Indian and the African. The latter has much larger ears and finer tusks, and its forehead is convex, while the Asiatic animal prefers to have it concave. The African elephant, however, is as amenable to discipline as the other. For there can be no doubt that it was the African elephant which charged with the armies of Hannibal and Pyrrhus, and danced before Nero and Galba.

He is, indeed, a truly splendid mammal, a remnant worthy of the great diluvian period when giant pachyderms divided among them the empire of a world of mud. He remains, like the one colossal ruin of the old Egyptian city, to remind us what the old Africa was like.

But the world of trade stands in need to-day of the African elephant; and out of his stately solitude, therefore, he must come to carry from the forest to the coast the produce which our markets demand. And for his capture the Arab and Zanzibari can have no more skilful assistants, or it may be teachers, than the veterans of the Indian khedda that have now gone out. Many a wild tusker, no doubt, has Beauty pommelled into servility, and many a one has Budding Lily coaxed by her treacherous blandishments into the toils of the Philistines. The tame females, it is well known, seem to take a positive delight in betraying the Samsons of the jungle into slavery; for, after lavishing their caresses upon them till they have tempted them within the fatal circle, they leave them, with a spiteful thump at parting, to the mercy of their captors.

When the Prince of Wales was in India, an elephant-hunt was among the amusements provided for his Royal Highness by that most royal of entertainers, and of murderers, Jung Bahádur, of Nepal, and in the contemporary records of the expedition, full justice has been done to that thrilling episode of the Prince's visit. The heroes of the capture were Jung Pershad and Bijli Pershad. The former, in height, weight, and courage, was superior to all the eight hundred elephants of the Nepalese stud, while Bijli, "The Lightning," had no match for speed and pluck combined. The first wild tusker sighted was a magnificent fellow, sulking and fuming in a clump of tall jungle grass, and whenever he charged out of it the ordinary fighting elephants brought up at first against him fled before him. Then, with all the leisurely solemnity befitting his renown, old Jung Pershad came swinging up. But, no sooner had the huge bruiser hove in sight than the wild giant, measuring him at a glance, confessed his master, and fled before the overpowering presence. The grand old gladiator did not attempt pursuit. His bulk forbade it, and so did the etiquette of his profession.

To his friend and colleague in many a previous fight, Bijli the swift-footed, pertained the privilege of pursuit, and from the moment when the quarry perceived the strangely rapid advance of his new antagonist, he reccognized the gravity of his peril. Flight from Bijli was as vain as contest with Jung. So he swung round in his stride, and for full two minutes the pursuer and pursued stood absolutely motionless and silent, face to face. And then, on a sudden and with one accord, " with their trunks upraised and their great ears spread, and with a crash like two rocks falling together, the giants rushed upon each other. There was no reservation about that charge: they came together with all their weight, and all their speed, and all their heart." But the skill that comes of practice gave the professional just the one point he needed to beat so splendid an amateur; and he beat him "by sometimes ramming him against a tree, sometimes poking him in the side so as almost to knock him over, sometimes raising his trunk above his head, and bringing it down on the poor tusker's neck. At last the wild elephant fairly gave up, surrendered, and made no further pretence of either fighting or flying."

Henceforth, in far other scenes, other Jung Pershads and other Bijlis, mighty in battle, will win renown, and, winning it, will do for Central Africa what the camel has done for Central Asia, and what ships have done for all the world's coasts. They will be the pioneers of trade, true missionaries, Asia's contingent in the little army that has set out to conquer, but without bloodshed, the desperate savagery of the Dark Continent.

At any rate it was a finely picturesque conception, this of compelling the Behemoths of the Indian jungles to serve in the subjection of the Titans of the African forests, and to bring face to face, in the centre of a continent, the two sole survivors of a once mighty order; and I could never look at Jumbo lounging along the path in the Zoölogical Gardens without thinking also of his noble kinsmen working their way in the cause of civilization and of man across the Dark Continent.

. . . .

Sagacity and docility are, no doubt, therefore, virtues which the elephant shares with man, but it is hardly fair to it to illustrate its intelligence by quoting the deplorable incident of the tailor, unless we are also prepared to illustrate the sagacity of men and women by referring to the performances of the Artful Dodger.

Let us rather generously forget that elephantine lapse, just as we remember that, after all, Noah — in that "aged surprisal of six hundred years" only got drunk once.

Nor, when we speak loftily of the elephant's docility, should we forget that the measure of this virtue may be gauged by the individual's capacities for the reverse. A white mouse is one of the most docile of animals, but what would it matter if it were not? A pinch of the tail would always suffice to frighten it into abject submission. But when the sagacious elephant decides for itself, as it often does, that docility is not worth the candle, that occasional turbulence, good-all-round rebellion, is wholesome for its temper and constitution, — who is going to pinch its tail? With one swing of its trunk it lays all the attendants flat, butts its head through an inconvenient wall, and is free! They are brave men who capture the wild elephants, but no one, however brave, tries to capture a mad one. It has to be shot in its tracks, dropped standing, for it is then something more than a mere wild animal. It has developed into a creature of deliberate will and, having in its own mind weighed the pros and cons, has come to the fixed conclusion that captivity is a mistake, and proceeds therefore on a definite line of intelligent and malignant action.

Indeed, among the episodes of Indian rural life there are few more appalling than such a one as that of the Mad Elephant of Mundla. It had been for many years a docile inmate of a government stud, but one day made up its mind to be infamous. Wise men have before now told the world that it is well to be drunk once a month, and others that we should not always abstain from that which is hurtful; so the elephant, determining upon a bout of wrong-doing, had some precedent to excuse him. The elephantine proportions of his misdemeanors, however, made his lapse from docility appalling to mere men and women whose individual wicked acts are naturally on so diminutive a scale; but, comparatively speaking, the gigantic mammal was simply "on the spree." Neverthless, it desolated villages with nearly every horrible circumstance of cruelty lately practised by the Christians of Bulgaria, and laid its plans with such consummate cunning that skilled police, well mounted and patrolling the country, were baffled for many days in their pursuit of the midnight terror. It came and went with extraordinary secrecy and speed from point to point, leaving none alive upon the high roads to tell the pursuers which way it had gone, and only a smashed village and trampled corpses to show where it had last appeared. It confused its own tracks by doubling upon its pursuers and crossing the spoor of the elephants that accompanied them.

It was not merely wild. It was also *mad*—and as cunning and as cruel as a mad man.

But insanity itself may be accepted, if you like, as a tribute to the animal's intelligence, for sudden downright madness presumes strong brain power. Owls never go mad. They may go silly, or they may be born idiots; but, as Oliver Wendell Holmes says, a weak mind does not accumulate force enough to hurt itself. Stupidity often saves a man from insanity.

It is also curious to notice how the size of Jumbo strikes so many as being somehow very creditable to Behemoth. But praise of such a kind is hardly worth the acceptance of even the hippopotamus. "The wisdom of God," says Sir Thomas Browne, "receives small honor from those vulgar heads that rudely stare about and, with a gross rusticity, admire His works;" and it is certainly gross rusticity to attribute credit to the elephant for being big. After all, he is not so big as other creatures living, nor as he himself might have been a few centuries ago. Moreover, though giants seem always popular, there is little virtue in mere size. The whale, driving along through vast ocean spaces, displaces, it is true, prodigious quantities of water, but the only admirable points about him, nevertheless, are his whalebone and his blubber. He is simply a wild oil barrel, and the more cheaply he can be caught and bottled off the better.

But speaking of personal bulk as a feature to be complimented, there is an illustration at my hand here in the next enclosure — for who could honestly congratulate the hippopotamus upon its proportions?

Men ought to have a grudge against this inflated monster, for it is one of the happiest and most useless of living things. Its happiness in a natural state is simply abominable when taken in connection with its worthlessness; and the rhinoceros, next door there, is no better. Providence, to quote the well known judge, has given them health and strength — "*instead of which*," they go about munching vegetables and wallowing in warm pools. They do absolutely nothing for their livelihood, except now and then affront the elephant. Even for this the hippopotamus is too sensual and too indolent; but the rhinoceros often presumes to hold the path against the King of the Forests. Their bulk, therefore, is either abused by them or wasted, so that their monstrous size and strength really become a reproach.

With the elephant it is very different. Every ounce of his weight goes to the help of man, and every inch of his stature to his service.

. . . . . .

I have said above that giants are always popular, and as perhaps the observation may be contested in the nursery, I would here, in the chapter on gigantic animals, interpolate my defence. Once upon a time, and not so long ago either, two bulky Irishmen were walking in San Francisco, when they met a foreigner sauntering along the street. Now they both hated foreigners, so they proceeded to assault him, whereupon the stranger took his hands out of his pockets, and, catching hold of the two Irishmen, banged their bodies together until they were half dead. The foreigner's performance drew the attention of passers-by to him, and they noticed, what the Irishmen had not discovered until too late, that the stranger was a man of gigantic physical strength. They also remarked that but for the feat he had performed this Hercules might have gone to and fro unsuspected, for not only was his demeanor modest and unassuming, but his face wore *a gentle and benevolent expression*. He was, in fact, of the true giant breed, reduced in proportions to suit modern times, but having about him, nevertheless, all the thews and the inoffensive disposition of the original Blunderbore.

To explain my meaning further I need only refer to the history of that overgrown but otherwise estimable person whose lodgings were burglariously entered by a young person named Jack, who for no apparent reason — such was the laxity of the public morals in those days — climbed up, so we are asked to believe, the stalk of a leguminous vegetable of the bean kind, and, having effected a forcible entry into the giant's premises, robbed the amiable but stertorous Blunderbore of the most valuable of his effects. Here, then, is a case in point of a person of retiring habits being assaulted simply because he was of gigantic size and strength, and of the public condoning the assault on that account alone. It is contended, I know, that Jack was incited to his crimes by a cock-and-bull story about the giant's castle having belonged to Jack's father, told to the boy by an old woman whom he chanced to find loitering about his mother's cottage, — with one eye, depend upon it, all the time on the linen spread out on the hedge. But it was just like the vagabond's impudence to foist her nonsense on a mere child. For after all, how could Jack's father have had a castle in the clouds, unless he had been a magician? — in which case Jack himself was little better, and his mother, by presumption, a witch; in which case they ought all to have been ducked in the horse-pond together.

Whether this Jack was the same person who, in after-life, settled down to industrious habits, and, presumably unassisted, built a House for himself, chiefly remarkable for the zoölogical experiences in which it resulted, I am unable to determine. But looking to the antecedents of the Giant-killer, his laziness at home, and his unthrifty bargain in that matter of his mother's cow, I should hesitate, even with the memory of Alcibiades's conversion to Spartan austerity in my mind, to believe in such a reformation as this, of a young burglar turning into a middle-aged and respectable householder. In the mean time it is noteworthy that the Jack of the Beanstalk was a boy of forward and larcenous habits, that he committed an unprovoked series of outrages upon a giant in whose house he had been well treated, and that the giant was an affable personage of great simplicity of mind and easily amused, kind to poultry and fond of string music.

Indeed, had he not been so excessively large it is probable he would have been a very ordinary person indeed. This, at any rate, seems certain, that if he had been any smaller he would not have been either so simple or so shabbily treated. It has always been the misfortune of huge stature to be taken advantage of, and so many men of strength have been betrayed and brought to grief by Jacks and Aladdins, Omphales and Delilahs, that it has come to be understood that when a man is preternaturally strong he should be also extremely unassuming in demeanor, and liable, therefore, to unprovoked aggression.

It has, I know, been gravely endeavored, by a certain class, to shake the world's belief in the existence of giants, but the attempt has been fortunately unsuccessful. No argument, however ingenious, erudite, or forcible, can knock out of sight such an extremely obvious fact as a giant; and I consider, therefore, that Maclaurin, who attempted to demonstrate, by the destructive method and mathematics, the impossibility of giants, might have saved himself the labor of such profane calculations. The destructive argument; however, I confess, has this much in its favor, that it explains why many of the Anakim are weak in the knees, for, inasmuch as the forces tending to destroy cohesion in masses of matter arising from their own gravity only increase in the quadruplicate ratio of their lengths, the opposite forces, tending to preserve that cohesion, increase only in the triplicate ratio. It follows, therefore, that if we only make the giant long enough he must, by mathematics, go at the knee joints.

Indeed, in our own modern literature will be found much excellent matter with regard to weak-kneed giants from which it appears that the show-frequenting public take no delight whatever in infirm Goliaths; and those who may have any to exhibit will do better to put the feeble-legged Gogs and Magogs to useful tasks about the house or back-garden than display them in public for gain. In one of these stories the giants, when they became decrepid, waited upon the dwarfs attached to the show. The tendency to mock at a giant becomes, among the lower orders, uncontrollable when Blunderbore is shaky in the lower limbs; and under these circumstances, as it is not legal to make away with giants when used up, he should be either kept in entire obscurity, or only have the uppermost half of him exhibited.

This inclination to make fun of men of exceptionally large stature or extraordinary strength may be due to a half-recognized impression on the mind that such persons are out of our own sphere, superhuman, and preposterous. They are out of date, too, being, as it were, relics of fables and the representatives of a past world, in which they kept the company of gnomes and dwarfs, ogres, hobgoblins, and other absurd gentry of the kind, living irregular lives, perpetually subject, from their great size, to dangerous accidents, and, as a rule, coming to sudden and ridiculous ends. It was very seldom, indeed, that a giant maintained his dignity to the last, and there hangs, therefore, a vapor of the ludicrous about the memory of the race, so that nowadays men speak of them all as laughable and rather foolish folk.

In the stories which are so precious to childhood,

giants, when they have not got ogresses as wives, are never objects of complete aversion. On the contrary, the young reader rejoices over the downfall of the bulky one, not on the score of his vices, or because he deserves his fate, but because the child's sympathies naturally incline towards the undersized personages of the story; and if the poor blundering old giant could be only brought up smiling over a hasty pudding on the last page, the story would not be thought, in the nursery, to be any the worse for that — so long, of course, as there was no doubt left in anybody's mind as to Jack being able to kill Blunderbore again, should Blunderbore's conduct again justify his destruction. Sometimes, I regret to remember, the giants went about collecting children for pies, and from such as these all right-minded men should withhold their esteem; but for the rest, the ordinary muscular and inoffensive giant, it is impossible to deny a certain liking, nor, when he is provoked to display his strength, a great admiration.

IV.

THE ELEPHANT'S FELLOW-COUNTRYMEN.

The Rhinoceros a Victim of Ill-Natured Personality. — In the Glacial Period. — The Hippopotamus. — Popular Sympathy with it. — Behemoth a Useless Person. — Extinct Monsters and the World they Lived in. — The Impossible Giraffe. — Its Intelligent use of its Head as a Hammer. — The Advantages and Disadvantages of so much Neck. — Its High Living. — The Zebra. — Nature's Parsimony in the matter of Paint on the Skins of Animals. — Some Suggestions towards more Gayety.

ELEPHANTS, there is no doubt, are favorites with the public, and they merit their popularity. It is difficult, perhaps, to say as much for their cousins, the rhinoceroses. For some reason or another, the public resent the personal appearance of these animals, and no one compliments them. Straightforward opprobrium is bad enough, no doubt, but depreciatory innuendo is still harder to bear, just as the old writer tells us, in the matter of the patient patriarch, that " the oblique expostulations of his friends were a deeper injury to Job than the downright blows of the Devil."

A rhinoceros, therefore, when he stands at the bars with his mouth open in expectation of the donation which is seldom thrown in, hears much that must embitter his hours of solitary reflection. The remarks of visitors are never relieved by any reference to his sagacity or docility, as in the case of the elephant; nor does any appreciation of usefulness to man temper the severity of their judgments upon him. That he is very ugly and looks very wicked is the burden of all criticism, and it is a wonder that under such perpetual provocation to do so he does not grow uglier and look wickeder than he is. No ordinary man could go on being called " a hideous brute " for any great number of years without assuming a truculent and unlovable aspect; and it would not, therefore, be much matter for surprise if the rhinoceros, although such conduct were altogether foreign to his character and even distasteful to his feelings, should develop a taste for human flesh.

As it is, he munches hay — not with any enthusiasm, it is true, but with a subdued satisfaction that bespeaks a philosophic and contented mind.

In the wild state, whether he be the African species or the Asiatic, the rhinoceros is a lazy, quiet-loving beast, passing his days in slumber in some secluded swamp of reed-bed, and coming out at night to browse along the wild pastures that offer themselves on forest edges or the water-side. In his caged condition his life is simply reversed, for his days are spent under the public eye, in wakefulness and mental irritation, while his nights are given unnaturally to repose and solitude. There are no succulent expanses of grass and river herbage to tempt him abroad with his fellows, as in the nights of liberty in Nubia or Assam ; and let the moonlight be ever so bright he cannot now, as once, saunter away for miles along the lush banks of some Javan stream, or loiter feeding among the squashy brakes of the Nile. But captivity, if it robs him of freedom, injures the rhinoceros less than most of the beasts of the field, for he was never given to much exercise, and his life was an indolent one. Now and again, it is true, the hunters found him out, and awakened him to an unusual vivacity, and on such occasions he developed a nimbleness of limb and ferocity of temper that might hardly have been expected of so bulky and retiring an individual. Sometimes also he crossed the elephant on his jungle path, and in a sudden rush upon his noble kinsman vindicated his right of way, and expended all the stored-up energy of many months of luxurious idleness. But such sensations were few and far between. As a rule, his company were diminutive and deferential — wading birds of cautious habits, and the deliberative pelicans, wild pigs, and creatures of the ichneumon kind. The great carnivora never troubled their heads about such a preposterous victim, and the nations of the deer kind, couching by day in the forest depths and feeding by night in the open plain, saw nothing of the bulky rhinoceros. He lived therefore in virtual solitude, — for water-fowl and weasels were hardly worth calling companions, — and was indeed so vigilant in guarding his concealment that he remained a secret for ages.

The rhinoceros, therefore, figures nowhere in folk-lore, and neither fairy tale nor fable has anything to tell us of it. Art owes little to it, and commerce nothing. It points no moral and adorns no tale. Unassisted by associations, and possessing neither a literature nor a place in the fauna of fancy, the monstrous thing relies for sympathy and regard simply upon its merits, and these have sadly failed to ingratiate it.

With the hippopotamus the case is somewhat different, for the apparently defenceless nature of the river-horse enlists public sympathy on his behalf, while the very absurdity of his appearance disarms ill-natured criticism. The horn of the rhinoceros is its ruin, for the popular esteem will never be extended to a creature that carries about on the tip of his nose such a formidable implement of offence. The hippopotamus, fortunately for itself, is unarmed, so that a certain compassionate regard is not considered out of place. Its skin, though ludicrous, looks smooth and tight, suggesting vulnerability, or even a tendency to burst on any occasion of violent impact with a foreign body, while the rhinoceros wears an ill-fitting suit of impenetrable leather, which hangs so easily upon its limbs as to lead the spectators to suppose the brute had deliberately put it on as a kind of overcoat for defence against any possible assailants. Thus prepared for emergencies, it carries its bulk about with a self-reliant demeanor that, taken in conjunction with the aggressive tone in which it grunts, alienates all tenderness of feeling, and makes sentiment impossible.

The hippopotamus, on the other hand, seems to have had all its arrangements made for it without being consulted beforehand, and to submit to the personal inconveniences that result with a mild and deprecatory manner that commends it to sympathetic consideration. Had proofs of its own future appearance been sent in to the hippopotamus to revise, it might have suggested several useful alterations, — a greater length of leg in order to keep its stomach off the ground, and a head on such a reasonably reduced scale that it could hold it up.

As matters stand, Behemoth lives under considerable disadvantages. It is true that he is amphibious, and that when tired of dragging his bulky person about on the land he can roll into the water and float there. But this dual existence hardly makes amends for the discomforts of such a bladder-like body. The world, however, owes both the hippopotamus and the rhinoceros a grudge, inasmuch as neither contributes to human welfare. That their hides make good leather is no adequate justification for such huge entities, and the fact of their teeth and horns being useful for paper-knives and walking-sticks hardly authorizes two prodigious creatures to occupy so much terrestrial space. It is centuries ago since the elephant made good its claim to be considered a friend and benefactor of the human race, but neither of its great companions has ever bestirred itself in the service of men. Their day, perhaps, is coming.

Immense tracts of country are being now opened up in Africa to the world's industries, and the highways of future commerce lie right through the homes of the rhinoceros and hippopotamus. How startling will be the effect upon the wild creatures of the forests and the rivers! Long-established nations of monkeys and baboons will be driven by the busy axe from the shades they have haunted for generations, and as, league after league, the creepers and undergrowth are cleared away, multitudes of animal life will have notice to quit. Progress will order them to move on, and so by their families and parishes they will have to go, — the sulky leopard-folk and solemn lemurs, troops of squirrel and wild-cat, and the weasels by their tribes. Diligent men will mow down the cane-beds that have housed centuries of crocodiles, and the exquisite islands will be cleared of jungle that human beings may take possession of the ancestral domains of the lizard kinds. Wildernesses of snakes will have to go, and out of the giant reeds flocks of great water-fowl will rush startled from their hiding-places. Advancing to where the older timber grows and the nobler plains are spread, the colonist will disturb the bulky rhinoceros and the lordly elephant; and in the creeks of river and lake that will come under man's dominion the hippopotamus will find its right of place challenged. The time, therefore, it may be, is not far distant when the present waste of traction power will cease, and the two monsters, hitherto useless, be trained to drag our caravans across the plains and our barges down the rivers of the Dark Continent.

From my speaking of the elephant as a Mammoth, of the rhinoceros as a Titan, and the hippopotamus as Behemoth, you might fairly charge me, reader, with having forgotten that these animals, big as we think them, are really after all only the pygmies of their species. But I had not really forgotten it, for before me lies a paragraph announcing the discovery, in Siberia, of one of those colossal animals, which nature is very fond of dropping in, in a casual way, every now and then, just to keep our pride down and to remind us, the creatures of a degenerate growth, what winter meant in the years gone by, and what kind of person an inhabitant of the earth then was.

He had to be very big indeed, very strong, and very warmly clad, to be called "the fittest" in the Glacial Period, and to survive the fierce assaults of the Palæolithic cold. This rhinoceros, therefore, exceeds by some cubits the stature of the modern beast, and is also by some tons heavier.

It appears that an affluent of the Tana River was making alterations in its course, and in so doing cut away its banks, revealing the embedded presence of a truly Titanic pachyderm, which, for want of a fitter name, has been temporarily called a rhinoceros. But it is such a creature that if it were to show itself now in the swamps of Assam or on the plains of Central Africa, it would terrify off its path all the species of the present day, whether one-horned or two-horned, and make no more of an obstinate elephant than an avalanche does of a goatherd's hut that happens to stand in the line of its advance. Its foot, if set down upon one of the rhinoceroses of modern times, would have flattened it as smooth as the philosopher's tub rolled out those naughty boys of Corinth, who had ventured to tickle the cynic through the bunghole with a straw. Besides its size, the huge monster in question asserts its superiority over existing species by being clothed in long hair, a fleece to guard it against the climate in which it lived, and from which even the tremendous panoply of the nineteenth-century rhinoceros could not sufficiently protect the wearer. Thus clad in a woolly hide and colossal in physique, the Siberian mammal not only lived, but lived happily, amid snowy glaciers that would have frozen the polar bear and made icicles of Arctic foxes.

Perhaps even man himself did not exist in the rhinoceros's day; at any rate, if he did, he had the decency to secrete himself in holes and burrows, and when the mammoths came along the road to get out of their way. He was a feeble creature at first, and his best accomplishments were those that taught him how to escape his many foes, for our ancestors had but little time for the cultivation of other arts and sciences when the best part of their days and nights had to be spent in scrambling up trees out of the reach of prowling carnivora, and running away from ill-tempered things of the rhinoceros and elephant kind. Gradually, however, he began to defend himself, and from defence he rose at last to the dignity of offence. Armed only with flint-stones, he had the audacity, this progenitor of ours, to attack the bulky pachyderms; and, if the testimony of the crags and clay may be believed, he actually overcame the Goliaths of the forest with his pebbles. Were it not, indeed, for these relics of the age of flint weapons, it might be doubted whether man was ever contemporary in Britain with the mammoth; but as matters stand, there is every reason for supposing that he was. Whether this juxtaposition of human implements and animal skeletons means that our ancestors slew the beast or that the beast ate our ancestors, it is impossible to say. Probably they both gave and took.

It was an age of silence and twilight and snow; an epoch of monsters.

In Australia a huge marsupial, with the head of an ox, and compared to which our kangaroo is only a great rat, straddled and hopped about as it pleased, in the company of wombats as big as bears; and in America the megatherian sloth crept browsing among the forests of the primeval continent, like some bulky thing of Dreamland, voiceless, solitary, and slow-footed; while the glyptodon — the wondrous armadillo of the past, that could have driven its way through a street of houses as easily as the mole tunnels through the furrows of a field — wandered with the same strange loitering pace along the river banks. In those days there was no need for the beasts to hurry, for life was long and there was nothing to harm them; so they crawled about on land and waded in the water as lazily as they pleased. It is true that the extinct kangaroo, as big as a hippopotamus in the body, had an enemy in the pouched lion; but there were twenty kinds of lesser kangaroos which the carnivorous beast could attack first; so the largest lived on in peace and flourished, growing more and more huge, until at last Man appeared in a spectral sort of way upon the scene, and annihilated the genus. For reptiles, our own colonies in Africa supply individuals worthy in every way to have been the contemporaries of these giants. Huge herbivorous dragons — two-tusked reptiles with the skulls of crocodiles — grazed along the rich pastures of the antediluvian Africa; and iguanadons, prodigious creatures of the lizard kind, with large, flattened, crushing teeth covering the palate above like a paving-stone, and working upon a corresponding breadth of surface in the lower jaw.

For birds, again, we need go no farther — for we should certainly fare no better — than our own colony of New Zealand, which monopolizes the wonders of the bird paradise, where a score of gigantic feathered things, as big as camels, had the islands all to themselves, feeding to their hearts' content on the nutritious fern-roots. The nurseries of the dinornis and the moa had, however, their *bogey* in the terrible harpagornis, a bird of prey far larger than the condor or the lammergeyer, and sufficient in itself to justify the old-world traditions of the roc, the simurg, and the other gigantic fowls of story. But the adult birds had no cause for fear even from such an eagle as this; and so the geese grew so big that they could not fly, and gradually dispensed with wings, and the coots became so prodigious that they, too, gave up flying as a troublesome and unnecessary method of locomotion; and everything at last came to waddling about together, too fat to go fast, and so secure from harm that they had no cause for haste.

It was a grand world in one sense, but a stupid, useless world in other respects. The leviathans and the behemoths of the time — creatures of unlimited space and time and food — prowled about, without any horizon to their migrations, cropping the herbage as they went and dying where they happened to be standing last. They would not even take the trouble to settle for posterity the question as to the exact limits of their habitation, but dropped their preposterous bones into snowdrifts, which melted and swept them off to distant sea-beds, or into rivers which tumbled their venerable remains along from the centres of continents to their shores, or left them stranded, with all sorts of incongruous anachronisms, to puzzle the ages to came.

. . . .

For ever so many centuries nobody with any pretensions to intelligence would believe that such a creature as the giraffe existed. It was its neck that did it, and a man who persisted in believing in that part of its body might have been sent to the stake for it. It was in vain that travellers tried to convince Europe that they had seen such an animal with their own eyes, for as soon as they came to the neck part of their description they were put out of court at once. Yet it was a case of "neck or nothing," and, as our forefathers would not have the neck at any price, they had nothing.

The idea of a zebra was difficult enough for them to entertain, but of a zebra *gone to seed*, in such a way as these travellers described the giraffe, appeared preposterous and impossible; so they said. Yet in earlier days the giraffe was known to Europe, for Imperial, wild-beast-killing Rome had not only known the camel-leopard, but had been much amused by it, for the giraffe has a method of fighting which is entirely original, and is a very pleasing illustration of the instinct which teaches wild animals to make the most of nature's gifts. The giraffe has neither claws nor tusks nor beak nor sting nor poison-fangs nor sharp teeth, nor yet hobnailed boots; so when it is out of temper with one of its own kind it does not fly in the face of Providence by trying to scratch its antagonist's bowels out, as a tiger might, or toss it like a rhinoceros, or peck its eyes out like a vulture, or sting it like a scorpion, or strike it like a cobra, or fly at its throat like a wolf, or jump on it as the costermonger does. The sagacious animal is conscious how foolish and futile such conduct on its part would be. On the contrary, the giraffe, remarking that it has been provided by nature with a long and pliable neck, terminating in a very solid head, uses the upper half of itself like a flail, and, swinging its neck round and round in a way that does immense credit to its organization, brings its head down at each swing with a thump on its adversary. The other combatant is equally sagacious, and adopts precisely the same tactics; and the two animals, planting themselves as firmly as possible by stretching out all four legs to the utmost, stand opposite each other hammering with their heads, till one or the other either splits its skull or bolts.

Their heads are furnished with two stumpy horn-like processes, so that the giraffes, when busy at this hammer and tongs, remind the spectators somewhat of two ancient warriors thumping each other with the spiked balls they used to carry for that purpose at the end of a chain. It is possible that the knowledge of this fact about giraffes would have gone far towards convincing our obstinate forefathers and foremothers of the creature's actual existence, and it is impossible, therefore, to deplore too sincerely the lamentable ignorance of natural history which deprived preceding generations of the enjoyment of this animal. To the Romans so eccentric a procedure in combat greatly endeared the giraffe; and it is within the limits of reasonable expectation to believe that our ancestors of the Dark Ages would similarly have appreciated it had they allowed themselves to be so far convinced of its entity as to get one caught.

For the giraffe is distinctly an enjoyment. It is a pity, perhaps, that it has not got wings; but we must accept things as we find them, and, taken all round, there is no doubt that the camelopard is a comfort and a pleasure. It gives us hopes of further eccentricities, and contracts the limits of the marvellous. It is about the best instalment of the impossible that has been vouchsafed us.

The hippopotamus is a great prodigy in its way, and the kangaroo is out of the common. But they are neither of them of the same class as this sky-raking animal, that passes all its life, so to speak, looking out of a fourth-story window. Think of the places it could live in! A steeple would be as comfortable as possible for it, or its body might be put into a back kitchen and its head up the chimney. The cowl at the top outside would keep the rain off its head, and, as the wind blew it round and round, the giraffe, from its sweep's eminence, would be gratified by a gyroscopic view of the surrounding country. It is the only animal that lives on the earth and never thinks about the ground it walks on.

It takes terra firma as a matter of course, and does

not even trouble itself to find out where the trees grow from. It browses on the tops of them without troubling itself to wonder how leaves got so high up in the air; and while other animals are snuffing about on the earth, and blowing up the dust to their own inconvenience, the giraffe reconnoitres the ceilings, and knows all about the beams. The hippopotamus in the next house would never even surmise that there was such a thing as a roof over him unless it were to fall on his head, but he thoroughly understands the bricks and flagstones with which his apartments are paved; but with the giraffe it is just the reverse. Spiders, as a rule, build their cobwebs in the cornices, in order to be out of harm's way; but in the giraffes' house, if they do not wish to be perpetually molested by sniffing, they have to build in the angles of the floor; and, in the countries where giraffes are common, we may similarly presume that little birds never sit and sing on the tops of bushes, but always about the roots, or else the giraffes might accidentally nibble them off the twigs. Sometimes, it is true, the giraffe stoops to mammalian levels; but there is something so lofty even in its condescension that the very act of bending enhances the haughtiness of its erect posture, and suggests that it does it from policy. To be always keeping state, and forever in the clouds, might make shorter animals accuse it of acting superciliously; so, remembering Bacon's maxim, that " amongst a man's inferiors one shall be sure of reverence, and therefore it is good a little to be familiar," it affably condescends at intervals. Its usual gestures are all cast in Alexandrines, and so, like the poets, it breaks a line every now and then to relieve the overstateliness of the measure.

It is difficult to believe that the giraffe finds much fun in life; for, after all, most of the fun of the animal world goes on upon the ground. Of course, if the giraffe thinks itself a bird, it may be contented enough all by itself in the air, but its aspect is one of subdued melancholy, such as appertains to all anomalous positions, whether those of queen-dowagers or dodos. The dodo, for instance, left all by itself as the last of its race (like Kingsley's poor old gairfowl on the All Alone Stone), must have had many sad moments. It was prevented, on the one hand, by the demise of all its kindred, from enjoying the society of its own species, and, on the other, by the dignity of being-about-to-become-extinct, from mingling in the social life of more modern fowls. The giraffe, in the same way, moves about with a high-bred, languid grace that has more than a suspicion of weariness about it.

Yet, taken all for all, it has not been hardly treated by nature. If its neck had been telescopic, like a turtle's, it would, indeed, have been unduly favored, but as it is it comes off impartially. Its long neck must necessarily betray it to its enemies, for no lion worth its salt could help seeing a giraffe as it lounged about, browsing in the middle of the sky, with its upper-t'gallant-stunsails set; but then again the giraffe, from such an elevated lookout, should be able to descry the prowling beast of prey at a greater distance. Its length of neck, again, so medical science assures us, secures it from all danger of apoplexy; but on the other hand, it is terrible to think what a giraffe's sore throat would be like. *Imagine seven feet of sore throat!* Again, the camelopard carries no water-butts inside it, as the camels do, although it lives in the plains of Africa, where water often fails; but in recompense it has a tongue about two feet long — no small comfort to it when thirsty — and eyes that project after the manner of a shrimp, so that, if it likes, it can look behind it and in front at the same time. Thus, counterbalancing defect and advantage, we find the giraffe very fairly off, while in the conditions of its wild life there is much to rank it among the happier of the beasts.

. . . .

Next door, so to speak, to the giraffes are the zebras, and, passing from one to the other, the thought occurs how pleasantly art might be made to supplement nature in the coloring of animals, or how agreeable it would have been if in the first instance Nature herself had painted a few more of the larger animals as she has decorated these two comrades of the African wilderness.

In the bird world, color has been lavished prodigally, and among insects we find hues of every tone and brilliance. The wicked caterpillar, for instance, is defended, from those who would take away his ill-spent life, by shades of green and brown that harmonize with the vegetables he ravages; and why was the same considerate anxiety for its welfare not extended to the gentle hippopotamus?

A pea-green river-horse, browsing among the reed-beds of Old Nile, would have added a charm to the scene; and Stanley would hardly have been so angry with the behemoths of Victoria Nyanza if he had found them floating among the lotus-pads, painted in imitation of water-lilies. The rhinoceros, again, is a hideous object, from its vast expanse of mud-colored skin; yet what a surface he presents for a noble study in browns!

What fine effects of shade might not be obtained

among those corrugated folds of hide; or let us for a moment consider what he would look like *burnished!* Nature has not stinted metallic tints in bird, or insect, or fish, or reptile; and yet in the mammals, where such magnificent results might have been attained, she withheld her hand. It is difficult, indeed, in these degenerate days to imagine such a superb spectacle as a herd of brazen elephants crashing their way through a primeval forest; or rhinoceroses, glittering like the dome of the Boston State House, wandering among the ruins of old Memphis; or hippopotamuses of mother-o'-pearl, sporting on the bosom of Old Nile with electro-plated crocodiles!

The carnivora advantage by the accident of their painted skins; but the zebra and the giraffe need no excusings for crime, for they commit none. They are innocent and beautiful at one and the same time. The hippopotamus, poor monster! is only innocent, and the rhinoceros is neither, and each, therefore, receives from the public its proportion of depreciative comment; the former being patronized for its helplessness, and bantered on its personal appearance; the latter being rudely spoken of, not only for the ugliness of its looks, but the wickedness of them, the malicious twinkle in its little eyes, and that offensive horn at the tip of its nose, which Pliny tells us he always sharpens upon an agate before attacking the elephant.

Now, if all were impartially adorned in colors, all would share more largely in public sympathy; for just as no one now would think of shooting the gold and silver pheasants, no one then would think of prodding a golden rhinoceros with his umbrella, or betraying the confidence of a silver hippopotamus with empty paper-bags or the innutritious pebble.

V.

CATS AND SPARROWS.

They are of Two Species, tame and otherwise. — The Artificial Lion. — Its Debt of Gratitude to Landseer and the Poets. — Unsuitable for Domestication. — Is the Natural Lion the King of Beasts? — The true Moral of all Lion Fables. — " Well roared, Lion!" — The Tiger not of a Festive Kind. — There is no Nonsense about the Big Cats. — The Tiger's Pleasures and Perils. — Its Terrible Voice. — The poor Old Man-Eater. — Caught by Baboos and Killed by Sheep. — The great Cat Princes. — Common or Garden Cats, approached sideways. — The Physical Impossibility of Taxing Cats. — The Evasive Habits of Grimalkin. — Its Instinct for Cooks. — On the Roof with a Burglar. — The Prey of Cats. — The Turpitude of the Sparrow. — As an Emblem of Conquest and an Article of Export. — The Street Boy among Birds.

CATS are of two kinds at least, — the common or garden pussy, and the wild or undomesticated felis.

The former is of various colors and qualities, the gray specimens being called tabbies and the larger ones toms. Both are equally fond of fish, and their young (which are born blind) are called kittens, and are generally drowned.

The latter, or undomesticated kind, is exactly like the former; but it is usually much larger, and when offered milk it does not purr. One of these cats is called the lion. The lion, to be precise, is also of two sorts — the natural and the artificial — and on the whole the latter animal is the better of the two. It is generous and brave, the King of Beasts, and one of the supporters of the British Arms.

Landseer has done a great deal for this lion, and in Trafalgar Square in London has left on record four specimens, which all other lions, *vel Africanus vel Asiaticus* should try and live up to. Other artists also, notably Doré on canvass, and Thorwaldsen in stone, have advantaged the artificial lion very considerably, and both poets and lion-slayers have done their best to elevate its moral and physical virtues in the public estimation, — the former from a mistaken estimate of this animal's character, derived from antiquity, the latter from a natural desire to represent themselves as being men of an extraordinary courage. These powerful agencies between them have succeeded in rehabilitating the artificial lion, who was at one time becoming rapidly absurd by the liberties taken with it in heraldry and on sign-boards.

A lion rampant, with his tongue lolling out, and two knobs at the end of his tail, is only one of a hundred heraldic aberrations from the normal type, which lovers of nature must agree in deploring; and the green, blue, and red lions of English inns were all such "fearful wild-fowl" as might make cats weep. There have even been *spotted* lions! It was high time therefore for the artistic champions of the great cat to come to the front, or we might soon have had Tabby and Tortoise-shell lions and Tom lions on our sign-boards.

What dignity after this would have attached to that haughty speech of the lioness who, being rallied by a grasshopper upon having only one cub, loftily replied, "Yes, true, I have only one — *but that one is a lion.*"

The story has long been popular, and often been applauded, but, as it seems to me, without sufficient judgment. What else could the lioness have expected to produce but a lion? Such was only to be anticipated.

Now if her cub had been a camel or a rhinoceros her pride would have been justified by the exceptional character of her performance; or if her offspring had been a hippopotamus or a giraffe, we might have accepted such complacency as not unnatural under the circumstances. But what are the facts of the case? Or if again it had been even a lion rampant, with its tongue out, or a green lion, or a spotted one, we might have understood the tawny mother's exultation. As it was, her *hauteur* was surely misplaced. A lioness gives birth to a cub and it turns out a lion — *voilà tout !* Yet she was pleased on this account to snub the prolific insect who addressed her, as if she herself had done something out of the common, rare and worth talking about. As a matter of fact, after all, it was only an ordinary, every-day lion. Moreover, it would have been quite within the grasshopper's right to retort, "A lion? Nonsense. It is only a cat — a kitten. I can hear it mewing." For the baby lion is faintly brindled, like the most ordinary of pussies, and mews precisely like the kitten in the nursery.

Nevertheless, the artificial (or supernatural) lion differs in many valuable respects from the natural animal. It is magnanimous, as witness that story of the mouse that released the lion from a net and was dismissed by the lion with thanks. Now in a wild state the lion would have eaten the mouse, for it has the usual cat's taste for mice and rats; and though, if the truth must be told, only an indifferent mouser, might no doubt be made useful in a kitchen. Besides clearing the domestic precincts of the cheese-nibbling folk, it would not be above catching the crickets on the hearth or the humble cockroach — and eating them. The lion in a wild state never disdains such small deer as insects. But whether our modern cooks and kitchen maids would care to have a promiscuous lion downstairs is another matter, and the doubt on this point suggests a very painful contrast between the manners of the larger and the lesser cats.

The lesser cat, it is only too true, is often so carried away by her feelings as to indulge in the surreptitious canary; and she has been known to forget herself so far during the night-watches as to skirmish on the window-sill, in the company of the cat from next door, with such vivacity and want of judgment as to upset flower-pots into the back-yard. The gravity of these misdemeanors cannot be slurred over, but, after all, to what do they amount compared to the havoc that would result from the domestication of some of the larger cats — such as lions?

Confessing his sins in a parliament of the beasts, the lion in the fable says: "J'ai dévoré force moutons; même il m'est arrivé quelquefois de manger le berger!" and from a shepherd to a cook is only a brief step. But between a canary and a cook there is a distance of many parasangs, and the enormity of the one offence is barely comparable to that of the other. Again, the light-hearted cat, when foregathering for frivolous converse with her kind, does damage, as has been said, to occasional flower-pots, and has even in her gayety been known to fall ruinously through the kitchen window. But supposing we tried to keep lions about the place, and our lion were to get on to the roof of the summer-house or on the garden wall with the lion from next door, what would be the result? The roaring of the lion when at liberty is said by those who have heard it to be something terrific. It lays its head, we are told, close to the earth, and in this position emits a tremendous utterance, which rolls growling along the ground like the first mutterings of a volcano. It could be heard all over the town, and we should never get a wink of sleep! But if the lions got frolicsome the consequences would be even more dreadful. The gardens, with their uprooted shrubs, twisted railings, and dilapidated walls, would look next morning as if some earthquakes had been on the premises overnight and got drunk before leaving.

This, however, is somewhat of a digression. To return to the artificial lion and the points in which it differs from the natural animal, we find, besides its magnanimity, that this species possesses an unusual sense of honor. It is said, for instance, by those who wish to magnify it, that it roars before entering a jungle — in order to give all the little creatures in it a chance of running away. The lion is too noble a beast, they say, to take a mean advantage of its neighbors, or to surprise any of them, even the humblest; so it gives warning to the bystanders, like Mr. Snodgrass in the "Pickwick Papers," that it is ": going to begin." But what are the facts? The lion when on the lookout for a meal is as stealthy as a cat when compassing the ruin of the garden sparrow. It crawls along on its stomach, taking advantage of every tuft of cover and inequality of the ground, and maintaining a perfect silence. More often still it lies in ambush for its victim; and those who have watched a lion under a tamarisk, waiting for the antelope to come browsing by, say there is no difference whatever between its tactics and those of Grimalkin when she lurks under a gooseberry bush for the casual robin. Another fact is that the lion is only bold in the dark. It becomes savage, of course, at all hours, if passers-by take the liberty of wounding it; but during the daytime and on moonlight nights it is, as a rule, so timid that travellers in the Lion-veldt of Africa never even trouble themselves to tether their wagon cattle. Yet this is the King of Beasts.

In what, then, is it kingly? Certainly not in generosity, nor yet in its habits. Kings do not go about catching rats and frogs and insects, nor in their own dominions do they skulk among the undergrowth when in search of a meal. Is it its size? Certainly not; for the elephant is its companion, and the lion never dares to cross the mammoth's path, confessing by its deference a sense of superiority which other beasts, the lion's subjects, refuse to entertain — notably the tiger, the wild boar, and the rhinoceros. These three do not hesitate to affront the elephant in broad daylight, and certainly would not turn tail for their "king" if they met him. Is it then in its appearance that this animal claims to be royal among the quadrupeds? It is true that in repose — notably in the splendid bronzes of Trafalgar Square — there is a surpassing majesty in the lions' heads. They have the countenances of gods. Their manes sweep down upon their shoulders like the terrible hair of the Olympian Zeus, and there is that in their eyes that speaks of a foreknowledge of things and of days, grand as fallen Saturn and implacable as the Sphinx.

But then this is in bronze. In Nature, only one half of the world's lions have any manes at all; and even of these, the African species, there are but few, so travellers assure us, that reflect in any considerable degree the dignity of Landseer's effigies, while one writer speaks of "the blandness of his [the lion's] Harold Skimpole-like countenance!"

Yet, after all, if we dethrone the lion, which of the beasts shall wear the crown? The elephant is infinitely superior, both morally and physically; but the ermine would hardly sit well upon the unwieldly pachyderm. The tiger is more courageous and as strong, but there is too much blood on its claws for a royal sceptre. Shall we give the beasts a dictator in the violent rhinoceros, or raise them an emir from the people by crowning the wild boar? But why have a monarchy at all? Let the quadrupeds be a republic.

But the suggestion is quite worthy of consideration, whether the modern ideal of the lion is not really due to a misconception of the object of our predecessors in making this animal so prominent. Originally, there is no doubt, the people fixed upon the lion as the king, *not* because he had any of the kingly virtues, but because he had all the kingly vices. They satirized monarchy under this symbol. By endowing him with royalty they intended, therefore, to mark him out for public odium, and not for public reverence, just as in more modern days the wolf has stood in Ireland for the landlord. With this explanation as a key, all the fables and stories told of the lion, which hitherto have misled the popular mind as to the regal qualifications of the lion, fall to pieces at once, and are seen to illustrate the failings and iniquities of the purple, and not its virtues or its grandeur.

Take Æsop alone, and translate his fables by this light. The lion and the boar fight, and the match is an equal one — king against the people; but seeing the vultures, a foreign enemy, on the lookout for the corpse of the vanquished, whichever it might happen to be, they make up their quarrel. . . . A lion (the king) saw three bulls (his turbulent barons) pasturing together, and he made them quarrel and separate, when he ate them up one after the other. . . . A lion (the king's army) made an alliance with a dolphin (the king's navy) in order to have everything their own way, and then the lion tried to oppress a wild bull (his people) and got the worst of it, and the navy could not help him a bit. . . . Two kings, a lion and a bear, fall to fighting over a kid, and are at length so exhausted with the combat that a passing fox carries off the kid. . . . A lion, an ass, and a fox went a-hunting, and on their return the king ordered the ass to apportion the spoil. The ass divided it carefully into three equal portions, which so enraged the lion that he devoured him on the spot, and ordered the fox to make a fresh partition. The fox put everything into one great heap as the king's half, and kept only an accidental fragment of offal for himself, upon which the lion commended his art in division, and asked him where he had learned it. "From the ass," replied the sycophant. . . . A great king, a lion, asked a humble neighbor for a favor, which was granted on condition that the lion would dismiss his armed followers — have his teeth drawn, in fact; and as soon as he had consented, the humble neighbor whipped the king off his premises. . . . The lion is represented as afraid of the crowing of the cock — the awaking of the people; as putting himself to great trouble to catch a mouse that had annoyed him; as the dupe of councillors; and as being constantly overmatched by his subjects.

These fables, therefore, and a hundred others, are not written to dignify the royalty of the lion among the beasts, but to depreciate royalty among men under the symbol of a lion, — an animal that has a majestic aspect and noble antecedents, but is both tyrannical and mean, mutton-headed and stealthy. His friends are always the cunning, and his natural enemies the courageous. The poets, however (of course), entirely misunderstand these parables of antiquity, and, having often heard and read of the king of beasts, they invest the lion with all the insignia of monarchy. But the poets, until the nineteenth century, were as a class curiously and ludicrously ignorant of natural history, — and more completely at discord with Nature generally, more unsympathetic, more imitative, and more incorrect, than could be supposed possible. So their championship of the lion goes for nothing, unless we are content to accept all their fictions in a lump together, and to think of bears ravaging sheepfolds, baboons swinging by their tails, and vultures chasing turtle-doves.

The travellers who seek a lion-slayer's fame are no less at fault, for they also misuse their facts. Other travellers on the same hunting-grounds have described the great cat to us too often to make the Bombastes Furioso of spurious adventures a reality. Instead of the huge beast standing erect on the plain in mid-day, and advancing with terrific roaring upon the hunter, every hair of the magnificent mane erect and the eyes flashing fire, we are introduced to a sulky cat that trots away round the corner on the first warning of man's approach; and which, so far from provoking conflict, takes advantage of every feature of the country that offers it concealment, or affords it a way of escape from its dreaded persecutor. The Dutchmen in Africa have named the districts in which this animal ranges, the Lion-veldt, and this is a splendid compliment. But they regard the king of beasts as a pest, and do not fear it as a danger, while the natives reverence it as *a voice*, and a terrible one, but *præterea nihil*. It was for this same majesty of voice that Ali the Caliph was named the Lion of Allah. In the "Pilgrim's Progress" it was the *sound* of the lions that first terrified Faithful and his party, for we are told it had "a hollow voice of roaring;" and it was the same roaring that frightened poor Thisbe to her death. Perhaps then, after all, it is with beasts as it is often with men, that he who roars loudest and oftenest is counted the best in the crowd, and that the lion's only claim to kingship is in the power of his lungs. If this be so, we can only say, with the duke in the play, "Well roared, lion!"

Another large cat is called the tiger. There is no nonsense about the tiger as there is about the lion. He is not an impostor. Wolves may go about pretending that they are only dogs that have had the misfortune of a bad bringing up, and the lion may swagger round trying to look as if he were something else than a cat; but the tiger never descends to such prevarication, — setting himself up for better than he is, or claiming respect for qualities which he does not possess. There is no ambiguity about anything he does. All his character is on the surface. "I am," he says, a "thorough going downright wild beast, and if you don't like me you may lump me; but in the mean while you had better get out of my way." There is no pompous affectation of superior intelligence about the tiger, no straining after a false reputation for magnanimity. If he is met with in a jungle, he does not make-believe for the purpose of impressing the traveller with his uncommon sagacity, or waste time like the lion in superfluous roaring, shaking of manes, and looking kingly. On the contrary, he behaves honestly and candidly, like the beast he is. He either retires precipitately with every confession of alarm, or, in his own fine outspoken fashion, goes for the stranger. Nor, when he makes off, does he do it as if he liked it, wasting his time in pretentious attitudes, or in trying to save appearances. He has no idea of showing off. If he has to go he goes, like lightning, and does not think for a moment of the figure he is cutting. But if, on the other hand, he means fighting, he gives the stranger very little leisure for misunderstanding his intentions. The tiger, therefore, deserves to be considered a model wild beast, and to be held in respect accordingly. He knows his station and keeps it, doing the work that Nature has given him to do with all his might.

The result of this honesty is that no one misrepresents the tiger. Exaggerated praise and slander are alike impossible of an animal that refuses to be misjudged. There is no opening for dishonest description, for he is always in the same character; no scope for romancing about a beast that is so consistently practical, or for fable when he does nothing in parables. Moreover, most of the other beasts play a second part in the world, and have a moral significance, — like the creatures grouped about Solomon's throne, or the standard-emblazonments of the tribes of Israel, or the armorial bearings of families and nations, or the badges of the Apostles. But no one uses the tiger in this way as a metaphor. There is not sufficiently subtlety in the emblem. It is too coarse, too downright. A tiger is a tiger, and nothing more or less. Once only it was made a royal emblem, — by Tippoo, the Sultan of Mysore, — but then professedly out of mere brutal ferocity. In the same vein that amiable prince constructed a mechanical toy, now in the South Kensington collection, which represented a tiger, life-size, mumbling the body of an English soldier; and when the machinery was in proper order, the tiger growled and the soldier groaned with considerable power. But Mr. John Bright, so they say, finding time heavy on his hands during the Sultan's ball, amused himself with Tippoo's toy, and by overwinding the machine, broke it. At any rate, the tiger goes through his growling performances now in a very perfunctory and feeble manner.

For the same reason, namely, that the tiger affords no room for the play of fancy, the poets prefer leopards to tigers. There is more left to the imagination in the sound of the smaller animal's name, and as it is not so well known as the tiger, they have wider margin for poetical license. The moralist, for a similar reason, avoids the tiger, for no amount of ingenuity will extract a moral out of its conduct.

In short, then, the tiger may be taken as the supreme type of the pure wild beast. Life has only one end for him — enjoyment; and to this he gives all his magnificent energies. Endowed with superb capabilities, he exercises them to the utmost in this one direction, without ever forgetting for an instant that he is only a huge cat, or flying in the face of Nature by pretending to be anything else.

Speed, strength, and cunning are his in a degree to which, in the same combination, no other animal can lay claim; in daring none exceed him, while for physical beauty he has absolutely no rival. A tiger has been known to spring over a wall five feet high into a cattle enclosure, and to jump back again with a full-grown animal in its jaws; and has been seen to leap, holding a bullock, across a wide ditch. As regards its speed, the first bounds of a tiger are so rapid as to bring it alongside the antelope; while for strength, a single blow of its paw will stun a charging bull. Its stealth may be illustrated by the anecdote of the tiger carrying away the bait while the sportsmen were actually busy putting up the shelters from which they intended to shoot it when it came; and its daring, by the fact that numbers do not appal it, that it will single out and carry off a man out of the middle of a party, and that it regularly helps itself to cattle in broad daylight, in full sight of the herdsmen or the whole village. I have not gone for my illustrations to any traveller's tale, but to records of Indian *shikar* that are absolutely beyond suspicion. To enable it to achieve such feats as these Nature has created in the tiger the very ideal of brute symmetry and power. The paws, moreover, are fitted with large soft pads which enable this bulky animal to move without a rustle over ground where the lizard can hardly stir without being heard; while its coloring, though it seems conspicuous enough when seen in a cage behind bars and against a background of whitewash, assimilates with astonishing exactness to its surroundings when the tiger lies in ambush under the overhanging roots, or crouches amongst the cane-grass.

For the tiger makes no pretence to invincible courage.

On the contrary, he prefers, as a rule, to enjoy life rather than die heroically. When death is inevitable he is always heroic, or even when danger presses him too closely. But, if he can, he avoids the unequal contest between brute courage and explosive shells, and makes off at once for more sequestered woodlands, where he can reign supreme and be at ease. It is indeed a splendid life that this autocrat of the jungle leads. The day commences for him as the sun begins to set, and he then stalks from his lair to drink at the neighboring pool, after which, his thirst slaked, he creeps out towards the glade where the deer are feeding. The vigilant, restless herd has need now for all its acuteness of ear and nostril, but it will certainly be unavailing, for the tiger is hungry, and, his prey once sighted, there is no gainsaying him. Using all the craft of his kind, the great cat steals upon his victims with consummate patience, and in such silence that even the deer have no suspicion how swiftly that stealthy death is approaching. It is like being killed by a shadow or a ghost, for not a sound of moving leaf or breaking twig has given them warning; and yet, all on a sudden, right in their midst it may be, there is an instant's swaying of the grass, and lo! the tiger.

The next instant he is flying through the air in a terrific bound, and as the herd sweeps away down the glade, one of their number is left behind, and is already dead.

The tyrant eats what he wants, and then strolls back into the jungle indolently and, so to speak, in good humor with all the world. We can then imagine him stalking a company of sambhur in fun, and afterwards see him standing up alone in the open space, laughing grimly, shaking his sides at the joke, as the antlered creatures fly terrified before his form revealed; or we may watch him insolently stretching himself in the full moonlight upon the ground near the favorite drinking pool, and daring all the beasts of the jungle to slake their thirst there so long as he remains. What strange wild scenes he must witness in the gray morning, as the world begins to wake up to life, and the night-feeding things go back to their lairs, with the bears shuffling along in good-humored company, the slinking wolves, and the careless trotting boars; and the multitude of smaller creatures, furred and feathered, going out for the work of the day, or coming home tired with the work of the night.

Nor is his life without brilliant episodes of excitement, for, apart from the keen triumphs that he enjoys whenever he seeks his food, there are thrilling intervals in each recurring summer when the hunt is equipped for his destruction, with all the pomp of marshalled elephants and an army of beaters.

The heat of May has scorched up the covert and the water, except in a few pools where a fringe of vegetation still lingers, and the tiger can still find a mid-day lair. Here the hunters seek him, and, whether we look at the quarry they pursue or the picturesque surroundings of the day's excitement, it must be confessed that tiger-shooting has no rival in all the range of sport. Even if no tiger is seen, if the elephant grass is beaten in vain, and the coverts of cane-clump and rustling reed are drawn without a glimpse of the great striped beast, there is such a multitude of incidents in the day's adventure that it is never a blank. As the drive comes on towards the ambushed rifles, the park-like glades that stretch away to right and left are never wanting in animal life. The pea-fowl and the wild pig, the partridges and grouse of several kinds, are all afoot, hurrying along before the advancing line. The jackals sneak from brake to brake, and, pacing out of the jungle that marks the watercourse, come the swamp deer and the noble sambhur. Here a wolf breaks cover sullenly, looking back over his shoulder as he goes, in the direction of the shouting beaters. There a bear goes by, complaining of his rest disturbed. The monkey-folk come swinging along in a tumult of the foliage overhead, and small creatures of the civet kind, with an occasional hare or wildcat, slip by, all wondering at the uproar, but all unmolested alike. For the honor of death is reserved to-day for the tiger only, and he, as a rule, is the last of all the denizens of the jungle to allow his repose to be broken, or to confess that he is alarmed. But even he has eventually to admit that this advancing line of noisy men means danger, and so he retires before them, creeping from clump to clump with consummate skill. Yet the swaying tassels of the tall plumed grass betray his moving, and on a sudden he finds himself in the ambush laid for him, and from the tree above him or from some overhanging rock the sharp cracks of the rifle proclaim that the tyrant of the jungle is dead.

When the tiger is followed up with elephants, fresh elements of adventure and picturesqueness are added to the day's sport — but the theme is an old one. The fact, however, remains that whatever the method employed for encompassing his death, or wherever he may be found, the tiger proves himself a splendid beast. If he can, he will avoid the unfair contest with bullet and shell; but let him only have his chance and he shows both man and elephant how royally he can defend his jungle realm against them.

His voice, it has been contended, is not regal. To dispute this one has only to go to any menagerie, where, though the lion's roar may be the loudest, the tiger's is not less terrific. Nor when he is heard roaming abroad in the jungles in the night can anything be imagined more terribly weird or unnatural than his utterances.

He has found, perhaps, that a pack of wild dogs — voiceless hunters of the forest — are crossing his path; and his angry protest, delivered in rapid, startling coughs, is certainly among the most terrifying sounds of Nature, while nothing can surpass the utter desolation that seems to possess the night when the tiger passes along the jungle to his lair, with his long-drawn, whining yawn. The lion's roar is, of course, unapproachable in its grandeur, but the tiger compresses into a cough and a yawn such an infinity of cruelty and rage, such unfathomable depths of fierce wild-beast nature as cannot be matched in forest languages.

Man-eating tigers and, even more, man-eating tigresses have always commanded among human beings a certain awful respect. Nor is this to be wondered at in India, when each year's returns tell us that about a thousand persons perish annually by these brutes. When, therefore, to the word "tiger" — itself a synonym in every language, civilized or savage, for stealthy, cruel, strong-limbed ferocity — is prefixed the aggravating epithet of "man-eating," the imagination prepares itself for the worst, and the great carnivore stalks past, in the mind's eyes, a very compendium of horrors, bearing about with it on its striped hide a Newgate Calendar of its many iniquities. But is it not just possible that the sensitiveness of humanity with regard to itself and all that pertains to its own security and dignity may have exaggerated the terrors of the man-eater? A lion-eating tiger would in reality be quite as fearful a thing as one that, with toothless jaws and unnerved limbs, falls upon miserable men and women; but a lion-eating tiger would not be considered an abominable monster. We should speak of it as a wise dispensation of nature for keeping the equilibrium among the carnivora, as a respectable and commendable beast that apologized for and justified its own existence by killing something else as noxious as itself; just as the cockroach has retained some shreds of reputation by eating mosquitoes. But alas for the tiger! the day comes when the wretched animal is so ill-conditioned that its kith and kin will not admit its relationship, and drive it forth; so feeble that the wild pig turns upon it and mocks it; so slow of foot that everything escapes from it; so old that its teeth fall out and its claws splinter; and, in this pitiful state, it has to go far afield for food. It has to leave the jungles it has lorded it over for so many years; the pleasant pools to which, in the evening, the doomed stag used to lead his hinds to water; the great beds of reed and grass in which, lazily basking, it heard the thoughtless buffaloes come grazing to their fate, crushing down the tall herbage as they sauntered on; the deep coverts of bamboo and undergrowth where the nylghai reposed his unwieldy bulk; the grand rock-strewn lair, whither he and his tigress used to drag the carcasses that were to feed their cubs.

But where is he to go in his old age? He must eat

to live, but what hope is there for such as he to earn an honest meal? With the best intentions possible, no one would believe him. His mere appearance in a village suffices to empty it of all but the bedridden. What is he to do? If the head men of the village would only stay and hear what he had to say, the tiger, it may be, would explain his conduct satisfactorily, and thenceforward might go decently, like any other hungry wretch, from hamlet to hamlet, with a begging-dish in his mouth.

Here, again, society is against him. In India the people do not eat meat, not enough of it, at any rate, to satisfy a tiger on their leavings; and to offer an empty tiger parched grain and vegetable marrows, wherewith to fill itself, is to mock the animal and to trifle with its tenderest feelings. So the tiger, despairing of assistance or even sympathy, looks about him in the deserted village, and, finding an old bedridden female in a hut, helps himself to her and goes away, annoyed, no doubt, at her toughness, but all the same, poor easy beast, glad of the meal.

Perhaps it is such a one as this that was caught not long ago by an old native in India, in a pit. A man-eating tiger that would fall into a pit could hardly have been in the enjoyment of the full complement of its senses; and when, having tumbled like a sack of potatoes into the hole, we hear that it did not jump out again, but permitted itself to be tied up and carted away, we must confess that something of the awesome terrors attaching by tradition to the anthropophagous cat fall away from it. An average sheep would have behaved with more spirit.

Meanwhile, it does not detract from the gallantry of

the capture, or the originality of the conception, that the tiger should have behaved so tamely. For the native, there can be only one feeling of respectful admiration. It would not occur to every one to dig a hole for a tiger, and sit by with a rope. But the capture, ridiculous as it was, has had some precedents, for the terror of the jungles has often, from pure rashness, stumbled into ridiculous positions with fatal consequences. Whether it is true that two British sailors once caught a tiger by tempting him into a barrel, and then, having pulled his tail through the bung-hole, tying a knot in it, I do not undertake to decide. But that a tiger has been taken prisoner in a blanket is beyond dispute; as also that a tiger, having thrust its head through a wicker crate which was filled with ducks, could not withdraw it, and in this ignominious plight, with the ducks making a prodigious noise all the while, blundered about the camp until, getting among the horses, it was kicked to death. Tigers have choked themselves by trying to swallow frogs, and in single combat with smaller animals been shamefully defeated.

Thus a man-eating tiger of immense proportions, at one time the pride of the Calcutta collection, was killed under circumstances that covered it with ridicule. It happened that a fighting ram belonging to a soldier in one of the regiments cantoned in the neighborhood, became so extremely troublesome that the colonel ordered it to be sent to the Zoölogical Gardens. Yet there it was as troublesome as ever, and being no curiosity, though excellent mutton, it was decided to give it to the great tiger. So ferocious was this creature supposed to be that it had a specially constructed cage, and its food was let down through a sliding grating in the roof. Down this, accordingly, the ram was lowered. The tiger was dozing in the corner, but when it saw the mutton descend, it rose and, after a long sleepy yawn, began to stretch itself. Meanwhile, the ram, who had no notion that he had been put there to be eaten, was watching the monster's lazy preparations for his meal with the eye of an old gladiator, and, seeing the tiger stretch himself, supposed the fight was commencing. Accordingly he stepped nimbly back to the farthest corner of the stage, just as the tiger, of course, all along expected he would do, — and then, *which the tiger had not in the least expected*, put down his head and went straight at the striped beast. The old tiger had not a chance from the first, and as there was no way of getting the ram out again, the agonized owners had to look on while the sheep killed the tiger!

Nor are such instances at all uncommon. Old cows have gored them, village dogs have worried them, horses have kicked their ribs to fragments, and even man himself, the proper lawful food of the man-eating tiger, has turned upon his consumer, and beaten him off with a stick. When a tiger can thus be set at naught by his supper, he hardly deserves all the reverent admiration with which tradition and story-books have invested him, and which an untravelled public has superstitiously entertained towards him.

"Generally speaking," says Dr. Jerdon, a great authority on Indian zoölogy, "the Bengal tiger is a harmless, timid animal. When once it takes to killing man it almost always perseveres in its endeavors to procure the same food; and, in general, it has been found that very old tigers, whose teeth are blunted or gone, and whose strength has failed, are those that relish human food, finding an easy prey."

Now, I would contend, there is no malignity here. The picture, indeed, is a pathetic one. Content, so long as it had good eyesight and sound teeth, to hunt wild beasts, the tiger, at an age when comfort and idleness should have been its lot, is compelled, poor wretch, to quit its natural haunts for the highways of men and their habitations. Its life becomes now a terror to itself; and the very quest for food is no longer the supreme pleasure it was in the days when it flashed like a streak of flame from its ambush upon the stately sambhur — or stalked with consummate skill the wary bison, and then plunging upon the great beast, bore it to the ground by the terrific impetus of its spring, and stunned it into beef with one tremendous blow. In those strong, fierce days, its roar silenced the many-voiced jungle; but now, as it creeps among the growing crops, or lurks in the shadow of the village wall, it has to hold its breath, lest a sound should betray it into danger. For everything is now a peril to it, even a company of unarmed men, or a pack of village curs, or a herd of kine. So it lays its helpless old body close along the ditch, where some weeds suffice to hide its terror-striking appearance, once its pride but now its ruin, and waits by the pathway for some returning villager, man, woman, or child, some belated goat or wandering calf. To be sure of its dinner it must be certain there will be no resistance, and every meal is, therefore, snatched with anxiety and fear. To such a life of degradation and shame does the splendid quadruped descend in toothless old age!

The lesser carnivora, as they are called, play a very important part in the political system of the beasts.

They are the great feudatory princes and independent barons of the wild world.

Claiming kinship with royalty, they possess within their respective earldoms all the privileges of independent sovereigns and the powers of life and death. At the head of fierce clans they defy the central authority, and retiring within their own demesnes maintain there almost regal state. Such are the puma, jaguar, leopard, and panther.

The puma, indeed, calls itself the lion in South America; the leopard, the tiger among the Zulus and throughout South Africa; and the panther is the tiger of Ceylon. But of these four furred princes, the jaguar rises most nearly to the standard of royalty, and it is certainly, both in appearance and the circumstances of its life, a splendid cat.

Unaccustomed to being annoyed, travellers see him in broad daylight lying stretched out at full length on the soft turf, under the shade of some Amazonian tree, thoroughly careless of danger, because so completely unused to being attacked. The explorer's boat passing along the river does not make him do more than raise his head, for the river is not in his own domain. It belongs to the cayman and the manatee, and it is their business, not his, to see to the boat. Wherever he goes animal life is so abundant that he finds no trouble in securing food, and, like the negroes of the Seychelles, he grows, from pure laziness and full feeding, sleek, large-limbed and heavy. His coat becomes strangely glossy, soft and close; the colors on it deepen and grow rich in sumptuous shades of velvety chestnut, brown and black; his limbs thicken, his body plumps out, and his jaws assume the full sensual contour characteristic of tropical man. He moves along with a lounging gait, often resting as he goes; and his eyes, as he turns his head incuriously to this side or to that, are large and soft and lustrous; while his voice, when he takes the trouble to warn away any incautious peccary or indiscreet capybara, is rich and low in tone. In every aspect, in fact, the jaguar presents himself to the mind as a pampered child of Nature, the representative in the beast world of the creole and negro of the Seychelles. In those wondrous islands the black man spends his day in utter idleness, lying on the white sea-beach or under the breadfruit trees, smoking the cigars his wife makes, watching the big fish chasing the little ones in the lagoon, or his fowls scratching among the wild melon beds. When he is hungry his wife goes down to the sea and catches a fish, one of his children plucks a pile of plantains and shakes down the green cocoanuts; and thus, indolent and full fed, he grows, like the jaguar, sleek and strong, with glossy skin and huge limbs.

The puma is a companion of the jaguar, but they seldom meet, for mutual respect defines for them their respective domains, and neither cares to trespass on the other. Nature has been equally kind to both, but the puma is of a restless temperament, and neither the abundance of food nor the temptations of the Brazils to idleness are enough to damp its energy. There is something of the immigrant and colonist about it. It is perpetually in quest of adventure or work to do, climbing about among the interwoven foliage, or prowling among the brushwood of more open country. Its one great object in life seems to be the chase, for the sport's sake, for it kills far more than it can ever eat, and often indeed does not attempt to consume its prey. This has given the puma a character for ferocity in works of natural history which its appearance in a cage would hardly justify, for its comfortable fur and sleek limbs might be thought to belong to a gentler creature.

The leopard and panther are to the east what the jaguar and puma are to the west; and their lives, whether we consider the kindliness of Nature to them or their strange immunity from harm, are equally to be envied. They live, it is true, within the empire of the tiger, but only, as in the days of the Heptarchy, the Mercian or the Northumbrian prince would have called himself within the realm of the Bretwalda; or as, in the early days of France, the dukes of Soissons or of Burgundy were subject to Paris; or, earlier still, only as Acarnania or Locris confessed the hegemony of Sparta. There is respect on both sides, and therefore a large measure of peace within the earldoms and duchies of the big cats.

. . . . . .

The domesticated cat is an animal that can be best approached sideways. Direct description, that is to say, does not bring out its peculiarities quite so well as the oblique form, which throws slanting lights upon the subject. To illustrate my meaning, let us take that frivolous proposition of the French to impose a tax upon cats; and following it out, note how the character of the animal develops itself by incidence.

How the tax is to be collected no senator ventured to explain, and when the project comes to the touchstone of practice we may confidently expect it to fall through. For the difficulties in the way of the collection of such a tax are immense. It is true they are not all on the surface, and so the impost may at the first glance pass as plausible; but, in reality, it would be hardly less easy to assess the householder on the mice that might infest his kitchen, or the sparrows that hop about on his window-sill, than upon the vagabond grimalkins that may choose to "squat" upon his premises. Putting on one side, however, the fact that both the social and the domestic systems would be shaken to their foundations by the exaction of such a duty, — that every cook would be set in opposition to her master by being called upon to pay the tax or dismiss her cat, — there remains this one great difficulty to a successful collection of a tax on cats, that no one would pay it. Some few eccentric persons — those, for instance, who pay "conscience money" — would, no doubt, come forward to be mulcted, but the vast majority of ratepayers would simply disclaim possession of cats, and throw the onus of proof upon the rate-collectors. "*My* cat!" the landlady would say to him, feigning astonishment, "Bless you, that's not *my* cat! It came in quite promiscuous one night, and I have been trying ever since to drive it away. If you don't believe me, sir, you can take it away with you now."

Under the circumstances, what could a collector, with ordinary human feelings, say or do? Is he to throw discredit upon a respectable person's statement, — supported, moreover, by her unmistakable sincerity in offering the cat there and then to the representative of Government, — by assessing her in spite of her protests?

Moreover, if the landlady, before his very eyes, should proceed to hunt the cat out of her parlor, should, farther, chase it downstairs into the kitchen with a duster, thence through the scullery into the back garden, and, not content with that, pursue it even to the uttermost angle of the garden wall, so that it should be entirely off her premises, the collector's position would be greatly aggravated; for what more could a person do than this to prove that there was no conspiracy in the matter, no attempt at fraudulent evasion of a legal demand? It is true that, if she were of a nimble kind, the landlady might prosecute her chase even farther, and not desist until she had seen pussy fairly out of the ward; but it surely has not come to this, in a free country too, that elderly ladies must satisfy tax-collectors by such violent exercise, to the detriment of their domestic and other duties; or, because a minion of the law insists upon it that wherever a cat is to be found there it is to be taxed, that females of all ages, delicately nurtured it may be, or otherwise incapacitated from rapid pursuit of animals, are to be set running about the streets and climbing trees, in order to rid themselves of importunate cats! The idea is preposterous.

Here, indeed, I have touched the very heart of the difficulty, for a cat does not of necessity belong to the place where she is found. Cats, in fact, belong to nowhere in particular. They are called domestic, I know, but they are really not so at all. They come inside houses for warmth, and because saucers with milk in them are more often found in houses than on garden walls, or in the roads, or up in trees; because street boys do not go about throwing stones in houses, and because there are no idle dogs there, looking round corners for something to hunt.

Besides, when it rains it is dry inside a house, as compared with out of doors, and sleep can be more comfortably arrived at in the daytime under a kitchen dresser than in such exposed and draughty spots as the roofs of outhouses or under the bushes in the garden of the square. The cat, therefore, comes into our midst from motives of pure self-interest alone, joins the domestic circle simply for the sake of the comforts it affords her, and seats herself upon our particular hearth and home only because she finds herself warm there, and safe.

But at heart she is a vagabond, a tramp, and a gypsy. She is always "on the patter." Our dwelling-places are really only so many casual wards to her, and she looks upon the basement floor of our houses as a fortuitous but convenient combination of a soup-kitchen and a lying-in hospital. When homeless she does not drown herself in despair, or go and buy poison from a chemist and kill herself. On the contrary, she avoids water with all the precaution possible, even so much as a puddle on the pavement, and carefully sniffs everything she sees lying about before she thinks of trying to eat it.

Nor does she, in desperation, go and steal something off a stall, in order to get locked up in shelter for the night, for she has instincts that teach her to avoid the coarse expedients with which homeless and starving humanity has so often to make such pathetic shift. The cat's plan is the simplest possible. She merely walks along the street as far as the first house, and, to guard against passing dogs, puts herself at once on the right side of the railings. Here she sits until the back-door opens, and as soon as she sees a domestic coming out she mews plaintively. If the domestic says *shoo* to her, she shoos at once, for she understands that there is one cat already in the house. But she only goes next door, and there repeats her manœuvre. The odds are that the next kitchen-maid does not say *shoo* to her, but only calls out to somebody else inside, "Here's a cat on the steps, a-mewing like anything." The adventurer, meanwhile, has got up and, still mewing, rubs herself suggestively on the post, arching up her back and leaning very much on one side — to show, no doubt, that she has no other visible means of support. The kitchen-maid duly reports the cat's proceedings, and some original-minded domestic at once hazards the suggestion that "the poor thing has lost hisself." This bold hypothesis is at once accepted as satisfying all the conditions of the problem, and ultimately, from one guileful gesture to another, the cat is found at last rubbing herself — still very much out of the perpendicular and still mewing — against the cook's skirts in front of the kitchen fire.

A cat has as keen an instinct for a cook as a policeman has, and makes straight for her. A strange dog, they say, will find out the master of a house at once, and immediately attach itself to him. The cat, however, does not trouble herself about such superficial differences of position as these, but goes without hesitation to the great dispenser of creature comforts, *the cook*. Masters, she says, are untrustworthy; they come and go, and in some houses do not even exist at all; but the kitchen fire is a fixed star, and the cook a satellite that may always be depended upon to be found revolving in her proper orbit. She attaches herself, therefore, to this important domestic at once, and forthwith becomes our cat.

Yet she is only our cat as distinguished from the cat next door. In no other sense is she ours at all. The chances are that the master of the house does not even know that there is such an animal on the establishment. Upon one occasion, certainly, he remembers

rudely expelling a cat, more in anger than in sorrow,
which he found in the library; but he had no idea, probably, when he had it raked out from under the furniture,
that it was a pensioner of his household, and a recognized retainer. Now, how can such a man be called
upon to pay a tax on a cat? The animal, by every one's
confession, quartered itself by guile upon the premises,
and belongs to nobody. The cook says it can go
(for she knows very well that it will immediately come
back again), and even the tax-collector could hardly,
under the circumstances of a general disclaimer, persist
in assessing the little animal. As I have already pointed
out, therefore, the presence of a cat in a house does not
imply ownership in the householder, for it would be just
as fair to infer from the presence of a tea-party of cats
in a back yard that they all belonged to the contiguous
house. A cat is at home nowhere, for she makes herself at home everywhere. All workhouses are much the
same to paupers. It is very difficult, therefore, to see
how the collector will collect his tax. His alternatives
will be equally disagreeable, for he must either refuse to
believe what he is told on oath by every person he calls
upon, or else he must remove the cats. For this purpose
he would have to go about accompanied by some conveyance not smaller in size than a train-car, for any
ordinary Square in the suburbs would supply enough
cats to fill a large vehicle. And when he has got them,
what will he do with them? Cats cannot be impounded
— except in a well, and even then it would be necessary
to keep the lid down; nor would it be permissible in
these days of advanced humanity to destroy them by
cremation as if they were so much condemned stores;
nor could they be served out to the parochial author-

ities for the sustenance of the aged poor. No decent person would consent to be a pauper and to live in a workhouse under conditions that involved cat soup. The question, in fact, is beset with immense difficulties; for one of two things must happen wherever the tax-collector calls, — either injustice must be perpetrated upon the householder, or the law be brought into contempt. Now, if some plan could be devised for ascertaining precisely whose cats they are that always pass the nights in such melancholy hilarity in their neighbors' gardens, and if these particular cats could be either heavily taxed or carted off — say, to the Canadian frontier — Government, I feel sure, and I speak for myself at all events, might depend upon the hearty co-operation of the public. As the project stands at present, however, a universal cat-tax appears to me impossible.

As another sidelong illustration of cat character, let us take the case of the gentleman found looking for a lost cat at one in the morning in a neighbor's till, — a proceeding which may be called, at any rate, curious. Whether he was really doing so or not, the magistrate before whom the case came had to decide for himself. The narrative itself is sufficient for my present purpose. Mr. James Cartwright, aged twenty-one, was charged, in a London police-court, with breaking into a rag-dealer's house at midnight, and stealing a gold mourning ring and twenty-six shillings, for after an exciting chase over the roofs of several outbuildings he had been caught, and the stolen property above referred to was found upon him. Mr. Cartwright, in explanation of his position, said that he was looking for a cat which he had lost. The simplicity of the defence is charming, and the readiness with which it was offered no less admirable, for it is one of the virtues of thought that it should be rapid, and one of the essentials in a hypothesis that it should be simple. Mr. Cartwright's mind must have flashed to its decision on the instant, and the only hypothesis that could possibly have covered all the suspicious circumstances — the hour of his capture, the position on the roof of an outbuilding, the headlong scramble over adjoining premises — was at once off his tongue. *He was looking for a cat.*

What more natural, he would ask, than that puss should have gone out at night, should have been on the roof of an out-building, and should have tried to elude capture by hasty flight over other roofs? Mr. Cartwright, no doubt, was much attached to his little friend — I can hardly call a cat a dumb companion — and having missed it from the hearth, braved the discomforts of the night air by going forth to seek it in its favorite haunts, which with cats are always a neighbor's premises. Failing to see it at the first cursory glance, he determined to go farther, but apprehending resistance from the cat, he armed himself with an iron bar which a neighboring rag-dealer used for securing a side-door, and, the door happening to open, Mr. Cartwright, naturally enough, went into the house to look for his pet. In his pathetic anxiety he searched every place, whether probable or improbable — and eventually the till.

The sight of the money in it probably suggested to him the feasibility of bribing the cat to return, and he took sufficient for the purpose — twenty-six shillings — and in his then forlorn and disconsolate condition the mourning ring naturally occurred to him as an appropriate and becoming possession. Had he found the cat he would, no doubt, have restored the ring and the money too, and mended the door as well; but, unfortunately, before his object was accomplished, and at the moment of hottest pursuit after the vagabond animal, he was himself captured, and, the circumstances looking suspicious (which it must be candidly admitted they did), he was taken up and committed for trial.

Looking for a cat at night requires good eyes, and might have been safely given to Hercules as an additional labor. For the cat is of an evasive kind. Its person is so inconsiderable that small holes suffice for its entrances and its exits, while a very trifling patch of shadow is enough to conceal a whole *soirée* of cats. Its feet, again, are so admirably padded that it makes no noise as it goes, and having been born to habits of sudden and silent escape, it vanishes from the vision like a whiff of mist. Terrier dogs think the cat a mean animal, and they have some reason on their side, for the cat never scruples to profit by every possible advantage which nature or accident may offer. Not content with having actually escaped, it perches itself comfortably upon a branch or roof just out of the pursuer's reach; and while the latter, frantic with tantalizing hopes, is dancing on its hind legs beneath it, the cat pretends to go to sleep, and blinks blandly upon the gradually desponding acrobat. Grimalkin has always this nice consciousness of safety, and does only just sufficient to secure it, enjoying for the rest the pleasure of watching its baffled adversary. Instead of disappearing altogether from sight through the kitchen window, the cat is content with squeezing through the area railings, and sitting on the window-sill in full view of the demented terrier, who can only thrust half his head through the bars, and stands there whimpering — " for the touch of a vanished cat and the sound of a puss that is still."

There is one more charge against the cat, that, though well cared for and well fed, she affects a homeless condition and, going out on the pantiles, foregathers with other vagabonds of her kind, and in their company indulges in the music of the future, expressive of many mixed emotions, but irregular and depressing.

Cats seem saddest when they trespass. At home they are silent, but entering a neighbor's premises they at once commence to confide their sorrows to the whole parish in melancholy dialogue, which in the morning are found to have been accompanied by violent saltations upon the flower-beds. Altogether, therefore, the cat out at night is one who deserves to be caught, and Mr. James Cartwright certainly had my sympathies in the object of his search. But for the means he employed to catch the cat it is impossible to entertain more than a very indifferent degree of respect. In the first place, he might have looked for his cat before one in the morning, which is an unconscionable hour to go running over the roofs of neighbors' outhouses. Nor in his search need he have wrenched off the iron bar which closed the rag-dealer's door, for it is not in evidence that his cat was of any extraordinary ferocity or proportions requiring so formidable a weapon of capture; nor, again, need he have looked in the till for his cat. Landladies' cats, it is notorious, go into remarkable places, and sometimes demean themselves in a manner quite surprising in such small animals; for they will play on the lodger's piano with dirty fingers, try on the lodger's bonnets, and eat prodigious quantities of the lodger's dessert, after taking the key of the chiffonnière out of the pocket of the dress that was hanging in the wardrobe in the bedroom. Mr. Cartwright's cat, however, does not appear to have been of this kind, and, unless its master meant to bribe the cat to return to him, all other methods failing, I do not see why he should have taken the twenty-six shillings. The mourning ring is more comprehensible, perhaps; but, on the whole, there was a doubtful complexion about that cat-hunt which certainly justified the severe view which the magistrate took.

The proper food of the cat, the common or garden cat, is the sparrow (*Spar. Britannicus*). The sparrow's favorite food is your garden seeds. When he sees you at work the ingenuous bird surveys your operations, and, pleased with the liberal feast prepared, informs his friends of the fact. As a rule they accept his invitation cordially. The diligence of the sparrow in eating what does not belong to him is very remarkable, and nowhere more conspicuous than in the back garden. Sitting on the spouts or chimney-pots of the houses round, he remarks all that goes on beneath, makes a note of the cat that has just gone under the currant bush at No. 25, and ponders at the top of his voice on the proceedings of the inhabitants of the row generally. Satisfied that seed-sowing is in progress in one of the gardens, he descends, and having collected his friends, remains with them upon the scene of operations, industrious to the last.

With one little black eye applied close to the surface of the soil, and the other doing general duty by keeping a watch upon the overlooking windows, whence sudden missiles might issue, he continues his patient but cheerful scrutiny until certain that nothing remains. It is of no use trying to tempt him from the larcenous repast by the exhibition of honest viands upon the adjoining path; for he knows, perhaps, that the bread will wait for him, but that if he does not eat the seed at once it will be grown beyond his powers of digestion. When he has nothing else to do, he will make fun of the crumbled loaf; will provoke his acquaintances to chase him by flying off with the largest lump; will play at prisoner's base with it, or drop it down gratings; will carry it up to the roof of a house and lose it down a spout; will do anything with it, in fact, but eat it in a proper and thankful manner.

The back-garden sparrow, indeed, is a fowl of very loose morality, but his habits of life have so sharpened his intelligence that the cats find it as difficult to catch him as the policemen do the urchins of the streets. Rustic sparrows, country-bumpkin birds, fall clumsily into the snares of the village tabby, but in the back gardens of urban districts the cat very seldom indeed brings the birds to bag. It is not that the quadruped has lost her taste for sparrows, or that she has forgotten all her cunning, for now that the shrubs are in leaf, and afford her convenient ambuscade, she may be seen on any sunny morning practising her old wild-life arts in order to circumvent the wily sparrow. But domestication blunts the feline intelligence, and after a long residence in kitchens, and daily familiarities with milkmen, the spell of civilization and its humdrum ways of life falls upon her, and, though she may hunt for sport, the comfortable assurance of a saucer daily replenished dulls her enthusiasm for strange meats; and, without forgetting that the sparrow is toothsome, she remembers more than she used to do that the sparrow is also nimble.

I have observed that the controversy as to whether sparrows are blessings or otherwise to the farmer, and whether, in these days of bad harvests, when almost every grain of corn is precious, the little birds should be encouraged or exterminated, is one that is regularly revived.

All the poets have formally denounced the sparrow, "the meanest of the feathered race," and how shall any one be found to speak well of him? The best that can be said in the defence of the familiar little fowl is very bad indeed, for no criminal code that yet exists would suffice to exhaust the calendar of his crimes and convict him for all his offences. Not only does the sparrow despise police regulations and make sport of by-laws, but he affronts all our standards of ethics, public morality, and religion. In a church he behaves with no more decorum than in a court of justice, and whether in the pulpit or the dock betrays an unseemly levity that will require the utmost extension of the Arminian doctrines of universal grace to compass his salvation. He is the street boy among birds, and his affronts are gratuitous and unprovoked. It is of no use to retort upon him, or threaten him with the law. The water-pipe suffices as an answer to every repartee, be it a gibe or a menace; and when a sparrow has hopped up a long spout, who would care to bandy arguments with him? Impervious to the battery of exhortation, he perches on the window-sill, invulnerable to the most formidable assaults of reason or the most ferocious onsets of sarcasm, and thoroughly comprehends upon which side of the glass he sits. Pelt him with hard names, and he only chirps monotonously; but if you throw a stone at him, you must pay for the damages.

The sparrow carries no purse, for he steals all he wants; and his name is in no directory, for he lives everywhere. His address is the world, and when changing his residence he apprises no one. There is no city whose freedom he has not conferred upon himself, and no corporation whose privileges he does not habitually usurp. Collectors of rates might well despair if directed to get their dues from him, and school boards need not hope for his reclamation. A long immunity from reprisals has so emboldened this feathered gamin that he seems now to fear nothing, riding on omnibuses free of charge, occupying tenements without paying rent, and feeding everywhere at no cost to himself.

Such, summarized, would stand the indictment against the sparrow, — a contemner of all law, and a rebel against all order, a criminal egotist of a very serious type. But what can be said for the defence? That he is consistently the friend of the farmer is still disputed, and that he fills any important place in the economy of nature, a close observation of his habits must make every one doubt. Imported into foreign countries as "the friend of man," the sparrow, in Australia as well as in America, has multiplied into a public nuisance; and in return for the gift of new worlds to colonize, the graceless birds have developed into a multitudinous evil. They have also been called "the nightingales of our roofs," and if they remained upon the roofs only they might be permitted to retain the flattering title of nightingales. Since, however, they come down off the slates into our houses and swagger about in our pleasure-grounds and business premises alike, giving us in return no pleasant song, their claims to the honor of "the queen of the feathered choir" cannot be gravely entertained. Upon the house-tops, if they always stopped there, we might extend to them a generous admiration; but when they contest with us the habitations which we have built for ourselves, and repay us for our protection with impudence only, such sympathy is difficult.

How then can he be defended, this chief vagabond of the air? On his merits he stands categorically convicted, and for his shortcomings it is difficult to find excuse or palliation. Did he ever suffer from winter as the wild things of copse and hedge do, or from drought, or from the encroachments of civilization, his small presumptions might pass unchallenged, as do those of the robins and the finches. But for him there is no frost so severe that it checks the supply of food in the streets, no snow so thick that it blocks up the sparrow's entrance to goods, sheds, and storehouses. His year has no Ramazan for him. For drought or flood he cares as little. His nurseries do not suffer by rising rivers, nor are his meals curtailed by any severity of the seasons. Nor yet when man, advancing, pushes back the domains of wild things in waste land and wood, does the sparrow share in the troubles which fall to the lot of the songsters of the countryside. Wherever man goes he follows him, a parasite of his grain bags; and no city in which our countrymen have settled is without him.

I remember myself noticing, during the late campaigns in Afghanistan and Zululand, how the sparrows went wherever the commissariat wagons went, and established a colony at every depôt. They crossed the Cabul River and the Buffalo with our armies, claiming at once privileges of conquest which our generals hesitated to assert. They levied instant toll on the grain fields, and billeted themselves upon the natives.

The area of their prevalence coincides with the empire of white men, for wherever, and as soon as, the flag goes up, in sign of the white man's rule, the sparrow perches on the top of it. Ships of all nations carry him as a stowaway from port to port, and, thus defrauding every company alike, these birds range the world, settling where they will. And everywhere the sparrow is safe alike.

And who cares to catch him? Youth, it is true, lays preposterous snares of bricks to entrap him, and sparrow clubs conspire against him; but no sportsman goes out to make a prey of him. Who, indeed, would expend time and patience in fetching a compass about a sparrow, or sit a summer's day with net and line, decoy-bird and call, with a sparrow before his mind as his reward?

Abroad, also, the sparrow's arrival is hailed with patriotic glee, and municipalities incontinently go to and legislate for his protection. The sparrow soon discovers that he is favored, and no sooner makes the discovery than he presumes upon it. Selecting prominent corners of public buildings, he stuffs rubbish into the crevices of the friezes, and advertises by long rags which he leaves fluttering and flapping outside that he has built a nest. Secure from cats and assured of man's patronage, he thrives and multiplies his kind, each generation adding to the general stock of effrontery and presumptuously acquired privileges, until nations turn in wrath upon their oppressors. Men hired for the purpose rake out the sparrows' nurseries from under the eaves of the churches, and purge the town-hall. But the sparrow cares little for such clumsy retaliation. One house is as good as another, and as for a nest being destroyed, he is glad of an excuse for beginning the honeymoon all over again.

And this reminds me that it is not only in his public character that this vagabond fowl calls for animadversion. In private life his conduct is disreputable. As a frivolous parent, given to rolling eggs out of the nest, and even also his infant progeny; as an unworthy spouse, transferring his affections lightly, and often assaulting the partner of his joys and sorrows; as a bad neighbor, scuffling with his kind wherever he meets with them, — in each aspect he presents himself to the moral mind as undeserving of respect. Yet, with something of that eccentricity of judgment which commends Punch, the immoral consort of Judy, to the public regard, we persist in looking upon the sparrow, with all his notorious faults, as a popular favorite, and resent any exposure of his obliquities.

The tyranny of the sparrow, in fact, is the price of civilization. Only savages are exempt.

VI.

BEARS — WOLVES — DOGS — RATS.

Bears are of three kinds, Big Bears, Middle-sized Bears, and Little Wee Bears. — Easily Provoked. — A Protest of Routine against Reform. — But Unreliable. — Unfairly Treated in Literature. — How Robbers went to steal the Widow's Pig, but found the Bear in the Sty. — The Delightful Triumph of Convictions in the Nursery. — The Wild Hunter of the Woods. — Its Splendid Heroism. — Wolf-men. — Wolf-dogs. — Dogs we have all met. — Are Men only Second-rate Dogs? — Their Emotions and Passions the same as ours. — The Art of Getting Lost. — Man not inferior to Dogs in many ways. — The Rat Epidemic in India. — Endemic in England. — Western Prejudice and Eastern Tenderness. — Emblems of Successful Invasion. — Their Abuse of Intelligence — Edax Rerum.

BEARS are of three kinds, as every child knows. There is the Great Big Bear, the Middle-sized Bear, and the Little Wee Bear. They are all of a domestic kind, and generally go out for a walk in the forest before breakfast, in order to give their porridge time to cool. When met with in a wild state they can be easily distinguished by their size, and by their subsequent conduct, for the bigger the bear is the more of you it will eat. If there is not much of you left when it has done, you may decide without hesitation that it was the Big bear you met: while if you are only moderately consumed, you may safely conclude it was the Middle-sized bear. The Little Wee Bear, or bear-kin, will only trifle with you, take a mere snack, as it were — make a trifling collation or luncheon, so to speak, off you.

But if still in doubt as to the species encountered, the Hindoo student's description of the bheel may assist the stranger in arriving at a correct conclusion, for the Big bear is black, " only much more hairy," and when it has killed you it leaves your body in a ditch. By this you may know the Big bear.

But, unless provoked to attack you, these creatures will not do so; so naturalists assure us. A bear's notions of provocation, however, are so peculiar that perhaps the safest rule for strangers to observe is not to let the animal see you. The bear never attacks any person whom it cannot see. This is a golden rule for persons who are in the habit of meeting bears to observe.

Otherwise there seem to be no limits to a bear's provocations. If it comes up behind you, and finds you not looking that way, it knocks off the back part of your head with one blow of its curved claws; and if it meets you face to face it knocks off the front part of your head. But there is nothing agreeable in this variety. Again, if it discovers you sitting below it on the same hillside as itself, it rolls itself up, and comes trundling down the slope upon top of you like an ill-tempered portmanteau; or if it is down below you, and becomes provoked, it comes scrambling up the hill with a speed that in a creature of such a shape is described, by those who have been charged, as quite incredible. Sometimes, on the other hand, bears receive very solid provocation without showing any resentment, for, as Captain Kinloch, a noted Indian Shikarry, has told us, the amount of lead which an old black bear will carry away in his quarters is amazing. But, as a rule, bears will not stand nonsense. It is well known how they behaved in the matter of Goldylocks, who, after all, had only eaten up the Little Wee Bear's porridge, and broken the seat of the Little Wee Bear's chair, and gone to sleep in Little Wee Bear's bed. Yet, if the family had caught her, poor Goldylocks would probably never have got home to her mother to tell the tale.

This characteristic animosity to man has given many writers on the bear a handle for great unfairness towards it.

I far prefer, myself, to see in the bear only some dull-witted, obstinate Mars, pathetic Jubal, or rough but staunch Sir Bors; some slumberous man of might, a lazy Kwasind, or sluggard Kambu Kharna; an easily befooled Giant Dumbledore or Calabadran; some loyal Earl Arthgal of the Table Round, or moody Margrave of Brandenberg — both of whom did not despise the fighting sobriquet of the Bear. For myself, I think no worse of the bear than Toussenel does, — indeed, hardly so badly; for I hesitate to agree with him that it symbolizes only the spirit of persistent savagery, the incorrigible protest of Routine against Reform; that it is the feral incarnation of hostility to progress, and the champion-in-arms of the pretended rights of the Beast against the authority of Man. Men of science assure us that it is one of the senior quadrupeds of the earth; and it was certainly the first among them that arrived at any idea of using fore paws as hands. But unfortunately for itself it has never raised itself any further in the scale; and now that it has been driven into the forest and wilderness, it seems to consider itself unfairly displaced, and sulkily maintains in the solitudes of the hills the character of a misanthrope, the *laudator temporis acti*, the Legitimist in retreat.

But, unfortunately for it, even in Russia, where the animal is held in semi-reverential awe, its flesh is considered a dainty by the hard-living races among whom it has raised its gloomy standard of protest, and its skin is valued everywhere; while its pomatum — the *pomade de lion* of Paris, the "bear's grease" of London — is alone sufficient for its utter ruin. Pretenders should be poor if they wish to be unmolested. Yet the bear obstinately maintains the unequal struggle, appealing to its semi-erect posture, its hand-like paws, its almost-absent tail, and its innocent tastes, for the clemency and consideration of man. It would, too, recall the facts of history, and remind us how, in the olden days of Roman beast-fights, the bear was hissed from the arena because it refused to fight with the Christians and other captives provided for it; and, pointing to the East, would remind us that there it is called a generous brute, because it will not molest the dead. If a man pursued by a bear feigns death, the bear passes on after a most cursory examination, generously preferring to be thus easily deceived rather than push examination beyond the limits of good taste. You shall also see in this way a truly benevolent man giving alms to a beggar sooner than scrutinize too narrowly the necessity for giving relief.

But I fear that none of these pleas avail the bear, for it is impossible to forget how lamentable are the exceptions to that innocent appetite for leaves and berries and roots which it displays in Europe, and how abominably carnivorous are the grizzly bear of America, and the polar bruin of the Arctic snows. These are facts beyond dispute — but I would not be unjust. I would not throw in their teeth, as some have done, the conduct of those she-bears of Judea, who avenged the touchy prophet by desolating the nurseries of all the countryside, for that was a miracle over which the she-bears had no control. Nor would I give credence to Daniel, when he takes the bear as an emblem of faithlessness; nor to the libellous narrative of Gesner, who tells us how bears make a practice of stealing young women; nor yet would I admit in evidence the mocking eulogies of Ælian. Pliny and Aristotle are of course to be discredited, and we must therefore come to modern times to find the bear justly judged. The delightful La Fontaine speaks of it as a blundering friend, and points the moral by the story of the bear who, wishing to brush away the fly that disturbed its master's slumbers, accidentally knocked off the top of its master's skull; and Artemus Ward tells us how it can be taught to do "many interestin' things, but is onreliable."

But, after all, this is no excessive disparagement, and within the moderate limits of justice.

. . . .

Among the stories which have delighted children of all countries, and probably from all time, is one that tells how certain evil-minded men went to steal a widow's pig, but how they found a bear in the sty instead, and how thereupon disaster, sudden and complete, overtook the robbers.

No child ever doubted the truth of that story; indeed how could it be doubted? It is well known that widows do as a fact frequently keep a pig, and where should they keep it but in a sty? Again, thieves are notoriously given to stealing, and what could be more advantageously purloined than a pig, — above all a pig belonging to a lone and unprotected widow? It is not with swine as with poultry or cattle, for the pig can be eaten up from end to end; even his skin makes crackling, and nothing need be left behind. There are no accusing-feathers to lie about the scene of larcenous revel, as is the case when hens have been devoured by stealth, and no bulky hide and horns to get rid of on the sly, as happens whenever robbers irregularly consume a neighbor's cow or calf. Again, a widow is, as a rule, a person who lives alone — I confidently appeal to all story-books to support this statement — and, except for such assistance as her cat can give her, is virtually defenceless at midnight against a number of armed and determined men. A widow's pig is therefore, and beyond all doubt, just the very thing to get itself stolen, and indeed we would venture to say that, as a matter of fact, it always *is* stolen.

Is it not natural, then, in children to believe implicitly the story we refer to? As for the other incidents of it — those in which the bear takes a prominent part — they, too, are exactly such as might be expected to occur frequently under similar circumstances.

A poor bear-leader on his way to the neighboring town is benighted, on a stormy evening, in a solitary place — just such a place as widows live in — and, knowing from a large and varied experience of men and cities that widows are kind of heart, he intercedes for a night's lodging for himself and his beast. It is no sooner asked than granted. The widow turns the cat off the hearth to make room for the man, and the pig out of his sty to make room for the bear. The cat and the pig grumble, of course, at having to make their own arrangements for the night; but, at any rate, the sacred duties of hospitality have been faithfully discharged, and, in the sequel, the widow is rewarded. The stormy night has suggested itself to certain good-for-nothing vagabonds — who, in their tramps along the road, have marked down the widow's pig for their prey — as an excellent opportunity of coming at some home-fed bacon cheaply; and, unconscious of the change of occupant, stealthily approach the sty, hoping, under cover of the night, high wind, and pelting rain, to carry off the porker in a sack which they have provided for the purpose. How differently the case falls out is quickly told. The bear, instead of allowing itself to be put into the sack like a lamb, gets up on its hind legs, and nearly kills the robbers.

From first to last the story has always been completely credible, for given a widow with a pig, a man with a bear, and robbers with a sack, the incident is one that might happen at any time.

Such being the story, so consistent in its circumstances and so complete in its action, it is very pleasing to find that the implicit faith of children in it has, after all, been rewarded by its actual occurrence. Everything is true that really happens, and it does not matter whether the story or the event comes first. Where the incidents have already actually transpired, and a writer sits down to describe them, the narrative is, no doubt, often excellent, vivid, picturesque, faithful, and so forth. Nevertheless, it is rather a commonplace performance after all, and depends for its virtues either upon the state of the narrator's eyesight and his propinquity to the scene of the event, or else to his judicial capacity for appraising the value of the evidence of others. But where the writer describes occurrences which have not yet occurred, the merits of his work are infinitely enhanced; and the wisdom of the prophets is nowhere more conspicuous than in their selection of this method of narration.

They made it a rule to speak before the event, instead of after it, and it is owing almost entirely to this that their utterances have been so highly spoken of.

Truth, it is said, is stranger than fiction; and so it is in a certain sense, because it is in the nature of fiction to be strange; but truth is a prosaic, every-day sort of thing, and when it is romantic it strikes the mind as being peculiarly wonderful. We do not as a rule expect facts to surprise us; so when they do, they startle us much more than any narrative ever created by novelist or poet. In that case they are more like fiction than fiction itself, and are therefore all the more charming. Thus, "The Bear in the Pig-sty" story may be considered admirable, while a pleasure is superadded by the reflection that the faith of childhood, which is at once the most solemn and the most fascinating attribute of that reverend and delightful age, has not been trifled with and betrayed. That the story was true the children have known all along, but now everybody knows it too, and acknowledges that the children were right.

At the village of Massegros, in France, only the other day, a bear-man came along the road with a bear, and asked for a night's lodging, and the bear was put into the pig-sty. At night three men came to steal the pig; but, on the contrary, one of the men died, the second very nearly, and the third went mad with fright. The bear did it — just as it was written in the story-book years upon years ago — and the pig is back in his sty again.

No wonder one man went mad from fright, for the difference between pigs and bears is very considerable;

and the thief putting out his arm to take hold, as he thought, of the sleek and inoffensive porker, might well be startled out of his senses to find himself handling the shaggy hide of a bear. The horror of the discovery, the utter impossibility of guessing what had happened, the first bewildering instant when Bruin rose with a roar from the litter, the next of horrid and inexplicable pain as the great brute closed with its assailant, combined to make such an experience as might well terrify the reason out of a man. Suddenness and darkness are the most awful allies of the dreadful, and when to these are added a consciousness of guilt and superstitious fear, the wits might easily take to flight, and a cunning thief go out a gibbering idiot.

For those who were hurt, — fatally, so the report says, — the horrors of the incident were in one sense even aggravated, as the bear is monstrously cruel in its attack. Thus natives of India look upon the wounds which it inflicts with even greater dread than they regard those from a tiger, for the latter are either clear gashes or bone-shattering blows; but, as a rule, the bear, standing erect before it closes with a man, strikes at the head and its huge blunt claws tear the skin down off the scalp, and over the face, or lay the throat bare, in either case blinding and stunning the unhappy wretch. The pain of even such an attack as that, however, could hardly increase for the unfortunate men the terrors of their position, when there rose up out of the pig's straw the giant apparition of a growling beast, a great black monster all hair and fury, that was upon them in an instant, roaring like an earthquake, and striking with the arms of a giant. No wonder that two of the three are dead, and the other one is mad!

But the triumph of virtue was delightfully complete, and the pig came by its own again. The widow who hospitably entertained the homeless bear-man, and the cat that surrendered her corner by the fire to the stranger were rewarded; the wicked men who went about stealing pigs were punished, and the story of the old fairy-tale book came true.

The moral of this evidently is that no one should refuse charity even to bears, and no one should steal pigs; for, though bear ham is good, it is not the same as pork ham, and it is better to save your own bacon than to steal your neighbor's. There is a second moral also, and that is that children are wiser than grown-up people, inasmuch as they believe that there is nothing so wonderful but it may really come to pass, and that everything which will happen has already happened before. Children never give over expecting and hoping, and this is why they alone are never disappointed, and why they deserve so thoroughly to enjoy the triumph of their convictions.

. . . .

The wolf is a creature of very bad character, and deserves most of it. Born of poor but dishonest parents, he inherits the family instinct for crime, and industriously commits it. No jury would recommend him to mercy, even on the score of youth, nor any chaplain pretend after execution that the deceased had died repentant.

Contrition, it is true, is a mandrake. It springs up under the gallows.

But the wolf, even in the very shadow of death remains a wolf still, and, according to the condition of his stomach, shows either one abominable phase of his character or the other. If hungry he is abject, and curls himself up meekly to receive the fatal blow, dying without half the protest that even a healthy lamb would make. But if he has just dined he snarls and snaps to the last. Yet even the wolf has found his apologists.

We have been told that he is only a dog gone wrong, that evil communications have corrupted his original manners, and that under more wholesome home influences he might have developed into a good dog Tray, instead of the bandit and assassin that he is.

The poetry of crime, however, is a dangerous theme, and when sentiment indulges itself upon the picturesqueness of a criminal's career, it is liable to degenerate into a whimsical justification of wrong-doing and its doer. I can appreciate the solemnity of the wolf's murders, supreme tragedies as they often are — or the splendor of its ravages when, Attila-like, it descends upon the fat plains to scourge the lowland folk — or the nobility of its recklessness as, from age to age, it challenges man to the unequal conflict — or the heroism which sends it out alone into the haunts of men to carry away a child, so that its own whelps may not starve. Nor in all the records of human violence is there to be found anything more tremendous than the deadly patience with which the trooped wolves pursue their victims, or the fierce *élan* with which they launch themselves from the forest depths upon the passing prey. A party of eighty Russian soldiers, fully armed, were moving in mid-winter from one post to another, when, just as the shades of evening were closing round them, an immense pack of wolves —scouring the black countryside for food — came suddenly across their line of march. Rather than swerve from their course, the intrepid brutes flung themselves upon the soldiers, and tore every man of the detachment to pieces.

This is literally an instance of that " Berserker rage," that fearless, unarmed rage of which the Scandinavian chroniclers tell us in terms of awesome admiration, so long as the heroes were the fair-bearded men who followed their Erics and Olafs to the sea. Now, for myself, I do not grudge the same admiration to the wolf when it acts as bravely as those old heroes of the Sagas, especially since the Norsemen themselves, to express the intensity of their valor and the surpassing ferocity of their attack, had to go to the wolf for a simile. But, after all, no pleading can avail the wolf, for the whole history of man — black or white, brown, red or yellow — convicts these animals of persistent and ineradicable wickedness — rising, often, it is true, to a considerable dignity in the proportions and manner of their crime, but as a rule taking rank only as misdemeanants of the lowest type.

Children looking at wolves always greet them as *bow-wows*, and in their pretty sympathy offer the wild hunter of the forest morsels of bun. Such cates, however, are not to the wolf's taste; he would far rather have the children themselves. But he knows that that is out of the question, so he blinks his eyes wearily, and with a sharp expression of discontent at his lot resumes his restless motion up and down the cage.

Only very young children, however, mistake the wolf for a dog, for there is that in its ugly eyes, set so close together and so sinister in their expression, that tells the elder ones that the creature before them is no dog, or, at any rate, not an honest specimen. Besides, nursery stories, fairy tales, and fables have taught them long ago the likeness of the wolf and its character, and the first look at the sharp snout set in gray fur reminds them of that face that little Red Riding Hood found looking out at her, one fine May morning, from under her dear old grandmother's nightcap. If the literature of the nursery has thus familiarized the wolf to the younger generation, their elders also, of whatever nation they may be, and whatever language they may speak, have continued to learn from a hundred sources of the implacable brute (the totem of the Pawnees) that makes the great highways of forest and plain in Northern and Eastern Europe and the mountain paths of the Pyrenees and Apennines so perilous to belated travellers, — that robs the Indian mothers of their children, or pulls down the solitary wood-gatherer as he goes trudging home at nightfall along the pathway that skirts the jungle. Tales of horror crowd into their memory as they look at the unkempt and restless creatures, condemned to-day to civilization and monotony, but once, perhaps, actors themselves in the very scenes that make the narratives of wolf adventure so appalling. In a bare cage, with iron bars before it, it is difficult to realize the full meaning of the thing before you.

There is nothing in its appearance, except that sinister proximity of its eyes, to betoken a creature so eminently dangerous when wild, no significance of cruel fury in its voice, no profession of murderous strength in its limbs. It looks like a shabby dog, and howls like an unhappy one. There is no fierce tiger-eloquence of eye, no ravening hyena-clamor in its voice, no lion-majesty of form. It seems a poor thing for any one, even a child, to be afraid of, for it appears half-fed and weak-limbed. As it trots backwards and forwards it is hard to believe that these pattering feet are really the same as those that can swing along the countryside in an untiring gallop, defy the horse and laugh the greyhound to scorn; or that the thin neck, craning out of the kennel there, could ever bear a dead child's weight. Yet this is indeed the very creature that has made countries ring with its dreadful deeds of blood, that has held mountain passes and lonesome wood-ways against all comers, has desolated villages and aroused the resentment of kings. There must, then, be something more, after all, in the thin-bodied thing than the eye catches at first sight, or why should England have had two monarchs that waged imperial war against it, or have had a month named after it, — the modern January, the old Wolf-monath, so called because the depredations of the beast were then especially terrible; or why should the wolf have been included in English litanies as one of the chief perils of life? "From caterans and all other kinds of robbers; from wolves and all other kinds of evil beasts, deliver us, O Lord!"

In other countries it has been at times a veritable scourge, and wherever this has happened local legend and folk-lore have invested the animal with strange, gaunt terrors. In the hungry North, where Arctic snows forbid the multiplication of small animal life, and the wolf would often be starved but for man and his domestic beasts, the wolf is the popular symbol of all that is tragic or to be dreaded, and signifies, in their superstition, the supreme superlative of ruin; for they say that when the last tremendous Night overshadows the earth, and our planet sinks out of the darkened firmament into eternal gloom, the Fenris-wolf and the Sköll-wolf will appear and devour the gods and the firmament! Further to the south, we find Scandinavian tradition replete with weird wolf-lore; and it is the same in Finland and all over Russia, Germany, and France, where the horrible fiction of the *loup-garou* — partly ghoul and partly wolf-man — still holds its own. Indeed, so terribly associated are the crimes of wolves and the sufferings of men that all over Europe, from the snows of Lapland to sunny Spain, the gruesome legend is a household story, and the wehr-wolf and wolf-children carry on the old Greek and Latin superstitions of the lycanthropes.

It is, however, in the East, in India, that the wolf attains the complete measure of its obliquities; for just as the korait snake kills a greater number of human beings than the far more deadly cobra, so the wolf takes infinitely more lives than the tiger. Thousands of adults fall victims annually to this animal's daring and ferocity, and the destruction of child-life by it is prodigious. It is not only in the remoter districts, where jungles and rocky wildernesses are found, that the wolves thus prey upon man, but in the very midst of busy towns.

They will creep, so the natives say, into houses, and lick the babies from the sleeping mothers' arms. The soft warm touch of the wild beast's tongue melts the guardian fingers open. One by one they loosen their hold, and, as the wrists sink apart, the baby slides gradually out of the protecting arms against the soft coat of the wolf. It does not wake, and then the brute bends down its head to find the child's throat. There is a sudden snap of closing teeth, a little strangling cry, and the mother starts to her feet to hear the rustle of the grass screen before the door as it is pushed ajar, and to feel her own feet slip in the blood at her side.

There are those who would gloss over the wolf's crimes by declaring it to be the brother of the dog, and it may be true enough that wolves learn to bark when fostered by canine mothers, that the dogs of the Arctic regions are in reality only wolves, and that till the white man came the Red Indian had no quadruped companion but the wolf. But, after all, such facts only amount to this — that though wolves are never fit to be called dogs, there are some undeveloped specimens of dogs only fit to be called wolves.

. . . .

I am very fond of dogs, and have indeed, in India had as many as seven upon my establishment at one time. Some I knew intimately, others were mere acquaintances; but speaking dispassionately of them, and taking one with another, I should hesitate to say that they were superior to ordinary men and women. It is, I know, the fashion to cite the dog as a better species of human being and to depreciate men as if they were dogs gone wrong. I am not at all sure that this is just to ourselves, for speaking of the dogs I have met — the same dogs in fact that we have all met — I must say that, on the whole, I look upon the dog as only a kind of beast after all. At any rate I am prepared to produce from amongst my acquaintances as many sensible men as sensible dogs, and if necessary a large number of human beings who if taken by accident or design out of the road will set themselves right again, who if separated for years from friends will readily recognize them and welcome them, who on meeting those who have done them previous injuries will show at once by their demeanor that they remember the old grudge, who will detect false notes in a player's performance, catch thieves, carry baskets to the butchers, defend their masters, and never worry sheep. On the other hand I will produce in equal number dogs who get themselves lost regularly and for good, until a reward is offered, who never recognize old acquaintances, but will fawn upon those who have injured them, who will sleep complacently through the performances of organ-grinders and never wake up when thieves are on the premises; who cannot be trusted with meat, and who will run away from their masters if danger threatens. Being quite certain of this, I think I am justified in maintaining that dogs are no better than men, and indeed I should not quarrel with him if any one were to say that but for man the dog would have been much worse than he is — probably, only a wolf still.

As a matter of fact, most of the dogs of my acquaintance have been positively stupid. One that I remember well was, however, considered by my friends of remarkable intelligence; but this story often told of him, to illustrate his intelligence, did not give me when I heard it, any high opinion of his intellect. But I may be wrong. He was accustomed, it appears, to go with the family to church. But one day the old church roof began to leak, so workmen were set at the job and the building was closed. But when Sunday came this intelligent dog trotted off as he was wont to do, to the church, and, composing himself in the porch as usual, remained there the customary time and trotted complacently home again. Now where does the intelligence come in, in this anecdote?

In a similar way stories are told in illustration of other feelings and passions, but most of them, so it seems to me, cut both ways. There are, indeed, many human feelings which the dog evinces in a marked way, and often upon very little provocation. The dog, for instance, expresses *anger* precisely as we do, and, in accordance with the human precept, "When the boy hits you, kick the post," will bite his friend to show his displeasure at a stranger. I had a little bull-terrier which went frantic if a pedlar or beggar came to the door, and, being restrained from flying at the innocent itinerant, would rush out as soon as released into the shrubbery and go for the gardener. The gardener knew the dog's ways, for he had had a sharp nip vicariously before, and when he saw Nellie on her way towards him, used to charge her with a lawn mower. Now at other times the gardener and Nellie were inseparable friends, and, weather permitting, the gardener's coat and waistcoat were Nellie's favorite bed. In human nature it is much the same, when the husband, because the news in the paper is disagreeable, grumbles at his wife's cap.

Hatred also the dog feels keenly, — in the matter of cats notably. I have seen one of the exceptionally intelligent dogs referred to above, stop and jump under a tree for an hour, and go back every day for a month afterwards to jump about ridiculously under the same tree, all because a cat which he had once been after, and wanted to catch, had got up that tree out of his way. There is no doubt in my mind whatever, from that dog's behavior, that he hated the cat.

Jealousy again is a common trait, and in Thornley's book there is an instance given of a dog that was so jealous of another pet that when the latter died, and had been stuffed, he always snarled if attention was drawn to the glass case from which his rival gazed with glassy eye upon the scene. The *envy* of the dog has given rise to the well-known fable of the dog in the manger; and the story told in " False Beasts and True " (in illustration of canine sagacity) exemplifies this trait in a striking way. Leo was a large and lawless dog, belonging to an establishment where lived also a mild Maltese terrier. The latter, however, fed daintily, and was clad in fine linen, whereas Leo got as many rough words as bones, and was not allowed in the pretty rooms of which the terrier was a favored inmate. From the reports furnished of the judicial inquiry which followed the crime, it seems that the lesser (very much lesser) dog had been missed for several days, and his absence bewailed, while something in the demeanor of the big dog suggested to all beholders that some terrible tragedy had occurred and that Leo was darkly privy thereto. A length a servant going to the coal-hole heard a feeble moaning proceeding from the farthest corner, and on investigating with a candle, the Maltese terrier was found buried under lumps of coal. The supposition was that Leo had carried his diminutive rival to the coal-hole, and there scratched down an avalanche of coals upon him; and the manners of the two dogs when confronted bore striking evidence to the truth of the theory. Of Leo's envy there can hardly therefore be a suspicion.

Gluttony is common to all dogs, but their general aversion to *drunkenness* is supposed, by their partial eulogists, to be demonstrated by the fact attested by the Rev. F. Jackson of a dog who, having been once made so drunk with malt liquor that he could not get upstairs without help, always growled and snarled at the sight of a pewter pot! To establish in a feeble way this individual's dislike of malt liquor, the eulogist, it seems to me, has trifled away the dog's intelligence altogether. Nor, as illustrating *sagacity*, is the following anecdote so very forcible at it might be. Begum was a small red cocker who, with a very strange perception of her own importance, engaged as her attendant a mild Pomeranian of her own sex, who having only three available legs, displayed the gentler manners of a confirmed invalid. Begum, several times in her long and respected career, became the joyful mother of puppies, and on all these interesting occasions her friend Rip (or Mrs. Gamp, as she came to be called) presided over her nursery, kept beside the mother in her temporary seclusion, exhibited the little strangers to visitors with all the mother's pride during her absences, and in short, behaved herself like a devoted friend. " Strange to say," says the author, " when the poor nurse herself was dying, and Begum was brought to her bedside to cheer her, the sagacious cocker snuffed her friend, and then leaping gaily over her postrate, gasping form, left the stable for a frolic, and never looked in again on her faithful attendant." This narrative, however, hardly illustrates the remarkable *gratitude* which may be almost said to be a dog's leading principle.

Regret and grief dogs no doubt share also with men, for my own terrier when he stands with sadly oscillating tail and his head stuck through the area railings, whimpering for " the touch of a vanished cat" and " the sound of a puss that is still," bears ample testimony to the former; nor when, out ferreting, the rabbit has mysteriously disappeared into an impassable earth, is there any room for hesitation as to Tim's grief. His regret at the rabbit's evasive habits is unmistakable. Mrs.

Sumner Gibson, to illustrate *joy*, tells us of her pet, which on seeing her unexpectedly return after a long absence was violently sick. I remember when at school seeing a violent physical shock, accompanied by the same symptoms, affect a boy when suddenly approached by a master while in the act of eating gooseberries in class. But none of us attributed the result to an excess of delight.

Laziness is a trait well exemplified in dogs. Thus Cole's dog of ancient fame was so lazy that he always leaned his head against a wall to bark. So did Ludlam's.

Courage is not more common among dogs than among men. I had once three dogs who accompanied me on a certain occasion to a museum. The hall at the entrance was devoted to the larger mammalia, and the dogs on passing the folding door found themselves suddenly confronted by the whole order of the carnivora, all drawn up according to their families and genera, ready to fall upon and devour them. With a howl of the most dismal horror, all three flung themselves against the door, and if I had not rushed to open it, would certainly have died or gone mad then and there from sheer terror. As it was they flew through the open door with every individual hair on their bodies standing out like a wire, and arrived at home, some three miles off, in such a state of alarm that my servants were seriously alarmed for my safety. One of the three always slept in my room at night, but on the night after the fright howled so lamentably, and had such bad dreams, that I had to expel him. Miss Cobbe, in her delightful book, illustrates this whimsical cowardice by a bull terrier, who, ready apparently to fight anything, went into paroxysms of hysterical screaming if an Indian-rubber cushion was filled or emptied with air in her presence; and the garden-hose filled her with such terror that on the day when it was in use, Trip was never to be found on the premises, nor would any coaxing or commands persuade her to go into the room where the tube was kept all the rest of the week.

Pride affects the dog mind, for who has not heard of Dawson's dog that was too proud to take the wall of a dung-cart, and so got flattened under the wheels? *Vanity* was admirably displayed by an old setter, who often caused us great inconvenience by insisting on following members of the family whenever they went out, usually most inopportunely. But one day the children, playing with it, tied a bow of ribbon on to the tip of its tail, and on everybody laughing at the dog's appearance, the animal retired under the sofa and sulked for an hour. Next day, therefore, when Nelson showed every symptom of being irrepressibly intent on accompanying the family to a croquet party to which he had not been invited, it occurred to one of the party to try the effect of a bow. The ribbon was accordingly brought, and Nelson being held quiet by two of the girls, the third decorated his tail. No sooner was he released, and discovered the adornment, than the self-conscious dog rushed into the house and hid under the sofa! An hour after the party were gone, he came out as far as the doorstep, and when the family returned there was Nelson sitting on his haunches with the most comic air of having something mortifying to conceal, and refraining from even wagging his tail, lest the hateful bow should be seen. Chivalry, magnanimity, treachery, meanness, a sense of propriety or utter absence of shame, humor, etc., may all in turn be similarly proved to be shared by the dog world; but it is a singular fact that so many of the anecdotes put forward to illustrate the virtues of this animal should, if read with a little irreverence towards the dogs, lend themselves to conflicting if not opposite conclusions.

Indeed, I look upon the woolly little white dog that is so common as a pet in England as absolutely criminal. You can see what a timid creature it is by the way it jumps when any cabman shouts, and yet its foolishness and greediness have got as many men into jail as a street riot would have done. You have only to look at it to see what an easy dog it is to steal. In fact, it was made to be stolen, and it faithfully fulfils its destiny. One man — the father of a young family, too — has been in prison twice for stealing that same dog. It is true that, on the other hand, he has sold it at a splendid profit on five other occasions, and has pocketed a handsome reward for "finding" it several times besides, but he nevertheless owes several weeks' incarceration to that same little dog's infamously criminal habit of looking so stealable. He can no more keep his hands off the animal than needles can help going to the nearest loadstone. It is of no use his trying to look the other way, or repeating the Lord's Prayer, or thrusting his hands right down to the bottom of his breeches' pockets, for as surely as ever that little dog comes by, Jerry will have to steal it. It is chiefly the dog's fault. It never follows its master or mistress for the time being like a steady dog of business, but trots flickeringly about the pavement, as if it was going nowhere in particular with nobody. It makes excursions up alleys on its own account, and comes running back in such a hurry that it forgets whether it ought to turn to the right or the left; or it goes half across a road and then takes fright at a cab, and runs speeding down the highway in front of it under the impression that the vehicle is in pursuit. Or it loiters at a corner to talk canine commonplaces to a strange dog, and then, like an idle errand boy, accompanies its new acquaintance a short way round several corners. Or it mixes itself up with an old gentleman's legs, and gets eventually trodden upon, and precipitately makes off squeaking down the middle of a crowded thoroughfare into which its owner cannot follow it. Of all these weaknesses Jerry and his comrades are perfectly well aware; and if you will only follow the dog for a quarter of an hour you will see the little wretch get "lost," as it calls itself—or as Jerry calls it, when the policeman inquires about the dog. There are some people who go through life leaving watches on dressing-tables and money on mantelpieces, and then prosecute the servants who steal them; others who lend strangers sovereigns in order to show their confidence in them, and then call in the police to get the stranger punished; others who post money in open envelopes, and are bitterly indignant with the authorities because it is never received by the addressee; many again who walk about with their purses in pockets placed where morality never meant pockets to be; who, in fact, are perpetually putting temptation into the way of their weak brethren, and then putting their weak brethren in gaol. And the foolish little white dog that is always getting itself stolen is exactly their representative in the canine society which, we are assured, reflects our own.

For myself, I think the dignified position which the dog fills in human society can be far more worthily treated, than by anecdotes of his various virtues and vices, for after all he is one of man's chiefest triumphs, and one of his noblest servants. "In the beginning Allah created Man, and seeing what a helpless creature he was He gave him the Dog. And He charged the Dog that he should be the eyes and the ears, the understanding and the legs of the Man."

The writer, Toussenel, then goes on to show how the dog was fitted for his important duties by being inspired with an overwhelming sense of the privileges of friendship and loyal devotion, and a corresponding disregard of the time-wasting joys of family and fireside pleasures, thinking, no doubt, with Bacon, that those without families — the discipline of humanity — make always the best public servants. "He that hath wife and children hath given hostages to fortune; for they are impediments to great enterprises, either of virtue or mischief." And again, "Charity will hardly water the ground where it must first fill a pool." The dog, therefore, was relieved of paternal affections in order that he might be able to give an undivided mind to the high task set before him, and thus afford primitive man, in the flock-tending days, the leisure necessary for discovering the arts and evolving the sciences.

If Tubal Cain, for instance, had had to run after his own herds he could never have got on with his panpipes; so the dog attended to the sheep and the goats, the kine and the camels, while his master sat in the shade by the river, testing the properties of reeds. Music was the result, thanks to the dog. In the same way, perhaps, we might trace all other great discoveries to the same canine source; and, really, seeing even nowadays, when man has become such a self-helping creature, how many dogs keep men and how many of them support old ladies, the philosopher would seem to have some basis for his fanciful theory that, but for dogs, men would still have been shepherds, and human society still in its patriarchal stage. The Red Indians keep no dogs; and what is the result? All their time is given up to dog's work, and they lead a dog's life doing it — chasing wild things about and holloaing after them. Other peoples, however, who started with them in the race of nations, and who utilized the dog, are now enjoying all the comforts of nineteenth-century civilization, hunting only for amusement and shepherding only on valentines.

Writers on the dog claim for it the noblest attributes of humanity, and share with it our meanest failings; and, although the vast majority of instances of canine mind may be classified under the phenomena of self-interest and imitation, it is humiliating to feel that, if the dogs were to give their opinions of men, the same classification would hold good, and that for each of their own weaknesses they could cite a parallel among men.

At present, as the matter stands, man seems in some danger of being reckoned only the second best of animals.

In a dispassionate view of the subject, however, the foibles of the dog should not be, as they so often are, overlooked.

Indeed, it might be well if some one would compile a counterblast of remarkable instances of the intelligence and docility of man, the human Trustys and good Dog Trays that abound in the world; the men who have been known to lose their friends in the streets and to find them again; who have been carried to immense distances by wrong trains, and turned up at home after all; who recognize acquaintances with every demonstration of delight after a long separation; who carry baskets from the bakers, and do not eat the contents by the way; who worry cats; who rescue men from drowning and from other forms of death; who howl when they hear street organs; who know a thief when he comes creeping up the back stairs at midnight, and hold him until help arrives; who fetch, and carry, and beg; who, in fact, do everything that a dog can do, and have died for all the world like Christians.

Such instances of intelligence in men, and even women, abound, and are amply authenticated by eyewitnesses.

Nor are any of the passions which move dogs unknown to human kind, for anecdotes illustrative of anger, fear, envy, courage, and so forth, are plentifully scattered up and down the pages of history and biography. In short, looking at the matter from both sides, I really think myself that there is no reason for supposing that man is in any way inferior to the dog.

In science the dogs go after the rats. So they do in nature. But in this book I was obliged to put the rats behind the dogs, as dogs grow so naturally out of wolves that I had it not in my heart to spoil the connection merely for the sake of being scientific. But the connection between rats and dogs, whichever way they come in a book, is none the less very intimate indeed, more so sometimes than the rats like.

But rats have a large history of their own, outside rat-pits. In Egypt and Chaldæa they were the symbol of utter destruction, while in India they are to-day the emblem of prosperous wisdom. The Romans took augury from rats, — happy indeed the man who saw a white one; and Apollo, the most artistic of the Greek divinities, did not scorn the title of the rat-killer. In this very England of ours, the hardy Norseman rats bore their share in the Conquest nobly, and on the continent they have ruined a city and a river. Rats, they say, have scuttled ships, and it is certain they once ate up a bishop.

Not long ago, rat-catching engrossed much of the attention of the Government of India. The emergency was as serious as it was preposterous, for among the great vermin plagues that have afflicted the world the rat-invasion that devastated the Deccan must take high rank. Indeed, since the croaking nuisance took possession of the halls of Pharaoh, there have been very few visitations that have so directly insulted the majesty of man's high birth, and so absurdly perplexed him.

Up and down the world at different times there have been many plagues — plagues of locusts and cockchafers, of mice and caterpillars, plagues that have ravaged the vineyards and the corn-fields, the pine-forests and the orchards, plagues that have afflicted the farmer and the merchant, the prince and the peasant, the tradesman and the manufacturer, plagues of beasts and birds and insects. Armies have actually marched against little things with wings, and senates have gravely sat in council over creeping creatures. The British force at Waterloo was not so numerous as that which the Moor sent against the advancing locusts; nor did the fathers of the city, fluttered by the news of Lars Porsena's approach, meet in more serious concern than did the French Assembly to concert measures, the State being in danger, to resist the *sauterelle vorace*. But in all these, quite apart from the gravity of the evil, there was a matter-of-fact sobriety about the circumstances of the impending danger, which separates them from the rodent visitation of the Deccan. Locusts are the avowed enemies of mankind, and their destruction has always been cheerfully assented to as a pleasing act of justice. No one when the *vastatrix* was at work among the vines held back the arm of retributive chemistry, nor when the *cynips* was vandalizing among our turnips was a kindly word spoken for the tiny foe. In India, however, everything, whether with fur or feathers, whether winged or wingless, finds a friend. Beautiful legends, orchid-like, have overgrown the old country, and so not only everything that moves, but every leaf that stirs, has a poem or a quaint conceit attached to it.

We in the West have flung our prejudices at even inoffensive creatures. Thus, the cormorant is abused by every poet who has mentioned the bird. The owl has no more friends than the toad; and the buzzard and the raven are as unpopular, and as heartily maligned by our imaginative writers, and in our proverbs and ballads, as the badger and the newt. Many others meet only with acidulated compliments, and some — like the glutton among beasts, the crow among birds — are ungenerously denied the possession of the most ordinary beast and fowl virtues. It is true that, on the other hand, we flatter unworthily the creatures of our own affection, embarrassing the pelican with our undeserved regard, and in the robin canonizing what in the sparrow we anathematize. But misplaced esteem does not compensate for wanton depreciation; nor does it affect our action when our prejudices are called into lively expression. Spiders fare ill with most of us, and no earwig of discernment comes for a holiday among us.

In India, however, everything alike is welcome at the fountain of superstitious tenderness, and where European influences have not penetrated, all creation seems to live in amity. The teaching of the compassionate Buddha, "the speechless world's interpreter," has elsewhere won for living things the same forbearance at the hands of other millions, and Asia thus stands apart from Europe as the refuge and asylum of the smaller worlds of creatures, harmful and harmless alike.

This pitifulness works often to strange results. A man-eating tiger establishes his shambles near a village, but the villagers, knowing him to be an old and esteemed acquaintance, lately deceased, steal away from their hamlet and deprecate any violent dislodgment of the human soul from its present tiger body. Monkeys rob the shops in the bazaar, but who could think of reprisals against such holy thieves? Snakes take human life, but pay none in penalty. Elephants and cuckoos, bulls and tortoises, quadruped and bird, fish and reptile, all come in for their special honors and special privileges, and, when danger threatens, for special immunity.

The rats in the Deccan in the same way enjoyed the full benefit of this delightful catholicity of benevolence, not from any virtues inherent in that forward rodent, or any tradition of good done to man in a former state, but simply from the Hindoo's tolerance of small life, and the contemporary growth of superstition.

The famines that laid waste some of the fairest provinces of India had stolen from every hearth one or more of the family circle, and the peasant mind, loyal to its teachings, refused to believe that the loved ones had been lost forever. Cruel drought bound the ground as with iron, and so the seed sown never gave its increase. Starvation crept round the hamlet, and one by one the weakest died.

Yet the wheels of time rolled on, and another harvest-time came round. The seasons were kindly, rain was abundant, and the ground returned to the sower's hand its hundred-fold. And back to the earth, glad with full harvests, crept the poor defunct. What more natural?

Not, of course, in the likeness of their old selves, for it is not given to man to live twice as man, nor yet in nobler form, for what had the pitiful starved dead given in alms to the Brahmins? So they came back to the world that had treated them so badly — as rats. Killed by the want of grain, they returned as grain devourers, and the round completeness of this retaliation sufficed to satisfy the Hindoo mind as to the iniquity of injuring the still hungry victims of the great famine. That they suffered from their depredations, their own memorials to the authorities attested amply. "We had promise of a good crop. But in came a multitude of rats, which have carried to their holes our ears of corn. Thus the morsel was taken from between our teeth, and the cornstalks stand headless in the fields." The government, in reply, assured them of its sympathy, assured them also of its knowledge of rat habits, and begged them to kill the rats. But there came the rub. Could a Hindoo who was about to be starved kill another Hindoo already once starved to death? Was it not just possible that when he himself had been starved he might return as a rat? To set such a precedent might be to commit suicide while committing murder; so they declined to kill the rats.

In England the rat plague is endemic. Only the other day the populousness of subterranean London was indicated by the disclosures connected with a case in a police court; for in the evidence taken against some men charged with damaging the bank of the Thames while digging for rats, it was alleged that these creatures swarmed " by tens of thousands " at the mouths of the sewers. Here they work to admirable purpose, in so far as they clear refuse from the river surface, but, in comparison with the mischief done in accomplishing it, their good offices are seriously depreciated. Few creatures have attained to such universal abuse as the rat, and few, perhaps, have deserved so much. It is true that its sagacity is prodigious, and every one knows that in the East it symbolizes Ganesha, the god of wisdom ; but its sagacity is so often displayed under compromising circumstances that the rat gains little respect for the possession of this valuable quality. It is very sagacious, no doubt, in an animal to dip its tail in a bottle of oil, and then carry its tail home to suck at leisure, but such larcenous refreshment will not commend itself to any but the disreputable. Nor is there much that is admirable in the wisdom which prompts the rat to make a wheelbarrow or truck of itself, for the greater convenience of removing stolen goods. It appears that, when a gang have come upon a larger plunder than they can carry away from the premises inside them, one of the number lies down on his back while the others load him up with the booty; that he balances the pile with four legs, and, to make matters extra safe, folds his tail over the goods and holds the tip in his mouth, and that his pals then drag him off along the ground by the ears and fur! This is excellent as far as the idea and its execution are concerned; but, after all, the end to which such means are adapted — the nefarious removal of another's property — is immoral, and unworthy of imitation. It is impossible to extend sincere admiration to so deplorable a misapplication of genius.

Nor can the other virtues attributed to rats, such as considerate treatment of the blind among them, their docility under domestication, and their industry, be regarded as unalloyed. Their industry, for instance, is shown by perpetual voracity, for the rat never ceases gnawing. It does not matter to the small beast what the substance may be, so long as its consumption does not immediately endanger its own person, for it takes a house just as it comes, and, beginning at the floor of the cellar, goes straight through to the slates. Yet this is not industry, although it may look like it, for the rat must either nibble or die. If it were to stop nibbling, and thus allow its teeth to grow unchecked, they would soon overlap each other, and cause lock-jaw, or, as from accident has sometimes occurred, would continue to grow in a curve until they pierced the eye or the brain.

On the rat's consideration for its kind, again, one might put a very sinister construction, for the knowledge of rat ways might prompt the belief that the infirm were only being cared for until they became fit to eat, and that the jealous solicitude apparently being displayed for the welfare of the afflicted relative was really only a series of selfish precautions to prevent others from surreptitiously making away with the object of their care before he was properly fattened for their own eating. The cannibal propensity is, indeed, grossly developed among rats. The parents eat their young, deciding for their offspring that death in infancy is better than a life of troubles: and the young who survive, seeing around them so much aged misery, and deploring such a future for their parents, piously consume their progenitors.

Thus too, among the earlier barbarians of the Oxus, did the Massagetæ who, if history has not traduced them, ate their infirm relatives, not from ill-will towards them, but as a public duty. Every man was expected to devour his own parents, and the interference of a stranger in the solemn rite might have been rudely resented. For a conscientious family, though they would not probably at other times have grudged him a seat at their board, might on such an occasion have misunderstood the stranger's offers of assistance, as reflecting upon their capacity to do their duty without outside help.

In its origin also the race of rats resembles exactly those successive waves of savage humanity that have swept westward over Europe, coming from the same Central Asian cradles, and tallying with them in the chronology of their invasions. Yet their great nation has also thrown out from time to time colonies of a far higher stamp of emigrant. Thus, though troops of rats followed and accompanied the Goth and the Hun and the Tartar, similar migrations marked also the Norman invasion and the Hanoverian accession. The rats, in fact, are the *doppelgängers* of invaders generally, following the provision chests of every human exodus, barbarian or otherwise; and are the emblem not only of determined incursion, but permanent occupation. They are the type of the successful invader, sagacious in forecast, fierce in attack, and tenacious in possession.

Wherever their colonies are planted, they take deep root at once and for ever, and the aborigines must either be absorbed into the conquering element, or disappear before it. Their motto is "Rats or nothing." Rat society, though thus maintaining with persistent ferocity the ground it has gained, and gradually extending its area, will be found, in its latest developments, to be everywhere representative of the most degraded classes of humanity.

VII.

SOME SEA-FOLK.

Ocean-folk. — Mermaids and Manatees. — The Solemnity of Shapelessness. — Herds of the Sea-gods. — Sea-things. — The Octopus and its Kind. — Terrors of the Deep Sea. — Sea-serpents. — Credible and Incredible Varieties. — Delightful possibilities in Cuttle-fish. — Ancient and Fish-like Monsters. — Credulity as to Monsters, Disastrous. — Snakes in Legend and in Nature. — Mr. Ruskin on Snakes. — The Snake-folk. — Shesh, the Snake-god. — Primeval Turtles and their Contemporary Aldermen. — Impropriety of Flippancy about Turtles.

MERMAIDS, though still reasonably abundant at country fairs in Europe, appear to have become extinct in the British Isles.

The latest authenticated appearance is that of the supposed mermaid which was discovered sporting in the sea off the Caithness shore, but which — by his own confession — turned out to be Sir Humphrey Davy bathing.

Since then, there have been several claimants to the title, but all have collapsed under the disintegrating touch of scientific inquiry, which, resolving the several compositions into their primal elements, classified them in detail as being part monkey, part salmon, and part leather.

Some no doubt — and I for one — regret the extinction of the mermaid, but the less superstitious majority will congratulate Science on having at last reduced to one or two facts all the miscellaneous congregation of sirens, mermaids, mermen, tritons, sea-cows, sea-swine, sea-horses, mer-devils, sea-lions, water-satyrs, and Undines, — all the wilderness of aquatic prodigies delineated in Aldrovandus his "History of Monsters," or spoken of from eye-witness by Maundeville, Olaus Magnus, and many another. The sub-order of the Sirenia now includes all those wonderful animals that have given the silly world so much pleasant fable, and wise men so much trouble, and they are now known as the Rhytinidæ and the Manatidæ. The first are extinct. Like the dodos, — which were so common in the Mauritius, when that island was first discovered, that the sailors chased them about by hundreds, knocking them on the head with stones, but of which now there are only two beaks, one foot, and a few feathers to bear witness that this great bird ever existed, — the Rhytina Stelleri, or Northern Manatee, was found swarming in 1741 upon the shores of an island in Behring's Straits. For ten months the shipwrecked sailors entirely supported life upon its flesh and oil, and so it happened that when, just twenty-seven years later, an expedition went out to inquire if a manatee fishery would be profitable, it was found that not a single specimen remained. The family of Rhytina had been actually extinguished from the world's list of living things in twenty-seven years, and the only remains of this astonishing animal at present known to exist are one skull and a few other fragments in European museums. Of the other sub-family, the Manatidæ proper, many species are known to naturalists, and the commonest of these, the manatee of the American coast, is called by showmen the "West India Mermaid."

Those who go to visit one, however, should dismiss from their minds all the fancies with which literature has invested these sea-folk, of rosy mermaids golden-haired, and jolly mermen with Bacchus faces, crowned with coral. Some, no doubt, expect a shapely Triton with flowing beard and his conch-shell slung by his side, or dainty lady of those siren islands

> "Whence fairy-like music steals over the sea,
> Entrancing the senses with charmed melody."

Others, on the other hand, visit it with preconceived ideas of some narwhal or whale creation, expecting a grampus-like thing, or anticipating a porpoise. But it is necessary to approach the mermaid with an imagination absolutely blank, for, whatever you try to imagine, you will be utterly discomfited by the reality.

Who, indeed, could soberly put before his mind the actual features of this sea-monster, so absurd in its shapelessness that if it were to be exhibited *dead* the most credulous rustic would sneer at it as a clumsy hoax? Even alive, the thing looks like a make-up, and a discreditable one; for in places the tail and paddling-paws — they are not fins nor yet legs — appear to have been injured, and the stuffing looks as if it was coming out. The ragged edges of the skin, if such an integument is to be called skin, frays away into threads, and, if it were not that the manatee winks occasionally, the spectator might be justified in asserting his own ability to make a better monster. But it is this very simplicity of its composition that renders the preposterous creature so astonishing and so absurd. Gustave Doré found out the secret, that, to depict the perfection of a monster only one element of incongruous monstrosity should be utilized at a time, and the result of his knowledge has been his incomparable creatures of fancy. On the other hand, from ignorance of this rule, the prodigious beings of Hindoo fable are habitually stupid and foolish, for the artist overlays his subject with such a multitude of deformities that the complete composition is silly and senseless. The Hindoos, therefore, should go to the manatee, and take a lesson in the wonderful effects to be produced by avoiding elaborateness of detail, for nothing in the animal world can be imagined less diversified in feature than this mermaid of the West Indies. In the lower world of creatures the slug alone presents us with an equally sober monotony of outline; and if a seven-foot slug were sewn up in an old tarpaulin, the result would be a tolerable reproduction of the manatee. One end would have to be flattened out into a gigantic beaver's tail, and the other be shaped snout-wise. The details of mouth, nose, eyes, and ears might be left to the creature's own fancy, or to accident.

Having no legs, it stands on its tail, and to keep its balance has to bend the head forward and bow the body. In this attitude of helpless humility the strange thing stands motionless many minutes together, and then, with a ghost-like, dreadful solemnity, it begins slowly to stiffen and straighten its tail, and thus, gradually rising into an erect posture, thrusts its nostrils above the surface. But only for an instant, for ere it seems to have had time to take a breath, the great body begins to sink back into its despondent position, and the small paddling-paws drop motionless and helpless as before. The deliberate sloth with which the manœuvre is executed has something of dignity in it, but otherwise the manatee is as ridiculous as it is helpless. The clumsy snout is constantly twitching like a rabbit's, but the gesture that seems so appropriate in the nervous, vigilant little rodent is immeasurably ludicrous in this huge monstrosity. The eyes, again, now contracted to a pin's point, now expanded full to gaze at you with expressionless pupils, seem to move by a mechanism beyond the creature's control. Voiceless and limbless, the bulky cetacean sways to and fro, the very embodiment of stupid, feeble helplessness, a thing for shrimps to mock at and limpets to grow upon.

A carcass of such proportions, such an appalling contour, should, to satisfy æsthetic requirements, possess some stupendous villany of character, should conceal under such an inert mass of flesh some hideous criminal instinct. Yet this great shapeless being, this numskull of the deep sea, is the most innocent of created things. *It lives on lettuce.* In its wild state it browses along the meadows of the ocean bed, cropping the seaweeds just as kine graze upon the pastures of earth, inoffensive and sociable, rallying as cattle do for mutual defence against a common danger, placing the calves in the middle, while the bulls range themselves on the threatened quarter. These are the herds which the poets make Proteus and the sea-gods tend, the harmless beeves with whom the sad Parthenope shared her sorrows! These are the actual realities that have given rise to so many a pretty fiction, the dull chrysalids from which have swarmed so many butterflies.

It is disappointing to those who cherish old-world fancies; but to Science the lazy, uncouth manatee is a precious thing. Science, indeed, has seldom had a more pleasing labor than the examination and identification of this animal; for, though so ludicrously simple in appearance, it is a veritable casket of physiological wonders.

It is the only creature known that has three eyelids to each eye, and two hearts. In most of its points it bears a close affinity to the elephant, but in others of equal importance it is unmistakably a whale! Its teeth, bones, and skin are all delightful studies to the naturalist, and he is thankful, therefore, that the manatee is what it is, and not the veritable mermaid that less prosaic minds would have it. Even these, however, may find some consolation for the loss of their ocean folk in learning of the strange ways of this strange beast, and its tranquil life below the sea, nibbling about in great meadows of painted seaweed. Some travellers have given it a voice. Captain Colnett has left it on record that one remained by his ship for three hours, "uttering sounds of lamentation like those produced by the female human voice when expressing the deepest distress;" and another mariner tells us how, when sailing in an open boat, they surprised a manatee asleep, and, thinking it to be a merman, they hesitated to harpoon it, and how on a sudden the creature awoke, and with an angry shout plunged into the depths! Anger, nevertheless, appears to be utterly foreign to its character, for among the Malays the name of the Eastern species is a synonym for gentle affection, and every writer, from Buffon to our time, bears evidence to its sociability and remarkable absence of fear of men. But, alas for the manatee! Its virtues are its bane, for whether among the West India islands or the creeks of the Guiana and the Brazilian coast, in the estuaries of the Oronoko and the Amazon, in the river-mouths of Western Africa, or in the archipelago of the Eastern seas, the same fearless confidence in man is rapidly hastening its extinction. The flesh is excellent food, the blubber yields a fine oil, the skin is of valuable toughness, and so before long the manatee of the warm seas may be expected to be as extinct as its congener of the cold North, — the lost rhytina of Behring's Straits.

. . . .

Victor Hugo, in his Guernsey romance, "The Toilers of the Sea," presented the world with a monster, a terror of the deep waters, something like the gruesome spider-crab of Erckmann-Chatrian, but even more horrible. It was the pieuvre, a colossal cuttle-fish, which had its den far down in the sea among the roots of the rocks; a terrible long-armed thing that lurked in the caverns of the deep, grappling from its retreat with any passing creature, paralyzing it by fastening one by one a thousand suckers upon it, and slowly dragging its victim, numbed with pain, towards the awful iron beak that lay in the centre of the soft, cruel arms. The novelist's pieuvre was hideous enough, and his description surpassing in its horrors, but in Schiller's poem of "The Diver," a thing of similar character, but rendered even more awful by not being described at all, compasses the death of the hero. He did not, like Victor Hugo's sailor, have a protracted struggle with the mysterious creature, and then come back to his friends with details of its personal appearance, but he dived out of sight and never returned. Schiller does not attempt, therefore, to describe the indescribable thing, but simply calling it *das*, throws the reader back in imagination upon all the horrible legends of the Mediterranean coasts and islands, to guess for himself the sort of monster it must have been that had seized the hapless diver and devoured him at its leisure in the twilight depths of the sea.

Such monsters as these, it has been dryly thought, belong only to legend and fable and poem, but this is not the case. Pieuvres of the Victor Hugo type, and "things" such as Schiller hints at, are, it is true, exaggerated specimens of the species, but their congeners — and dreadful ones, too — do actually exist, for they have been seen and fought with and described, and scientific conditions are all amply satisfied by those descriptions. Not long ago, a government diver at Belfast, Victoria, had a narrow escape from losing his life in the clutch of a huge octopus. It had seized his left arm, causing dreadful agony by the fastening of its suckers upon the limb; but the diver had an iron bar in his right hand, and, after a struggle that seemed to him to last twenty minutes, during which the monster tried hard to drag him down, he battered his assailant into a shapeless mass, and freed himself from its horrid grasp. Schiller's "Taucher" had no iron bar, and his bones, therefore, went to increase the heap which pieuvres, so Victor Hugo says, accumulate at the mouths of their deep-sea dens.

It is all-important, for the existence of these monstrous poulpes, cuttle-fish, octopuses, or sepias, that Science should countenance them; for, so long as professors array their calmly sceptical opinions on the one side, no number of sworn affidavits from the public as to personal encounters with the pieuvre will suffice to establish the creature as a verity. In the case of that other terror of the ocean, the sea-serpent, science goes dead against its existence, and Professor Owen speaks far too weightily for even sober official accounts of the great snake to be accepted as convincing evidence in its behalf. Thus Captain M'Quhae, of Her Majesty's ship "Dædalus," declared, in a report to the Admiralty thirty years ago, that he and his officers had seen sixty feet of a marine monster, with the head of a snake, under conditions which, taken with the trustworthiness and sobriety of his evidence, places the record of his encounter with "the great sea-serpent" above all others that either preceded or followed it. Yet even this account, so cautious in its language, and given by men so eminently capable of judging of objects seen at sea, was completely met at every point by the scientific verdict of "impossible."

That sixty-foot monsters besides whales may exist Professor Owen does not deny, for have we not already seals of thirty feet and sharks of forty, besides congers of unknown lengths? But he says this: if sea-serpents have been in the seas from the first, and are still there in such numbers as reports would have us believe, how is it that no single fragment of one, fossilized or not, has ever yet been washed ashore or dug up? The negative evidence from the utter absence of any remains weighs, therefore, with the scientific mind, and ought also with public opinion, against even such positive evidence as that of the commander of the "Dædalus;" for, after all, just as positive evidence from just as trustworthy witnesses abounds for the proof of ghosts. So the grand old kraken, the great sea-worm, remains still without identity; and though I trust humanity will never abandon any of its "glorious old traditions," especially such a fascinating one as the sea-serpent, I would caution it in the matter of any kraken professing to be more than a hundred yards long, lest it should be said of them that they prefer "the excitement of the imagination to the satisfaction of the judgment."

For monster cuttle-fishes, however, the public has the permission of science to believe anything it likes; and, in fact, the more the better. It may swell out the bag-like bodies of the poulpe to any dimensions consistent with the containing capacities of an ocean, and pull out their arms until, like Denys de Montford's octopus, they are able to twist one tentacle round each of the masts of a line-of-battle ship, and, holding on with the rest to the bottom of the sea, to engulf the gallant vessel with all sail set. Science is helpless to oppose the belief in such monsters, for they are scientifically possible, and, from the sizes already recorded, there is no limit reasonably assignable to their further extension, so that everybody is at liberty to revel "by authority" in cuttle-fishes as big as possible. The Victorian octopus referred to above measured only eight feet, but this proved almost sufficient to kill a strong man, while the body belonging to a specimen of such dimensions would have been quite heavy enough, had the arms once fairly grappled the victim, to sink him to the bottom of the sea, where, anchoring itself by its suckers to a rock in the sea-bed, the monster could have eaten its prey at leisure. The octopus, moreover, is very active, as the nature of its usual food — fishes and crustaceans — requires it should be; and the danger, therefore, to man, from the huge specimens which travellers have recorded — that of M. Sander Rang, for instance, the body of which was as large as "a large cask" — would be very terrible indeed; but fortunately gigantic specimens, though indisputably existing, are not common on populous coasts.

In a paper once read to the British Association by Colonel Smith, the writer adduced many instances of colossal sepias, among them an enormity of forty feet, and another, hardly less, of which fragments are preserved in the Haarlem Museum. General Eden records one of over twenty feet in length, and another creature of the same order, taken up on a ship at sea, which had arms that measured no less than thirty-six feet. In this way, increasing foot by foot, each enlarging specimen becomes a possibility, until at last there would be no reason for disbelieving even that wonderful story of Captain Blaney, who mistook a dead cuttle-fish for a bank, and landed on it with sixty men! But this was of course very long ago indeed, and may now be relegated to the limbo of Pontoppidan's famous monsters, — the krakens with lions' manes, that got up on end and roared, and pieuvres that hunted ships at sea. If ever, however, the cuttle fish should reach its fullest length and greatest bulk, the sea-serpent itself would have but a poor chance with it, so that we have, after all, the satisfaction of knowing that, though science forbids us to possess a kraken, we do possess in actual fact another monster which, if the kraken did exist, could probably catch it and eat it up.

· · · · · · ·

Sea-serpents, in spite of repeated efforts to obtain respectable recognition, have been hitherto regarded as mythical. For one thing, they showed no judgment in the selection of individuals to whom to exhibit themselves; and the testimony of their existence afforded by the masters of ships unknown on Lloyd's registers, and by American captains " of undoubted veracity " served only to plunge the monsters of the deep seas more profoundly into the obscurity of fable. Their opportunities for declaring themselves have been many, but they have preferred to come to the surface only when unscientific and untrustworthy witnesses happened to be passing overhead. A score of appearances of the sea-serpent have been recorded in as many years, but not one has gained credence, because, in the first place, of this defect in the credibility of the narrators, and in the next, because each man described such a different monster.

The whole marine fauna, from the narwhal to the octopus, was drawn upon for contributions to the hybrid thing which we were asked to believe was the veritable kraken; but when all the tusks and tails, legs and manes, fiery eyes and scales, horses' heads and wings came to be fitted on to a serpentine form of prodigious bulk and length, the miscellaneous result was so outrageous that credulity was staggered, and men, in despair, refused to believe even in a decent sea-serpent, or any sea-serpent at all.

A moderate animal of about fifty or a hundred feet in length, with the girth of an average barrel or two, and, say, half-a-dozen plausible propellers or even a twin screw, with a respectable snake's head at one end and coming to a proper point at the other, — such a creature would have been admitted into every household as an article of belief, and have largely assisted in developing the young idea as to Behemoth and Leviathan and the other wonders of the sea, which, in default of a definite beast, have so long loomed hazily in the child-mind as mere figures of speech. When, however, we were gravely asked to introduce to the notice of our school-children a heterogeneous patchwork monstrosity that stood up from its middle to rest its chin on the topgallant-stunsail-boom of a three-masted ship; that spouted and roared at one end and lashed up the sea into little bubbles at the other; that reared horned heads out of water, glaring the while with eyes of flame upon the trembling mariners, shaking aloft a more than leonine mane of hair, and paddling in the air with great uplifted paws, — parents, I think did well to warn off so disreputable an apparition from the sacred ground of infant schools and nurseries, and the scientific world showed judgment in withdrawing its approbation from such a disorganizing beast.

Nature insists upon her proprieties being observed, and so long as man remembers this, his zoölogical beliefs will remain fit to lie upon every breakfast table.

But if once we fall from the strict paths of possibility, our facts become improbable, and there will be an inrush of creatures trampling across, flying over, and swimming through every rule of natural history, every law of creation. If once the key is turned to let in these disturbing dualities, a mob of indeterminate things — gryphons and sphinxes, basilisks and dragons, wolf-men and vampires, unicorns and cockatrices — will crowd into the orderly courts of knowledge, and, breaking down all the bulwarks of our rational beliefs, will seat themselves triumphantly among the ruins of science!

No such dismal prospect of scientific chaos need, however, be entertained from the latest appearance of the sea-serpent, an animal which, from its description, would seem one that may be confidently admitted into the best conducted families as an article of household faith. Captain Cox, master of the British ship "Privateer," states that a hundred miles west of Brest, at five o'clock on the afternoon of a fine, clear day, he saw, some three hundred yards off, about twenty feet of a black snake-like body, three feet in diameter, moving through the water towards his ship. As it approached, he distinctly perceived its eel-like head and its eyes; but the sea-serpent, when it got so close as this, took fright and plunged with a great splash under the water, and then, turning itself round with a mighty disturbance of the sea, made off, raising its head frequently as it went. Now, here there is no extraordinary demand made upon credulity, for the merest infant can comfortably entertain the idea, in twenty-foot lengths, at any rate, of a snake as thick as an eighteen-gallon cask. The color, too, is simple black, and the head has no features more surprising than eyes.

The great sea-serpent, therefore, is, after all, found to come within the compass of the ordinary human understanding, and we are not asked to believe in more than a somewhat magnified conger-eel. In behavior, also, the present animal differs agreeably and rationally from all preceding *avatars* of the great sea-worm, as the Danes call it; for except that it splashed extravagantly when it turned round in the water, it did not demean itself otherwise than might respectably be permitted to a snake of such dimensions. At the same time, however, such is the weakness of human nature, there will be vestiges of regret for the turbulent, ill-behaved monstrosity that has hitherto done duty as the sea-serpent. The present worm is perhaps just a little too tame. If it had only shown a scale or two, or sparkled slightly at the nostrils, or betrayed some tendency towards horns or claws, shaken just a little mane, — not too much, of course, — or snorted, or brayed, or even squeaked moderately, we should have been better satisfied. We should have felt that we had got something. As it is, we have got only a huge eel, — no crest of hair, no flames, no ravening jaws, — a dull eel, too, that behaved with disappointing respectability, not even rising to a spout or a roar. It kept itself horizontal on the water, instead of standing on one end, and when it wished to go in the opposite direction, did so by the ordinary process of moving round, instead of leaping dolphin-wise or turning a prodigious somersault. All this is discouraging, but it is an ill-conditioned mind that cannot accept the inevitable with composure, and, after all, half a sea-serpent is better than none.

For until his latest revelation, we had really no sea-serpent to speak of; and now that we have at least twenty feet well authenticated, we may rest for the time contented. The only consolation is that the rest of the Soe Ormen may one day more completely fulfil our aspirations for something to wonder at and disbelieve in; for who can tell what singularities of contour remained hidden in the sea when the commonplace head and shoulders were exposed, or who even can guess at the length of the whole? Delightful possibilities, therefore, still remain to us; and, while we can safely add one end of the new monster to our marine zoölogy, we can cling with the other to all the fauna of old-world fancy. Twenty feet of an eel need not prevent us hoping for another hundred of something else; nor are we compelled from so commonplace a commencement to argue a commonplace termination. Meanwhile, we have a solid instalment of three fathoms of a sea-serpent to work upon, and it will be discreditable to national enterprise if something more — and a great deal more, too — does not come of it before long.

Favorable to such discovery is the habitat now assigned to the great conger, for it lies on the highway of our commerce. Hitherto, fiords on the Scandinavian coast, the headlands of Greenland, and other unfrequented waterways have been selected by krakens and aaletusts for their exhibitions; and though Danes, Swedes, and Norsemen generally have long believed in the existence of these monsters of the deep, their haunts were so much out of the way of regular sea traffic, that only fishermen, the most superstitious and credulous of mankind, could say they had actually seen them. Now and again a glimpse was said to have been caught in more accessible waters of some bulky thing answering in length of body to the description of a serpent, but flaws in the evidence always marred the value of the great vision. Six hundred feet of one, was, for instance, recorded off the English coast, but here the length alone sufficed to quench belief; while the other, with eyes "large and blue, like a couple of pewter plates," found basking off the shore of Norway, was discredited by its possessing legs. Exactly a hundred years ago a whole ship's crew vouched for the following awful apocalypse of the terrors of the sea: " A hundred fathoms long, with the head of a horse ; the mouth large and black, and a white mane hanging from the neck. It raised itself so high that it reached above the top of the mast, and it spouted water like a whale;" and, what is more, the skipper shot it!

Captain Cox, then, will have to work hard before he can bring his worm abreast of so thrilling a creature; but, meanwhile, he has commenced well. To him we owe the latest confirmation of one of the oldest of the world's superstitions, and though, in confirming it, he has divested the thing of our fancy of all that made it precious, he has given us in place of the rampageous sea-serpent of our ancestors, tinkered out of scraps from half the beasts in nature, a plausible and well-conducted eel. As a first attempt at a sea-serpent fit to be figured in a standard book it is commendable, but what I should like to see now is — the other end of it.

. . . . . .

It is one of the disappointments of my life that I have never heard Mr. Ruskin lecture on Snakes. Both the subject and the lecturer present to the imagination such boundless possibilities that no one could guess where the snakes would take Mr. Ruskin before he had done with them, or where Mr. Ruskin would take the snakes. Without a horizon on any side of him, the speaker could hold high revel among a multitude of delightful phantasies, and make holiday with all the beasts of fable. Ranging from Greek to Saxon and from Latin to Norman, Mr. Ruskin could traverse all the cloud-lands of myth and the solid fields of history, lighting the way as he went with felicitous glimpses of a wise fancy, and bringing up in quaint disorder, and yet in order too, all the grotesque things that heraldry owns and the old world in days past knew so much of: the wyvern, with its vicious aspect but inadequate stomach; the spiny and always rampant dragon-kind; the hydra, that unhappy beast which must have suffered from so many headaches at once, and been racked at times, no doubt, with a multitudinous toothache; the crowned basilisk, king of the reptiles and chiefest of vermin; the gorgon, with snakes for hair, and the terrible echidna; the cockatrice, fell worm, whose first glance was petrifaction, and whose second, death; the salamander, of such subtle sort that he digested flames; the chimæra, shapeless yet deadly; the dread cerastes; the aspic, pretty worm of Nilus, but fatal as lightning and as swift; and the dypsas, whose portentous aspect sufficed to hold the path against an army of Rome's choicest legions. All these, and many more, are at the lecturer's service as he travels from age to age of serpent adoration, and turns with skilful hand the different facets of his diamond subject to the listener's ear. From astronomy, where Serpentarius, baleful constellation, glitters, and refulgent Draco rears his impossible but delightful head, the speaker could run through all the forms of dragon idealism, recalling to his audience as he went on his way, beset with unspeakable monsters, the poems of Greek and of older mythologies, and touching on our own fictions of asp and adder, and other strange reptile things, — defining, however, all the while, with the bold outlines of a master-hand, the vast scheme of creation, wherein the chain of resemblance is never snapped and like slides into like, until the whole stands revealed complete, a puzzle for the grown-up children of men to put together in a thousand different ways, but one which will never fit in properly, piece to piece, unless the ultimate design be a perfect circle, a serpent with its tail in its mouth, a coil without a break. Fresh, racy morals, too, are to be drawn from the reptile kind; so that, though on an excursion into strange lands, and seeing only the strangest creatures in them, an audience might understand, even in such fantastic company, that the whole of them — the flowers that were snakes, and the birds that were beasts, and many things that were neither one nor the other — fitted in somehow or other, by hook or by crook, by tooth or by nail, into a comprehensive scheme of unity.

What a subject, indeed, for such a lecturer to choose; Professor Huxley once selected the snake theme, and, bringing to bear on it all the vast resources of his scientific mind, made the topic instinct with interest. There yet remained, however, for Mr. Ruskin's magic, ample space and verge for holiday-making, for just as it was with the chimæra in Coleridge's problem, that went bombonating, (booming like a bumble-bee) in space, so there is such a prodigious quantity of room to spare in the realms of snake fancy that no lecturer need fear to come into collision with any solids, let him dissipate as he will. Again, it happens that nearly all the world of myths converges upon, or radiates from, the great serpent fact; so that Mr. Ruskin, sitting in the very centre of the fairy web, could shake as he liked all the strands to its utmost circumference. Seated by the shores of old romance, he could at any time have thrown his pebbles where he would, certain of raising ripples everywhere, and of disturbing from each haunted reed-bed flocks of fabled things. But how much greater was his power of raising these spirits of past story when he circled over the same regions of imagination bestriding a winged snake — churning up the old waters with a Shesh of his own, and summoning into sight at the sound of his pipe all the mystery-loving reptiles of mythology, like one of the old Psylli or the Marmarids, or one of the Magi, sons of Chus, " tame, at whose voice, spellbound, the dread cerastes lay."

Eastern charmers, with their bags of battered snakes, not a tooth among them all, become very poor impostors indeed, compared with our modern master of reptile manipulation. The Hindoo's snakes are feeble, jaded vermin, sick of the whole exhibition as mere ill-timed foolery, tired of the everlasting old pipe that they have to get up to dance to, and weary of longing for just one hour of vigorous youth, when their poison fangs were still in their jaws, that they might send the old man who charms them to his forefathers in exactly twenty minutes by the clock. But Mr. Ruskin works only with fresh-caught subjects, or, at any rate, with old subjects so revivified that they leap from under his hand, each of them a surprise. The wise snakes of Colchis and of Thebes and of Delphi — I need not identify them more exactly — fall briskly into their places in the ring of the creative system, and every flower furnishes forth a Pythonissa to tell our new Apollo the secrets of a new cult. Does genius feed on snakes, that it never grows old? The ancients said that the flesh of the ophidians, though the deadliest of created things, gave eternal youth, and even cured death itself; and, though fatal as the shears of Atropos, the poison of asps was the supreme drug in the cabinet of the God of Doctors.

Even to our own day the legend comes down, tamed of course to suit the feeble representatives of the serpent kind that are found in this country; for in English folk-lore it is an article of belief that the flesh of vipers is an antidote to their poison, and that, though "the beauteous adder hath a sting, it bears a balsam too." All dangerous swellings also, such as erysipelas and goîtres, may be cured, it is satisfactory to know on rustic authority, by eating a viper from the tail upwards, like a carrot; or, simpler still, by rubbing the affected part with a harmless grass-snake, and then burying the worm alive in a bottle. But the justice here appears to me very defective, and will no doubt recall that duel the other day, where two women went out to fight "for all the world like men." They exchanged shots, and one bullet taking effect on a neighbor's boy, as he was scrambling through the hedge, and the other having hit a cow that was looking over the gate, the seconds declared that honor was satisfied. I recommend, therefore, that when the snake has effected the cure, it should not be bottled and buried, but should be put back into some bank or hedgerow to carry on its useful war against snails and slugs and worms.

There are few things a snake has not been found at one time or another to resemble, and there is nothing apparently that a snake is not able to do — except swallow a porcupine. One species, a native of Assam, is in itself an epitome of all the vices; for in its vindictive ferocity it not only stalks its prey and pounces upon it, but chases it swiftly, and tracks it like a bloodhound, relentlessly, drives it up trees, and climbs after it like a squirrel, hunts it into rivers, and dives after it like a seal, gets up on one end to pick it off a perch, or grovels like a mole after it if it tries to escape by tunnelling in the earth. So, at any rate, the Assamese say, and their word is as good as that of the Greeks in the matter of snakes. What awful parallels in the past, again, can be found in Nature adequate to the tales of terror that travellers have had to tell of the python which arrests in full career the wind-footed bison, of the boa-constrictor, that hurls itself from overhanging rocks and trees in coils of dreadful splendor upon even the jaguar and the puma, of the anaconda, the superb dictator of the Brazilian forests! Do the hydras, dragons, or chimæras of antiquity surpass these three in terrors? Nor among the lesser evils of the serpent folk of old, the cockatrices, basilisks, and asps, do we find any to surpass our own life-shattering worms, the cobra or the rattlesnake.

The snakes of antiquity, it is true, have come down to us dignified and made terrible by the honors and fears of past ages, when the Egyptians and the Greeks bound the aspic round the heads of their idols as the most regal of tiaras, and crowned in fancy the adder and the cerastes; when nations tenanted their sacred groves with even more sacred serpents, entrusted to their care all that kings held most precious and the gems that were still undug, confided the diamond mines to one and—more valued then than diamonds—the carbuncle to another, deifying some of their worms, and giving the names of others to their gods. But the actual facts known to science of modern snakes, the deadlier sorts of the ophidians, invest them with terrors equal to any creatures of fable, and with the superstitious might entitle them to equal honors with the past objects of Ammonian worship and still the reverence of all Asia, the central figures in the rites of Ops or Thermuthis, or whatever we may call the old gods now.

Science has now driven out Superstition, planting a more beautiful growth of beliefs in its place, and of these beliefs Mr. Ruskin is the trustee and the python, the oracle, the artistic Apollo.

. . . .

It is one of the penalties of extended empire that frontiers shall be constantly vexed, just as the sea along its margin is forever astir. But it is seldom that duties as a Great Power bring a nation into reluctant collision with such a strange, half-mythical folk as the Nagas of the northeastern frontiers of India with whom the English have periodically to fight. The Afghan hills were picturesque enough, and the rolling grass lands of Zululand were instinct with romance; yet neither Afghan nor Zulu can claim a tithe of the superstitious obscurity of the dwellers on the Naga hills, or affect pretensions to half their traditions. Indeed, what people on earth would dare to measure pedigrees with the snake-folk, or count ancestors against a race who claim to have a lineal descent from before the creation of man?

There are gaps, it is true, in the chain that would suffice to break even a herald's heart; but what else could be expected in the family trees of tribes that were old when the children of the Sun and the Moon, in the first generation, found them possessing the earth? Their progenitors flourished even before time and space had established their empire, and they count among the events of their national history the birth of the Creator.

Before history commences, and when gods were half men, and men were demigods, the Nagas inhabited India. They were contemporaries of the pygmies who fought with the partridge-folk for possession of the Ganges' banks; contemporaries of the monkey races that furnished long-tailed contingents to the conquering army of Rama, and gave deities to India; contemporaries of Garud, king of the bird-gods, and of Indra and Krishna, and all the merry-making pantheon of Vedic Hindostan. But there came from over the hill passes on the northwest, which nowadays men call the Khyber and the Kurram, nation after nation of Aryans, who, as moon-children and sun-children, fell upon the aborigines, and drove them from every spot worth possessing.

They hunted them to the tops of the mountains, and

into the very hearts of the forests, and, adding insult to injury, nicknamed the dispossessed people snakes, monkeys, and devils, representing them in their history as only half human, and thus hoped, no doubt, to justify their ill-treatment of them. Here and there these aboriginal tribes are still to be found in fragments, as primitive to-day as they were when first the Aryan invaders pretended to mistake them for wild beasts and vermin. Thus, in the northeastern corner of India are the Nagas, the Snakes, a medley of small tribes without cohesion, or even the power of cohesion, professing allegiance, in this nineteenth century of ours, some of them to potentates long ago extinct, others to the Empire of Burmah. The authority of British India is, of course, gradually becoming familiar to them and, very gradually also, being admitted; but it is probable that when the Afghan hills have become as settled as the Punjab, and Zululand as commonplace as Natal, the Nagas will still be found cherishing those wild notions of aboriginal independence that have made their reclamation seem so hopeless.

How can they ever consent to the dry formalities of civilization and the reign of law so long as they believe that Shesh, the great serpent, lies coiled under their hills, — governing the upper earth through his snake-limbed lieutenants, and recording his impressions of terrestrial affairs by the lustre of a great gem, the kanthi-stone, which he has erected in insolent revenge to light up his subterranean kingdom when he was driven from the sunlight by the more powerful gods of the Aryans?

This Shesh is a reptile worthy of homage, and may be accepted without hesitation and in defiance of all sea-serpents, past and future, as the greatest snake on record. When Vishnu and the gods met to extort from the sea the ichor of immortality, they plucked up from the Himalayan range the biggest mountain in it, and this they made their churn, while round it, as the strongest tackle they could think of, they bound the serpent Shesh. And the gods took hold of the head and the devils took hold of the tail, and, alternately tugging, they made the mountain spin round and round until the sea was churned into froth, and from the churning came up all the treasures of the deep, and the most precious possessions of man, and last of all immortality. The gods and the devils scrambled for the good things, but nothing more is said of the serpent who had been so useful, nor what he got for his services. Antiquaries in the West incline to think that he remained in the sea and became the kraken, but the Nagas believe him to be still under their hills, dispensing fate by the light of a diamond. When this misconception is removed from their minds the Nagas may be able to remark other errors of their beliefs and ways; but meanwhile they are in utter heathendom, and as delightfully free from misgivings with regard to their methods of asserting their liberty as are the tigers, rhinoceroses, elephants, buffaloes, or wild pigs that share their beautiful country with them.

While disciplined troops were being equipped with scientific weapons, and the machinery of a great government was slowly set in motion, the naked Nagas were squatting on their hillsides, taking augury from the flight of jungle-cocks. The British soldiers marched as military science dictated, but the Nagas shaped their course from or towards us at the dictation of their omeus — passing deer or falling reeds. On the one side there were Sniders and mountain guns, and on the other spears and daos. So it took little prophesying to foretell, that, let the cocks fly as they would, and the reeds fall to the right or to the left, the snake-men had a troubled season before them, and Shesh another sad experience to record on his gem-lit page.

* * * * * * *

Much has been written and said about the amiable reptile which men call a turtle; but many, I regret to say, have approached the subject in a spirit of levity which is very unbecoming. To be flippant about turtles is as intolerable as if one were to be frivolous about aldermen.

Even in his native waters the turtle is not of a light-hearted kind, for his gestures are solemn and his demeanor circumspect. His spirits never rise to the frolicking point. In captivity the creature assumes a sepulchral deliberation in manner, and his natural sobriety deepens at times into positive dejection. He prowls about on tip-toes as if contemplating a burglary, and never betrays any symptoms of alacrity or enthusiasm.

Death, however, gloriously transfigures the turtle. The poor, moping thing which when alive ate even grass apologetically, which seemed always pleading for forbearance and proclaiming itself humble, is at once canonized by the simple process of cooking. The despised worm that yesterday nibbled the herbage at our feet soars to-day a butterfly above our heads. The martyr has become a saint. Festivity and luxury hasten to greet when dead the creature they laughed at when living; and the modest turtle which in the morning was the sport of children is in the evening the favorite dish of princes. The lesser planets of the culinary firmament revolve round it in deferential orbits, confessing that their light is borrowed, that a greater attraction than their own holds the guests in station and regulates the festive board. No wonder, then, that the East believes this creature is an embodiment of the Divinity, and that the world rests upon a tortoise! The splendid significance of the Vedic legend is not less striking than its beauty, for here we see at once that the alderman keeps up the price of turtle, which keeps up the weight of the earth, and so the alderman himself becomes an avatar of the solar myth. Thus does history work in cycles and a pagan religion stand revealed.

It would be a nice point to decide whether the alderman was created for the turtle or the turtle for the alderman. Much is to be said on both sides. It is difficult to imagine either of them preceding the other in point of time, and equally difficult to consider them as eternally co-existent in point of space. Yet they must have been both contemporary and contiguous from the beginning of time, or else we are confronted with the preposterous problem of aldermen apart from turtles. Who knows when either began; or, if they proceeded from matter at different spots on the earth's surface? Who can tell us what natural forces first brought them into contact?

For myself I dare not trust my imagination in such depths of conjecture, but prefer, more comfortably, to avoid the difficulty, and to believe that aldermen and turtles were simultaneous. The primitive alderman, it is certain, could not have eaten up the original turtle, or the species would then and there, in that one disastrous meal, have become extinct. He spared it until it laid eggs, and then he ate it. When he died he bequeathed the secret to his son, who, becoming an alderman in due time, ate turtles likewise, and so on to the present day. The civic soup may therefore be added to the many other remarkable survivals of instinct in a species long after the necessity for its exercise has died out.

We, for instance, see the pensive bear dancing in public places, lifting up its hind feet one after the other in mechanical alternation, and holding its fore paws off the ground altogether, and we forget perhaps at first why it does so. The truth is that dancing is associated in Bruin's memory with the hot plates on which he was taught to dance, and no sooner therefore does he hear the tune played which once was the signal for the fire to be lit beneath him, than by instinct he gets up on his hind legs and keeps moving them one after the other off the surface which he still imagines is being heated. It does not matter to him that neither the country green nor the provincial market-place is fitted up with ovens for baking bears, for the original association of a certain tune with certain hot sensations on the soles of his feet is too strong for him, and he proceeds to dance. In the same way the alderman, feeling hungry, looks round for a turtle. It is not because this excellent reptile is the only edible thing obtainable, but because hunger, an inherited sensation, is associated in his mind by indissoluble bonds of memory with turtle fat.

Once upon a time, in the age of Diluvia and Catastrophe, the primeval alderman, being unclothed, fled the vertical rays of the sun, and, seeking shelter in the umbrageous swamp, saw there the pristine turtle. Sitting aloof he watched the creature crawling painfully about, and noted that it was a thing of inconsiderable agility, and suitable, therefore, to be a easy prey. Being himself of aldermanic proportions, he was averse to arduous exercise; so he surveyed the turtle, pleased. Anon he grew hungry, and hunger arousing him to comparative activity, he circumvented the unsuspecting turtle, that is to say, he got between it and the water, and soon made a prisoner of the slowly moving thing. Examination increased his satisfaction, for he found the turtle carried its own soup tureen on its back, and there and then, gathering in his simple way a few sticks from the adjoining brake, this primeval alderman enjoyed the delights of green-fat soup, — calling it, in his barbarous but expressive dialect, callipee, and the outer integuments of more solid meat which he found upon the stomach, callipash. So ever afterwards when he felt hungry, and too lazy to pick acorns, he circumvented a turtle.

Since then, of course, many years have past. Aldermen now wear clothes, and need not go about catching their meals, and the umbrageous swamps of a tertiary Britain are now the site of the city of London; but the old instinct, as we perceive, still survives, and the hungry alderman always calls for turtle.

Nor could the civic magnate do better. Some viands that have long been traditional for their excellence have ceased to be paraded on high days, and, to omit the more recondite, I need only cite the swan, once the dish of honor at every public feast; the hog barbecued; the ox roasted whole; the peacock garnished with his tail and russet pippins; the sturgeon and the stuffed pike; the bedizened boar's head. Each had conspicuous merits, and there are still those who maintain that the new meats cannot compare with the old. Let this be as it may, the turtle need never fear rivalry, and the alderman need never dread its extinction. In the seas of Florida alone it swarms in such prodigious quantity that well-authenticated cases are on record of small craft having to heave to until a shoal had passed, while in the remoter corners of the earth it still luxuriates in all its pristine multitudes, unthinned by capture and unmolested by man.

So long, therefore, as the alderman will remain constant to his soup, his soup will never desert him.

It is touching but strange that two species so widely separated, or, at any rate, so distantly connected as the common councilman and the common turtle, should display this mutual sympathy.

The latter is rather an ungainly animal, full in the stomach and short-legged, moving on rough ground with great difficulty. It is described in works on natural history as having a short round snout, a wide mouth, and a body very wide across the shoulders. It is further described as being very voracious. Yet there is nothing in these traits of person and character to detract from its estimable properties as an article of diet; and so long as it continues to secrete green fat, aldermen should not quarrel with the turtle either for the shortness of its legs or the rotundity of its body or the gluttony of its appetite.

PART IV.

IDLE HOURS UNDER THE PUNKAH.

PART IV.

IDLE HOURS UNDER THE PUNKAH.

I.

THE MAN-EATING TREE.[1]

PEREGRINE ORIEL, my maternal uncle, was a great traveller, as his prophetical sponsors at the font seemed to have guessed he would be. Indeed he had rummaged in the garrets and cellars of the earth with something more than ordinary diligence. But in the narrative of his travels he did not, unfortunately,

---

[1] Before committing this paper to the ridicule of the Great Mediocre — for many, I fear, will be inclined to regard this story as incredible — I would venture on the expression of an opinion regarding credulity, which I do not remember to have met before. It is this. Placing supreme Wisdom and supreme Unwisdom at the two extremes, and myself in the exact mean between them, I am surprised to find that, whether I travel towards the one extreme or the other, the credulity of those I meet increases. To put it as a paradox — *whether a man be foolisher or wiser than I am, he is more credulous.* I make this remark to point out to those of the Great Mediocre, whose notice it may have escaped, that credulity is not of itself shameful or contemptible, and that it depends upon the manner rather than the matter of their belief, whether they gravitate towards the sage or the reverse way. According, therefore, to the incredibility found in the following, the reader may measure, as pleases him, his wisdom or his unwisdom.

preserve the judicious caution of Xenophon between the thing seen and the thing heard, and thus it came about that the town-councillors of Brunsbüttel (to whom he had shown a duck-billed platypus, caught alive by him in Australia, and who had him posted for an importer of artificial vermin) were not alone in their scepticism of some of the old man's tales.

Thus, for instance, who could hear and believe the tale of the man-sucking tree from which he had barely escaped with life? He called it himself more terrible than the Upas. "This awful plant, that rears its splendid death-shade in the central solitude of a Nubian fern forest, sickens by its unwholesome humors all vegetation from its immediate vicinity, and feeds upon the wild beasts that, in the terror of the chase, or the heat of noon, seek the thick shelter of its boughs; upon the birds that, flitting across the open space, come within the charmed circle of its power, or innocently refresh themselves from the cups of its great waxen flowers; upon even man himself when, an infrequent prey, the savage seeks its asylum in the storm, or turns from the harsh foot-wounding sword-grass of the glade, to pluck the wondrous fruit that hang plumb down among the wondrous foliage." And such fruit! — " glorious golden ovals, great honey drops, swelling by their own weight into pear-shaped translucencies. The foliage glistens with a strange dew, that all day long drips on to the ground below, nurturing a rank growth of grasses, which shoot up in places so high that their spikes of fierce blood-fed green show far up among the deep-tinted foliage of the terrible tree, and, like a jealous body-guard, keep concealed the fearful secret of the charnel-house within, and draw round the black roots of the murderous plant a decent screen of living green."

Such was his description of the plant; and the other day, looking it up in a botanical dictionary, I find that there is really known to naturalists a family of carnivorous plants; but I see that they are most of them very small, and prey upon little insects only. My maternal uncle, however, knew nothing of this, for he died before the days of the discovery of the sun, dew, and pitcher plants; and grounding his knowledge of the man-sucking tree simply on his own terrible experience of it, explained its existence by theories of his own. Denying the fixity of all the laws of nature except one, that the stronger shall endeavor to consume the weaker, and holding even this fixity to be itself only a means to a greater general changefulness, he argued that — since any partial distribution of the faculty of self-defence would presume an unworthy partiality in the Creator, and since the sensual instincts of beast and vegetable are manifestly analogous — the world must be as percipient as sentient throughout. Carrying on his theory (for it was something more than hypothesis with him) a stage or two further, he arrived at the belief that, given the necessity of any imminent danger or urgent self-interest, every animal or vegetable could eventually revolutionize its nature, the wolf feeding on grass or nesting in trees, and the violet arming herself with thorns or entrapping insects.

"How," he would ask, "can we claim for man the consequence of perceptions to sensations, and yet deny to beasts that hear, see, feel, smell, and taste, a percipient principle co-existent with their senses? And if in the whole range of the animate world there is this gift of self-defence against extirpation, and offence against weakness, why is the inanimate world, holding as fierce a struggle for existence as the other, to be left defenceless and unarmed? And I deny that it is. The Brazilian epiphyte strangles the tree and sucks out its juices. The tree, again, to starve off its vampire parasite, withdraws its juices into its roots, and piercing the ground in some new place, turns the current of its sap into other growths. The epiphyte then drops off the dead boughs on to the fresh green sprouts springing from the ground beneath it, — and so the fight goes on. Again, look at the Indian peepul tree; in what does the fierce yearning of its roots towards the distant well differ from the sad struggling of the camel to the oasis, or of Sennacherib's army to the saving Nile?

"Is the sensitive plant unconscious! I have walked for miles through plains of it, and watched, till the watching almost made me afraid lest the plant should pluck up courage and turn upon me, the green carpet paling into silver gray before my feet, and fainting away all round me as I walked. So strangely did I feel the influence of this universal aversion, that I would have argued with the plant; but what was the use? If only I stretched out my hands, the mere shadow of the limb terrified the vegetable to sickness; shrubs crumbled up at every commencement of my speech; and at my periods great sturdy-looking bushes, to whose robustness I had foolishly appealed, sank in pallid supplication. Not a leaf would keep me company. A breath went forth from me that sickened life. My mere presence paralyzed life, and I was glad at last to come out among a less timid vegetation, and to feel the resentful spear-grass retaliating on the heedlessness that would have crushed it. The vegetable world, however, has its revenges. You may keep the guinea-pig in a hutch, but how will you pet the basilisk? The little sensitive plant in your garden amuses your children (who will find pleasure also in seeing cockchafers spin round on a pin), but how could you transplant a vegetable that seizes the running deer, strikes down the passing bird, and once taking hold of him, sucks the carcass of man himself, till his matter becomes as vague as his mind, and all his animate capabilities cannot snatch him from the terrible embrace of — God help him! — an inanimate tree?

"Many years ago," said my uncle, "I turned my restless steps towards Central Africa, and made the journey from where the Senegal empties itself into the Atlantic to the Nile, skirting the Great Desert, and reaching Nubia on my way to the eastern coast. I had with me then three native attendants, — two of them brothers, the third, Otona, a young savage from the gaboon uplands, a mere lad in his teens; and one day, leaving my mule with the two men, who were pitching my tent for the night, I went on with my gun, the boy accompanying me, towards a fern forest, which I saw in the near distance. As I approached it I found the forest was cut into two by a wide glade; and seeing a small herd of the common antelope, an excellent beast in the pot, browsing their way along the shaded side, I crept after them. Though ignorant of their real danger the herd was suspicious, and, slowly trotting along before me, enticed me for a mile or more along the verge of the fern growths. Turning a corner I suddenly became aware of a solitary tree growing in the middle of the glade — one tree alone. It struck me at once that I had never seen a tree exactly like it before; but, being intent upon venison for my supper, I looked at it only long enough to satisfy my first surprise at seeing a single plant of such rich growth flourishing luxuriantly in a spot where only the harsh fern-canes seemed to thrive.

"The deer meanwhile were midway between me and the tree, and looking at them I saw they were going to cross the glade. Exactly opposite them was an opening in the forest, in which I should certainly have lost my supper; so I fired into the middle of the family as they were filing before me. I hit a young fawn, and the rest of the herd, wheeling round in their sudden terror, made off in the direction of the tree, leaving the fawn struggling on the ground. Otona, the boy, ran forward at my order to secure it, but the little creature seeing him coming, attempted to follow its comrades, and at a fair pace held on their course. The herd had meanwhile reached the tree, but suddenly, instead of passing under it, swerved in their career, and swept round it at some yards distance.

"*Was I mad, or did the plant really try to catch the deer?* On a sudden I saw, or thought I saw, the tree violently agitated, and while the ferns all round were standing motionless in the dead evening air, its boughs were swayed by some sudden gust towards the herd, and swept, in the force of their impulse, almost to the ground. I drew my hand across my eyes, closed them for a moment, and looked again. The tree was as motionless as myself!

"Towards it, and now close to it, the boy was running in excited pursuit of the fawn. He stretched out his hands to catch it. It bounded from his eager grasp. Again he reached forward, and again it escaped him. There was another rush forward, and the next instant boy and deer were beneath the tree.

"And now there was no mistaking what I saw.

"The tree was convulsed with motion, leaned forward, swept its thick foliaged boughs to the ground, and enveloped from my sight the pursuer and the pursued; I was within a hundred yards, and the cry of Otona from the midst of the tree came to me in all the clearness of its agony. There was then one stifled, strangling scream, and except for the agitation of the leaves where they had closed upon the boy, there was not a sign of life!

"I called out 'Otona!' No answer came. I tried to call out again, but my utterance was like that of some wild beast smitten at once with sudden terror and its death wound. I stood there, changed from all semblance of a human being. Not all the terrors of earth together could have made me take my eye from the awful plant, or my foot off the ground. I must have stood thus for at least an hour, for the shadows had crept out from the forest half across the glade before that hideous paroxysm of fear left me. My first impulse then was to creep stealthily away lest the tree should perceive me, but my returning reason bade me approach it. The boy might have fallen into the lair of some beast of prey, or perhaps the terrible life in the tree was that of some great serpent among its branches. Preparing to defend myself I approached the silent tree, — the harsh grass crisping beneath my feet with a strange loudness, the cicadas in the forest shrilling till the air seemed throbbing round me with waves of sound. The terrible truth was soon before me in all its awful novelty.

"The vegetable first discovered my presence at about fifty yards distance. I then became aware of a stealthy motion among the thick-lipped leaves, reminding me of some wild beast slowly gathering itself up from long sleep, a vast coil of snakes in restless motion. Have you ever seen bees hanging from a bough — a great cluster of bodies, bee clinging to bee — and by striking the bough, or agitating the air, caused that massed life to begin sulkily to disintegrate, each insect asserting its individual right to move? And do you remember how without one bee leaving the pensile cluster, the whole became gradually instinct with sullen life and horrid with a multitudinous motion?

"I came within twenty yards of it. The tree was quivering through every branch, muttering for blood, and, helpless with rooted feet, yearning with every branch towards me. It was that terror of the deep sea which the men of the northern fiords dread, and which, anchored upon some sunken rock, stretches into vain space its longing arms, pellucid as the sea itself, and as relentless — maimed Polypheme groping for his victims.

"Each separate leaf was agitated and hungry. Like hands they fumbled together, their fleshy palms curling upon themselves and again unfolding, closing on each other and falling apart again, — thick, helpless, fingerless hands (rather lips or tongues than hands) dimpled closely with little cup-like hollows. I approached nearer and nearer, step by step, till I saw that these soft horrors were all of them in motion, opening and closing incessantly.

"I was now within ten yards of the farthest reaching bough. Every part of it was hysterical with excitement.

The agitation of its members was awful — sickening yet fascinating. In an ecstasy of eagerness for the food so near them, the leaves turned upon each other. Two meeting would suck together face to face, with a force that compressed their joint thickness to a half, thinning the two leaves into one, now grappling in a volute like a double shell, writhing like some green worm, and at last, faint with the violence of the paroxysm, would slowly separate, falling apart as leeches gorged drop off the limbs. A sticky dew glistened in the dimples, welled over, and trickled down the leaf. The sound of it dripping from leaf to leaf made it seem as if the tree was muttering to itself. The beautiful golden fruit as they swung here and there were clutched now by one leaf and now by another, held for a moment close enfolded from the sight, and then as suddenly released. Here a large leaf, vampire-like, had sucked out the juices of a smaller one. It hung limp and bloodless, like a carcass of which the weasel has tired.

"I watched the terrible struggle till my starting eyes, strained by intense attention, refused their office, and I can hardly say what I saw. But the tree before me seemed to have become a live beast. Above me I felt conscious was a great limb, and each of its thousand clammy hands reached downwards towards me, fumbling. It strained, shivered, rocked, and heaved. It flung itself about in despair. The boughs, tantalized to madness with the presence of flesh, were tossed to this side and to that, in the agony of a frantic desire. The leaves were wrung together as the hands of one driven to madness by sudden misery. I felt the vile dew spurting from the tense veins fall upon me. My clothes began to give out a strange odor. The ground I stood on glistened with animal juices.

"Was I bewildered by terror? Had my senses abandoned me in my need? I know not — but the tree seemed to me' to be alive. Leaning over towards me, it seemed to be pulling up its roots from the softened ground, and to be moving towards me. A mountainous monster, with myriad lips, mumbling together for my life, was upon me!

"Like one who desperately defends himself from imminent death, I made an effort for life, and fired my gun at the approaching horror. To my dizzied senses the sound seemed far off, but the shock of the recoil partially recalled me to myself, and starting back I reloaded. The shot had torn their way into the soft body of the great thing. The trunk as it received the wound shuddered, and the whole tree was struck with a sudden quiver. A fruit fell down — slipping from the leaves, now rigid with swollen veins, as from carven foliage. Then I saw a large arm slowly droop, and without a sound it was severed from the juice-fattened bole, and sank down softly, noiselessly, through the glistening leaves. I fired again, and another vile fragment was powerless — *dead*. At each discharge the terrible vegetable yielded a life. Piecemeal I attacked it, killing here a leaf and there a branch. My fury increased with the slaughter till, when my ammunition was exhausted, the splendid giant was left a wreck — as if some hurricane had torn through it. On the ground lay heaped together the fragments, struggling, rising and falling, gasping. Over them drooped in dying languor a few stricken boughs, while upright in the midst stood, dripping at every joint, the glistening trunk.

"My continued firing had brought up one of my men

on my mule. He dared not, so he told me, come near me, thinking me mad. I had now drawn my hunting-knife, and with this was fighting — with the leaves. Yes — but each leaf was instinct with a horrid life; and more than once I felt my hand entangled for a moment and seized as if by sharp lips. Ignorant of the presence of my companion I made a rush forward over the fallen foliage, and with a last paroxysm of frenzy drove my knife up to the handle into the soft bole, and, slipping on the fast congealing sap, fell exhausted and unconscious, among the still panting leaves.

"My companions carried me back to the camp, and after vainly searching for Otona awaited my return to consciousness. Two or three hours elapsed before I could speak, and several days before I could approach the terrible thing. My men would not go near it. It was quite dead; for as we came up a great-billed bird with gaudy plumage that had been securely feasting on the decaying fruit, flew up from the wreck. We removed the rotting foliage, and there among the dead leaves still limp with juices, and piled round the roots, we found the ghastly relics of many former meals, and — its last nourishment — the corpse of little Otona. To have removed the leaves would have taken too long, so we buried the body as it was with a hundred vampire leaves still clinging to it."

Such, as nearly as I remember it, was my uncle's story of the man-eating tree.

II.

EASTERN SMELLS AND WESTERN NOSES.

IN his essay showing that a certain nation — contrary to the generally applauded notion — "do not stink," Sir Thomas Browne uses with effect the argument that a mixed race cannot have a national smell. Among a mongrel people he contends no odor could be gentilitious; yet he nowhere denies the possibility, or even impugns the probability, of a pure people having a popular smell, a scent in which the public should share alike, an aroma as much common property as the National Anthem, a joint-stock fragrance, a commonwealth of odor, — a perfume with which no single individual could selfishly withdraw, saying, "This is my own, my proper and peculiar flavor, and no man may cry me halves in it," as Alexander or Mahomet might have done, who, unless history lies, were divinely scented. Not that individual odors, as distinct from those of the species, have been uncommon in any times. Many instances may be found, if examples were required, to support "a postulate which has ever found unqualified assent."

"For well I know," cries Don Quixote, "the scent of that lovely rose! and tell me, Sancho, when near her, thou must have perceived a Sabean odor, an aromatic fragrance, a something sweet for which I cannot find a name, — a scent, a perfume, as if thou wert in the shop of some curious glover."

"All I can say is," quoth Sancho, "that I perceived somewhat of a strong smell."

It would, however, be pure knavery to argue from the particular fragrance of Don Quixote's lady that all the dames of La Mancha could appeal to the affections through the nose. Equally dishonest would it be to disperse Alexander's scent over all Macedon, or with a high hand·conclude that all Romans were "as unsavory as Bassa." On the other hand, to argue, from the existence of a scentless individual, the innocence of his brethren, is to suppose that all violets are dog-violets, or that the presence of a snowdrop deodorizes the guilty garlic: whereas, in fact, the existence of such an individual enhances the universal fragrance; as Kalidasa says, "one speck of black shows more gloriously bright the skin of Siva's bull." If a number of units produce an aroma, it will be hard to believe that each is individually inodorous, in which argument from probabilities I have to a certain degree the countenance of the Pundits in their maxim of the Stick and the Cake. What is more to the point, we have on the globe at least one fragrant people, for (leaving Greenlanders out of the question) no one denies that Africans are aromatic. This is no novel suggestion, but an old antiquity; it is a point of high prescription, and a fact universally smelt out. If, therefore, one nation can indisputably claim a general odor, it is possible another may; and much may be found to support any one who will say that in this direction "warm India's supple-bodied sons" may claim equality of natural adornment with "the musky daughter of the Nile." If it were not for the blubber-feeding Greenlanders, I might contend that "it is all the fault of that confounded sun," for heat expresses odor elsewhere than in Asia and Africa, and I can keep within "Trismegistus his circle" and "need not to pitch beyond ubiquity" when I cite Pandemonium as an instance of unity of smell in a large population. We read in Byron's "Vision of Judgment" that at the sound of Pye's heroics the whole assembly sprang off with a melodious twang and a variety of scents, some sulphureous, some ambrosial; and that the sulphureous individuals all fled one way gibbering to their own dominions, that odorous principality of the damned whither in old times the handsome minstrel went in quest of his wife. That the infernal fraternity is uni-odorous we know, on the authority of the immortal Manchegan Squire, who says: "This devil is as plump as a partridge, and has another property very different from what you devils are wont to have, for it is said they all smell of brimstone," that is, like the Vienna matches — *ohne phosphor-geruch* — that Wendell Holmes hates so honestly.

To return to India, it is very certain that a single Hindoo is not always perceptibly fragrant; yet it is equally certain that if, when a dozen are together, an average be struck, each individual of the party must be credited with a considerable amount. In any gathering of Orientals the Western stranger is instantly aware of a circumambient aroma; he becomes conscious of a new and powerful perfume, — a curious *je ne sais quoi* scent which may possibly, like attar of roses, require only endless dilution and an acquired taste to become pleasant, but which certainly requires dilution for the novice. No particular person or member of the public seems to be odorous beyond his fellows, but put three together, and they might be 300. Perhaps this is produced by sympathy, by some magnetic relation between like and like, the result of natural affinities. It may be that each Hindoo is flint to the other's steel, and that more than one is requisite for the combustion of the aromatic particles; and that, as evening draws the perfume from flowers, and excitement the "bouquet" from a muskrat, contiguity and congregation are required for the proper expression of the fragrance of Orientals. Cases of individuals innocent of all savor carry therefore no weight, unless to those who believe that all asses can speak because Balaam's quadruped was casually gifted with articulate utterance, or that fish as a rule possess stentorian lungs because Mr. Briggs once caught a pike that barked.

A notable point about this Eastern savor is that, though it approaches many others, it exactly resembles none. Like Elia's burnt pig, it doesn't smell of burnt cottage, nor yet of any known herb, weed, or flower. Though unique, its entity is intertwisted with a host of phantom entities, as a face seen in a passing train, instantly recognized but never brought home to any one person from its partial resemblance to a hundred; and they say that no number of qualified truths can ever make up an absolute verity. By smelling a musk-rat through a bunch of garlic an idea of it may be arrived at, but hardly more; for the conflicting odors hamper the judgment by distracting the nostrils, keeping it hovering in acute uncertainty between the components without allowing it to settle on the aggregate — "so blended and running into each other, that both together make but one ambrosial result or common substance." This seems to be affected not by an actual confusion of matters but by parallel existence; rather by the nice exactitude of balance than mutual absorption; not so much by a mingled unity as from our impotence to unravel the main threads, to single out any one streak of color. It is like a nobody's child, a Ginx's baby, with a whole parish for parents; or one of those puddings which at every mouthful might be sworn to change its taste, and which when finished leaves one indelible but impalpable fragrance on the memory of the palate, that may be called up by every passing odor, but is never in its composite singularity again encountered. It is a lost chord.

In the West no such community of fragrance obtains, and the great science of perfume, though exquisitely perfected in certain details, does not command as in the East the attention of the masses. With us it is the exception to use scent, but with them the singular person is the scentless one. The nose nevertheless plays an important part even in Europe, and it is well, therefore, that this feature has at last found one courageous apostle.

Dr. Jäger, a professor of Stuttgart, has, after most patient experiments with his own nose, proved it to be the seat of his soul. Simply with the nose on his face the learned professor is enabled, eyes shut and ears stopped, to discriminate the character of any stranger he may meet, or even that he has passed in the street. He can, then, by merely putting his nose to the keyhole, tell what the people on the other side of the door are doing; and, more than this, what they have just been doing, can assure himself whether they are young or old, married or single, and whether they are happy or the reverse. Proceeding upon the knowledge thus acquired by a process which we may call successful diagnosis, the professor argues, in a lecture which he has given to the world on this fascinating subject, that if different scents express different traits of character, each trait in turn can be separately affected by a particular scent; and his experiments, he gravely assures us, prove him here as right as before. For not only can Dr. Jäger smell, for instance, bad temper or a tendency to procrastination in any individual, but by emitting the counteracting antidote odor, he can smooth the frown into a smile, and electrify the sluggard into despatch. Yet Dr. Jäger does not claim to possess within himself, his own actual body, more perfumes than any of his neighbors. He does not arrogate to himself any special odors, as did Mahomet and Alexander the Great, or ask to divide honors with the civet-cat or musk-deer. There is no insolent assumption of this kind about the professor, no unnatural straining after the possession of extraordinary attributes. He merely claims to have discovered by chemical research certain preparations, which, when volatilized, produce certain results upon the nostrils. There is no o'er-vaulting ambition in this. The merest tyro can compass as much with a very few ingredients; and, as a matter of fact, any boy of average, or even the meanest, capacity can, by a courageous combination of the contents of his chemical chest, produce such effluvia as shall at once, and violently, affect the nostrils of the whole household, not excluding the girl in the scullery or the cat on the nursery hearthrug. But the boy's results are miscellaneous and fortuitous. He blunders upon a smell of extraordinary volume and force by, it may be, the merest accident, and quite unintentionally, therefore, lets loose upon himself the collective wrath of his family circle. Dr. Jäger, however, has brought the whole gamut of smells under his own control; and so, by letting out from his pocket any one he chooses, he can at once dissolve an assembly in tears or make every face in it ripple with smiles. The great secret of composition once attained, care in uncorking is all that is demanded; and the professor, with his pocket full of little bottles, can move about unsuspected among his kind, and, by his judicious emission of various smells as he goes along, can tranquilize a frantic mob, or set the passing funeral giggling, or a Punch-and-Judy audience sobbing.

Hitherto the nose has been held, as compared with the other organs of sense, in very slight account indeed. It has always been looked upon as the shabby feature of the face, and, in public society, has been spoken of with an apology for mentioning it. Many attempts have been made to render it respectable, but the best-intentioned efforts of philosophers have been thwarted by the extremes to which their theories have been pushed by the longer-nosed individuals of the public. The nose may be really an index of character, but the amount of nose does not necessarily imply, as some people contend, a corresponding pre-eminence of genius or virtue. Many great and good men have had quite indifferent noses, while the length of the proboscis of more than one hero of the Chamber of Horrors is remarkable. The feeling against this feature has, therefore, been irritated rather than soothed by the well-meant efforts of theorists. When the urchin, innocent of art, wishes, with his simple chalk, to caricature the householder upon his gate-post or garden-door, he finds in the nose the most suitable object for his unskilled derision. Grown up, the same urchin, exasperated with his neighbor, seizes him by the nose. This ill-feeling against the feature admits of little explanation, for it seems altogether unreasonable and deplorable. It is true that the nose takes up a commanding position on the face, and does not altogether fulfil the expectations naturally formed of so prominent a member. Vagrant specks of soot settle upon it and make it ridiculous, An east wind covers the nose with absurdity. It is a fierce light that beats upon a throne, and the nose, before assuming a central place, should perhaps, remarking the fact, have been better prepared to maintain its own dignity. But beyond this, impartial criticism cannot blame the feature. On the other hand, much can be said in its favor, and if Dr. Jäger is right, a great future lies before the nose. Lest it should be thought I exaggerate the importance of Dr. Jäger's discoveries, I give the learned professor's own words. "Puzzled as to the meaning of the word *soul*," says he, "I set myself to inquire, and my researches have assured me that the seat of the immortal part of man is in his nose. All the mind affections are relative to the nasal sensations. I have found this out by observing the habits of animals in the menagerie; and, finding how exquisite was their sense of smell, I conceived my great idea, and experiment has proved me right. So perfect can the perceptions by the nose become that I can discover even the mental conditions of those around me by smelling them; and more than this, I can, by going into a room, tell at once by sniffing whether those who were last in it were sad or mirthful. Aroma is in fact, the essence of the soul, and every flavor emitted by the body represents a corresponding emotion of the soul. Happiness finds expression in a mirthful perfume, sorrow in a doleful one. Does not a hungry man on smelling a joint of meat at once rejoice? I myself have been so overcome by the scent of a favorite fruit that, under an uncontrollable impulse, I have fallen upon and devoured the whole plateful! so powerful is the sense of smell." To present the different perfumes accurately and easily to the eye, the professor, when first delivering his lecture, drew upon a blackboard a number of diagrams showing the various curves taken by the scent atoms when striking upon the soul-nerves, and explained briefly certain instruments he had constructed for registering the wave motion of smells, and the relative force with which they impinged upon the nose of his soul or the soul of his nose. The audience meanwhile had become restless and agitated, and the professor therefore hurried on to the second section of his discoveries — those for counteracting the passions detected by the nose. "I have here," he said, "a smell-murdering essence, which I have discovered and christened Ozogene, and with which I can soothe the angry man to mildness or infuriate a Quaker." But the audience, such is the bigoted antipathy to the exaltation of the nose, would not stand this on any account, and the professor, in obedience to the clamor, had to resume his seat.

Dr. Jäger did not, therefore, secure a patient hearing; but he should remember how at all times the first apostles of truth have been received, and live content to know that posterity will gravely honor his memory, though contemporary man makes fun of his discoveries. Indeed, posterity will have good cause to honor the great man who shall thus have banished from among them strife and anger. The Riot Act will never have to be read to an excited populace, since a squirt of perfume will suffice to allay their fury. The comic lecturer or charity-sermon preacher may assure themselves of the sympathy of his audiences quite apart from the matter of their discourse. Science will have new fields opened to it, and humanity take a new lease of its pleasures. The nose, hitherto held of little more account than the chin, will supersede all the other features, and, like Cinderella, rise from the kitchen ashes to palace dignities, developing under the Darwinian theory into proboscidian dimensions of extraordinary acuteness. The policeman will need no evidence but that of his nose to detect the thief, actual or potential, and the judge, unhampered by jury, counsel or witnesses, will summarily dispense a nasal justice. Diplomacy will be purged of its obscurities, and statesmen live in a perpetual palace of truth. Conscious of each other's detective organs, men will speak of their fellows honestly, and hypocrisy will cease from society. How will war or crime be able to thrive when the first symptom of ill-temper in a sovereign or of ambition in a minister can be quenched at the will of any individual ratepayer? And thus a universal peace will settle upon a sniffing world.

III.

GAMINS.

ANTHROPOLOGY, no doubt, is a great science, but still it is merely an infant, — a monster baby, I confess, but scarcely past the age at which Charles Lamb liked sucking-pigs and chimney-sweeps. Toddles and Poddles, as readers of Dickens will remember, used to go on buccaneering expeditions, but they were only across the kitchen-floor, and often ended in the fireplace. Anthropology, in the same way, makes only short excursions, and these even are not always marked by judgment in direction. At any rate, there can be no doubt that anthropology has not as yet paid any consideration to the great co-ordinate science of "lollipopology" of which one sub-section concerns itself with the phenomena of gamins.

This subject has perhaps been touched upon in ephemeral literature, but it was a mere flirtation, a flippant butterfly kind of settling. The intentions were not matrimonial; there was no talk of taking the house on a lease. And yet the subject of gamin distribution is worthy investigation. Why are there no gamins in India, with their street affronts and trivial triumphs? Pariah dogs are scarcely an equivalent for these unkempt morsels of barbarism, these little Ishmaels of our cities. What is the reason, then, for their absence? Can it be too hot to turn three wheels a penny? Surely not; for dust is a bad conductor of heat, and what gamin is there — pure-minded, a gamin *nomine dignus* — that would not rather turn thirty somersaults in a dust-bin than three on a pavement? Why, my "compound"[1] alone would tempt to an eternity of tumbling. And yet no Hindoo of my acquaintance has even offered to stand on his head! Can it be that there is no ready means of causing annoyance? What! Is there not that same dust? Would not any gamin, unless lost to all sense of emulation and self-respect, rejoice in kicking up dust if he saw the remotest glimpse of even the chance of molesting anybody? Again, why do not little Hindoos throw stones about? Because there is nothing to throw at? Hah! Put one vulture down in Islington, and mark the instant result. Nothing to throw at? *Mehercule!* Any member of a large family will remember the tumultuous uprising and stair-shaking exit of the junior olive-twigs if even a wagtail came into the garden. A cat on the lawn was convulsions. Imagine, then, those same impetuous juniors surrounded by blue-jays, bee-eaters, and gray squirrels! And yet the young Hindoo sees an easy mark for any of the stones lying at his feet, and passes on. Perhaps it is something in the shape of the stones? The argument is plausible; for Indian stones, it is true, are of hideous shapes, angular and unprovocative. The fingers do not itch to throw them. But European gamins will throw brick in scraggy and uncompromising sections, *rebarbatif* and volcanic in appearance, — at, when other targets fail, a curbstone. A London gamin would heave his grandmother, if he

---

[1] A word of vexed derivation, but meaning in India (and Batavia, I believe) the precincts of a dwelling-house, — premises, in fact. — P. R.

could, at a mungoose. Are Hindoos forbidden to throw stones? Perhaps they may be, but imagine forbidding a gamin to throw stones, or forbidding a gamin to do anything! When England sells Gibraltar it will be time to think of that; or when, as Wendell Holmes says, strawberries grow bigger *downward* through the basket. It is evident, then, that none of these are the right reasons, so it only remains to conclude that Hindoos were not designed in the beginning for gamins. Boys, they say, are the natural enemies of creation, but Young India contradicts this flat. "Boys will be boys" has stood most of us in good stead when brought red-handed before the tribune; yet Young India needs no excusings for mischief. He never does any. He has all the virtues of his elders, and none of their vices, for he positively prefers to behave properly.

Perhaps as a last resource the absence of gamins in India might be accepted as a key to the theory of climates, for we know that Nature never wastes. Nature is pre-eminently economical. What, then, would have been the use of giving Bengal ice and snow, since there are no gamins to throw it about, or to make slides on pavements?

In England the small boy begins to throw stones as soon as he can crawl to one, and continues to do so until he takes to gloves, or is taken up by the police; and there are tolerable reasons why he should thus indulge himself. Take, for instance, the case of a passing train. The boys see the train coming and a lively interest is at once aroused in its approach; the best places on the bridge are scrambled for, and the smaller children, who cannot climb up for themselves, are hoisted on to the parapet and balanced across it on their stomachs to see the train pass. As it comes puffing and steaming up, the interest rises into excitement, and then, as the engine plunges under the bridge, boils over in enthusiasm. How are they to express this emotion in the few seconds at their disposal? They must be very quick, for the carriages are slipping rapidly past one after the other. It is of no use shouting, for the train makes more noise than they, and they, unfortunately, have no handkerchiefs to wave. But the crisis is acute, and something has to be done, and that promptly. There is no time to waste in reflection, or the train will be gone, and the sudden solitude that will follow will be embittered to them by the consciousness of golden opportunities lost for ever. They wave their arms like wild semaphores, scream inarticulately, and dance up and down, but all this is manifestly inadequate. It does not rise to the occasion, and they feel that it does not. The moment of tumult, with the bridge shaking under them, the dense white steam-clouds rushing up at them, and the roar of the train in their ears, demands a higher expression of their homage, a more glorious tribute from their energy. Looking round in despair, they see some stones. To grab them up in handfuls is the work of an instant, and in the next the missiles are on their way. After all, the moment had been almost lost, for the guard's van was just emerging from under the bridge, as the pebbles came hurtling along after the speeding train; but the youngsters rejoice, and go home gladdened that they did not throw in vain, for the guard, hearing the pattering upon the roof, looked out to see what was the matter and shook his fist at them, and the boys feel that they have done their best to celebrate the event, that their sacrifice has been accepted, and that they have not lived and loved in vain. For it is, undoubtedly, a sacrifice that they offer, — a sacrifice to emotions highly wrought, to an ecstasy of enthusiasm suddenly overwhelming them and as suddenly departing, to the majesty of the train and its tumultuous passage.

Boys do not, it will be noticed, throw stones at passing wheelbarrows or at perambulators, or even at cabs. Neither the one nor the other excites sufficiently. They belong more to their own sphere and their own level in life, are viewed subjectively, and seem too commonplace for extraordinary attentions. The train and the steamboat, however, are abstract ideas, absorbing the human beings they carry into their own gigantic entity, so far removed from the boys' own lives that they do not fall within the pale of ordinary ethics, and have to be viewed from a higher objective platform. Besides, the driver and guards of the train, being in a hurry, have no time to get down and catch the pelters, and therefore it is safe to pelt — so the boys think.

Whether magistrates have ever studied, or should study, the matter from any other than a police-court point of view I should hesitate to affirm. But in the ordinary cases where lads fling pebbles at a steamboat or train, their parents are fined, with the option of the culprits going to prison, and as the parents no doubt always give the urchins their full money's worth in retribution, justice is probably dealt out all round fairly enough. The boys, it generally appears, hit "an elderly passenger" with one of the stones which they throw; and there matters culminate, as the original act of stone-throwing, had the missiles struck no one, might have passed by as a surviving remnant of some old pagan ceremony.

Indeed from the very first, the youngsters have had bad examples before them; and if in such matters we are to go back to the original offenders, we must confess that Deucalion and his wife have much to answer for. Their descendants have been throwing stones ever since; and, whether in fun or in earnest, in the execution of criminal sentences or the performance of religious rites, men have never given over pelting each other. Whatever part of the world we go into, we find it is the same; for in the wilds of America the Red Indian shies flints at his spirit stones; all over Europe the devil is exorcised with stones; and in Asia, whether it is the Arab pelting the Evil One from the sacred precincts of the Holy City, or the Hindoo dropping pebbles into the valleys of enchantment, a similar tendency in race prevails.

As an instance of the innocent view taken of the practice by a distinguished Englishman, De Quincey, I would quote the incident of his meeting the king in Windsor Park. De Quincey was then a lad, and, walking with a young friend, was, he tells us, "theorizing and practically commenting on the art of chucking stones. Boys," he continues, "have a peculiar contempt for female attempts in that way. For, besides that girls fling wide of the mark, with a certainty that might have won the applause of Galerius,[1] there is a peculiar sling and rotary motion of the arm in launch-

---

[1] "Sir," said that emperor to a soldier who had missed the target in succession I know not how many times (suppose we say fifteen), "allow me to offer my congratulations on the truly admirable skill you have shown in keeping clear of the mark. Not to have hit once in so many trials, argues the most splendid talents for missing."

ing a stone, which no girl ever *can* attain. From ancient practice" (note this) "I was somewhat of a proficient in this art, and was discussing the philosophy of female failures, illustrating my doctrine with pebbles, as the case happened to demand, when —" he met the king, and the narrative diverges from the subject.

Nor is stone-throwing without some dignity in its traditions, for it has happened probably to many of us ourselves, and it has certainly been a custom from time immemorial, to take augury more or less momentous from this act, and make oracles of our pebbles. Among the many cases of this species of divination on record, none is more notable than that of Rousseau's, where he put the tremendous issues of his future state to the test of stone-throwing. "One day," says he, "I was pondering over the condition of my soul and the chances of future salvation or the reverse, and all the while mechanically, as it were, throwing stones at the trunks of the trees I passed, and with all my customary dexterity, — or in other words never hitting one of them. All of a sudden the idea flashed into my mind that I would take an augury, and thus, if possible, relieve my mental anxiety. I said to myself, I will throw this stone at that tree opposite. If I hit it, I am to be saved; if I miss it, I am to be damned eternally!" And he threw the stone, and hit it plumb in the middle, — "ce qui véritablement n'était pas difficile; car j'avais eu soin de choisir un arbre fort gros et fort près."

It is very possible, moreover, that the English boy throws stones from hereditary instinct; that he bombards the passing locomotives even as in primeval forests the ancestral ape "shelled" with the cocoanuts of his native forests the passing herds of bison. It would therefore be rash, without research into the lore of stone-throwing, and a better knowledge of the Stone Age, to say that the urchin who takes a "cockshy" at a steamboat does so purely from criminal instinct; for it is repeatedly in evidence that he takes no aim with his missile at all, but simply launches it into space, and, generous and trustful as childhood always is, casts his pebbles upon the waters in hopes of pleasant though fortuitous results.

Again, as I have already said, there is often no malicious motive. To pelt the loquacious frog is, in my opinion, a cruel act, but the criminality lessens, at least to my thinking, if the same stone be thrown at a hippopotamus. Similarly, we might recognize a difference between flinging half a brick at an individual stranger and throwing it at a mass-meeting or at a nation, or at All the Russias; while, if a boy threw stones at the Channel Squadron, he would be simply absurd, and his criminality would cease altogether. Where, then, should the line be drawn? The boy would rather pelt an ironclad than a penny steamboat, for it is a larger and nobler object to aim at; but, though he could do "H.M.S. Devastation" no harm, the police could hardly be expected to overlook his conduct. Stone-throwing has therefore come to be considered wrong in itself; just as the other day a wretched old bear, found dancing for hire in the streets, was astonished to learn from the police magistrate that bears are not permitted to dance in England. What his hind legs were given him for the quadruped will now be puzzled to guess, and in the same way the boy, finding he must not throw them, will wonder what stones were made for.

A very small cause, indeed, may have immense effects; and this holds good with national character as well as with natural phenomena. A little stone set rolling from the top of the Andes might spread ruin far and wide through the valleys at their feet, and the accident of Esau being a good marksman has left the Arabs wanderers and desert folk to the present day. The English character has itself been formed by an aggregation of small causes working together, and it will perhaps be found that one of the most important of them was the abundance of stones that lie about the surface of the ground in England. In India the traveller, may go a thousand miles in a straight line, and except where he crosses rivers, will not find anything on the ground which he can pick up and throw. The Bengali, therefore, cannot throw, and never could, for he has never had anything to practise with; and what is his character? Is he not notoriously gentle and soft-mannered? His dogs are still wild beasts, and his wild birds are tame. What can explain this better than the absence of stones? We in England have always had plenty of stones, and where the fists could not settle quarrels our rude ancestors had only to stoop to the ground for arms; and it is a mere platitude to say that the constant provision of arms makes a people ready to pick a quarrel and encourages independence in bearing. From the same cause our dogs obey our voices, for the next argument they know will be a stone; while, as for our wild birds, let the schoolboys tell us whether they understand the use of pebbles or not. In Greece the argument of the *chermadion* is still a favorite, for the savage dogs are still there that will recognize no other, unmindful of that disastrous episode in the history of Mycenæ, which all arose from Hercules's young cousin throwing a paving stone at a baying hound. These same boys of ours, therefore, have this argument also in their favor, that they are obeying an hereditary instinct and developing the original plan of nature, when they throw stones.

I doubt if the police will attend to this. It is better, perhaps, they should not, or at any rate, that they should whip the boys first and discuss the instinct afterwards. A reformatory, except at Stoney Stratford, for such offenders would not, so to speak, be out of place, and a penitentiary at Stonehenge would be delightfully apposite, for the urchins could not throw it about, however much they might pine to do so. If exile be not thought too harsh for such delinquents, punishment might be pleasantly blended with consideration, if our stone-throwing youth' were banished to Arabia Petræa. We would not go so far as to recommend stoning the urchins, for the ceremony which goes by that name was not the promiscuous casting of stones at a criminal, as is generally supposed. The guilty person, so the Talmud enacts, was taken to the top of an eminence of fifteen feet, and violently pushed over the edge. The fall generally broke his back, but if the executioners, on looking over, found their victim was not dead, they fetched one large stone and dropped it down from the same eminence upon the body. Such a punishment as this would not be suitable for the modern offence of pelting trains and steamboats. Nevertheless severity is called for; as, in spite of the hereditary and legendary precedent which the gamin of the period has for his pastimes, he cannot, even as the representative of the primeval ape, be permitted to indulge his enthusiasm at the sight of the triumphs of science in a manner that endangers the elderly passenger.

IV.

OF TAILORS.

THAT superstition is hateful, merely because it is superstition, is an inhuman doctrine. Yorick was superstitious, and so was Martin Luther. That a man should hesitate to shoot a raven lest he kill King Arthur unawares, can scarcely be held a criminal cunctation. Was ever man more superstitious than the silly knight of La Mancha, the sweet gentleman who loved too well; but did ever the man soil earth who hated Don Quixote? Cervantes, when he limned him, might laugh away the chivalry of Spain; but he did not, nor did he wish to, draw a knave. And yet in nothing do we find more to hate, with the honest hatred of an Esau, than in this same superstition. Heaven-born, it has bred with monster fiends. True superstition is reverent, and from it, like orchids from an old tree-trunk, spring blossoms of rare beauty. But as the same tree feeds noisome fungi, the vampire epiphyte and slab lichens, so from the grand old trunk of superstition has sprung out a growth of unwholesome fictions. What miscreant first said that a tailor was the ninth part, and no more, of a man? By what vile arithmetic did the author of the old play arrive at his equation of tailors to men when he makes his hero, on meeting eighteen of them, call out, "Come on, hang it, I'll fight you both!" Why a ninth, and why a tailor?

The tailor is the victim of misconstruction. Remember George Eliot's story of a man so snuffy that the cat happening to pass near him was seized with such a violent sternutation as to be cruelly misunderstood! Let Baboo Ishuree Dass say, "Tailors, they are very dishonest"; he is speaking of *natives*. Let Burton say, "The tailor is a thief"; he was fanciful. And let Urquiza of Paita be detested; he was only a half-bred Peruvian. Remember the regiment of London tailors; De Quincy's brave journeyman tailor; M. Achille Jules Cesar Le Grand, who was so courteous to Marguerite in the "Morals of May Fair"; the tailor of Yarrow who beat Mr. Tickler at backgammon; the famous tailor who killed seven at one blow and lived to divide a kingdom, and to call a queen his stepmother. Read "Mouat's Quinquennial Report of the Lower Provinces," and learn that the number of tailors in prison was less by one half than that of the priests. They were, moreover, the only class that had the decency to be incarcerated in round numbers, thereby notably facilitating the taking of averages and the deduction of most valuable observations.

Tailors, the ninth part of a man! Then are all Æthiops harmless? Can no Cretan speak a true word, or a Bœotian a wise one? Are all Italians blaspheming, and is Egypt merry Egypt? Nature, and she is no fool, has thought good to reproduce the tailor type in bird and insect: then why does man contemn the tailor? Because he sits cross-legged? Then is there not a whole man in Persia. Why should our children be taught in the nursery rhyme, how "nine-and-twenty tailors went out to kill a snail, but not a single one of them dared to touch his tail"? Or why should the world exult over the tailor, whom the elephant, as we learn from Mrs. Gurton's "Book of Anecdotes," squirted with ditch-water? We know the elephant to have been the aggressor; but just as we rejoice with Punch over the murder of his wife, and the affront he offers to the devil, so we applaud the ill-mannered pachyderm. "The elephant," we read in childhood, "put his trunk into a tailor's shop," thrust his nose, some four feet of it, into a tailor's house, his castle, writing himself down a gross fellow and an impertinent. For the tailor to have said, "Take your nose out of my shop" would have been tame; and on a mammal ill-conditioned enough to go where he was not bidden, such temperance would have been thrown away. When the Goth pulled the beard of the Senator, the Roman struck him down. Did Jupiter argue with Ixion, or Mark bandy words with the lover of Isolt? The tailor did not waste his breath, but we read "pricked the elephant's nose with a needle." Here the story should end. Jove's eagles have met at Delos. But no. "The elephant," we are told, "retired to a puddle and filled his trunk with water, and returning to the shop, squirted it over the tailor." It was sagacious, doubtless, to squirt water at the tailor, and to squirt it straight; but such sagacity is no virtue, or the Artful Dodger must be held to be virtuous. The triumph of the elephant was one of Punch's triumphs; Punch, who beats his wife past recovery, hangs an intimate friend after stealing his dog, and trifles with the devil,—Punch the incorrigible homunculus who, fresh from murder (his infant being thrown out of window), and with the smell of the brimstone of Diavolus still clinging to his frilled coat, complacently drums his heels upon the stage and assures his friends in front that he has put his enemies to flight. *Root-a-too-it! Root-a-too-it!* It is a great villain; yet the audience roar their fat applause. So with the elephant. Yet Mrs. Gurton has handed him down to future childhood as a marvel of sagacity, to be compared only with that pig who tells the time of day on playing-cards; the cat in Wellingtons who made his master Marquis of Carabas, and rose himself to high honors; and that ingenious but somewhat severe old lady who labored under the double disadvantage of small lodgings and a large family. Of all these Mrs. Gurton, in her able work, preserves the worthy memories; but that episode of the high-handed elephant and the seemly tailor should have been forgotten — irrecoverably lost like the hundred and odd volumes of Livy, or Tabitha Bramble's reticule in the River Avon. But the blame of perpetuation rests not with Mrs. Gurton, but with her posterity. They admired the work and reprinted it, not like Anthon's classics, expurgated, but in its noisome entirety. The volume before me is now a score years old — one year younger than was Ulysses's dog, and two years older than Chatterton; so perhaps it may not be reproduced in our generation, and the mischievous fable may die out before the growth of better reading, as the scent of a musk-rat killed over-night fades away before the fumes of breakfast. Then let us hope, the tailor — the only story which reflects contempt on him being abolished — will assume his proper position between the angels and the anthropomorphous apes.

V.

THE HARA-KIRI.

THE Hara-kiri is a universal custom, for there is no passion in the mind of man so weak but it masters the fear of death. So said Lord Bacon; and he illustrates his text, as also does Burton, in his "Anatomy," with many notable examples of revenge triumphing over death, love slighting it, honor aspiring to it, grief flying to it, fear ignoring it, and even pity, the tenderest of affections, provoking to it. When Otho the Emperor committed suicide, many, out of sheer compassion that such a sovereign should have renounced life, killed themselves. Indeed it requires no strong passion to take the terrors out of death, for we know how frequently suicides have left behind them, as the only reason for their act, that they were "tired of life," weary, perhaps, of an existence monotonous with poverty or sickness, or even simply borne down by the mere tedious repetition of uneventful days. In spite, however, of the multitude of examples which past history and the records of our own every-day life afford, that death wears for many of all classes and both sexes a by no means fearful aspect, the human mind recoils from the prospect of digging, as it were, one's own grave, and shudders at the thought of being the executioner of one's own body.

Apologists have, however, been found for suicide, not

only in antiquity, but in modern days; some, like Dr. Donne, claiming for the act the same degrees of culpability that the law attaches to homicide, others founding their pleas on the ground that Holy Writ nowhere condemns the crime, and one profanely arguing that his life is a man's own to do with as he will. Goethe may be called an apologist for suicide, and so may all those historians or novelists who make their heroes "die nobly" by their own hands; and De Quincey himself seems to have been at one time inclined to excuse under certain circumstances the act of " spontaneous martyrdom."

Pity at first carries away the feelings of the sympathetic, but there are few healthy minds to which, on the second thought, does not come the reflection that suicide is, after all, an insult to human nature, and, for all its pathos, cowardly. There are, indeed, circumstances, such, for instance, as hideous, incurable disease, that tend to soften the public verdict upon the unhappy wretch, who, in taking his own life, had otherwise committed a crime against humanity, and played a traitor's part to all that is most noble in man. But these, as actually resulting in suicide, are very exceptional and infrequent. In most cases life is thrown away impatiently and peevishly, a sudden impulse of remo se or grief nerving the victim to forget how grand life really is, with its earnest aims and hearty work, and how bright it is with its every-day home affections and its cheerful hopes of better things and better times. Our courts of law generalize such impulses under the term " temporary insanity," and the world accepts the term as a satisfactory one, for it is not human to believe that a sane person would under any circumstances throw up life. Races, our own notably, conspicuous wherever found in the earth for their active, hearty, healthful pursuit of work or pleasure, refuse to believe that any but the mad, whether permanently or for the time only, would wilfully cut short their life's interests, and exchange sunlight and manly labor, all the ups and downs that make men brave and hopeful, for the gloomy ignominy of a premature grave. "Above all," says Lord Bacon, "believe it, the sweetest canticle is 'Nunc Dimittis, when a man hath obtained worthy ends and expectations;'" but death in the prime of life, "Finis" written before half the pages of the book had been turned, must always present itself to the courageous, cheerful mind as the most terrible of catastrophes.

In its most terrible form, the Hara-kiri is of course a Japanese evil; but suicide, alas! is not peculiar to any one country or people. In the manner in which they view it, nations differ, — the Hindoo, for instance, contemplates it with apathy, the savage of the Congo with pride, the Japanese with a stern sense of a grave duty, the Englishman with horror and pity, — but the crime has its roots in all soils alike, and flourishes under all skies. But that really grand system of legalized self-murder which was for ages the privilege of all who felt wounded in their honor, gives the Japanese a horrible pre-eminence in the Hara-kiri, and crime though we call it, there was much to admire in the stately heroism of those orderly suicides, notable for their fine appreciation of the dignity of Death, their reverent courtesy to his awful terrors, and sublime scorn for pain of body. From their infancy they looked forward to suicide as a terrible probability, the great event for which through the intervening years they had to prepare themselves. They learned by heart all the nice etiquette of the Hara-kiri: how they must do this, not that, stab themselves from left to right, and not from right to left. Strangely fascinating, indeed, are the "Tales of Old Japan," and among them most terrible is the account of "the honorable institution of the Hara-kiri." I will try to describe it, keeping as well as I can the tone of Japanese thought: —

In the days of Ashikaga the Shiogun, when Japan was vexed by a civil war, and prisoners of high rank were every day being put to shameful deaths, was instituted the ceremonious and honorable mode of suicide by disembowelling, known as Seppuku or Hara-kiri, an institution for which, as the old Japanese historian says, "men in all truth should be very grateful. To put his enemy, against whom he has cause for enmity, to death, and then to disembowel himself, is the duty of every Samurai."

Are you a Daimio or a Hatamoto, or one of the higher retainers of the Shiogun, it is your proud privilege to commit suicide within the precincts of the palace. If you are of an inferior rank, you may do it in the palace garden. Everything has been made ready for you. The white-wanded enclosure is marked out; the curtain is stretched; the white cloth, with the soft crimson mats piled on it, is spread; the long wooden candlesticks hold lighted tapers; the paper lanterns throw a faint light around. Behind yon paper screen lies hidden the tray with the fatal knife, the bucket to hold your head, the incense-burner to conceal the raw smell of blood, and the basin of warm water to cleanse the spot. With tender care has been spread the matting on which you will walk to the spot, so that you need not wear your sandals. Some men when on their way to disembowel themselves suffer from nervousness, so that the sandals are liable to catch in the matting and trip them up. This would not look well in a brave man, so the matting is smoothly stretched. Indeed it is almost a pleasure to walk on it.

Your friends have come in by the gate Umbammon, "the door of the warm basin," and are waiting in their hempen dresses of ceremony to assist you to die like a man. You must die as quickly too as possible, and your friends will be at your elbow to see that you do not disgrace yourself and them by fumbling with the knife, or stabbing yourself with too feeble a thrust. They have made sure that no such mishap shall befall. They will be tenderly compassionate, but terribly stern. They will guard you while your dying declaration is being read; if you are fainting, they will support you, lest your enemies should say you were afraid of death. But do not trust to your old friendship with those around you; do not try to break away from the sound of those clearly spoken sentences; for if you do, your friends will knock you down, and while you are grovelling on the mats, will hew your head off with their heavy-handled swords. They will hold you down and stab you to death. Remember this,— *you are to die, but you will not be allowed to disgrace yourself.*

You are here an honored guest. The preparations for your death are worthy of a Mikado. But you must not presume upon the courtesy shown you. It is merely one half of a contract, the other being that you shall die like a Samurai. If you shirk your share of the contract, your friends will break theirs, and will strike you to the earth like the coward you are.

See, the tapers are lit! Are you quite ready to die? Then take your way along that spotless carpet. It will lead you to the " door of the practice of virtue." Yours is the place of honor on the piled rugs — in the centre of your friends. How keenly they fix their eyes upon you. It is their duty to see that you are dead before those tapers are out. Those tapers cannot last another fifteen minutes. Be seated. Here is your old schoolmate, Kotsuké, coming to you with the dreadful tray. How sternly his lips are closed! You must not speak to him. Stretch out your hand to the glittering knife. Behind you, your relatives are baring their strong arms. You cannot see them, but they are there, and their heavy-handled swords are poised above you. Stretch out your hand. Why hesitate? You *must* take the knife. Have you it firmly in your grasp? Then strike! Deep to the handle, let the keen blade sink — wait a minute with the knife in the wound that all your friends assembled in the theatre before you may see it is really there — now draw it across your body to the right side — turn the broad blade in the wound, and now trail it slowly upwards.

Are you sickening with pain? ah! your head droops forward, a groan is struggling through the clenched teeth, when swift upon the bending neck descends the merciful sword of a friend!

A Samurai must not be heard to groan from pain.

How different from the respectful applause that greets the Japanese self-murderer is the first sentiment of healthy aversion that is aroused in English men and women by the news of a suicide. It is true that sometimes, at the first glance, the preceding circumstances compel our scorn or provoke us into only a disdainful commiseration with the victim, but pity is sure to follow. For the Hara-kiri is always pathetic; and if the suicide be a woman, how tenderly the feeling of pity is intensified!

Take such a case, for instance, as that of Mary Aird. Happily married, a loving mother, she yet threw her young life away in a sudden impulse of groundless apprehension for the future.

Mary Aird's letter, in which she announced to her husband her dreadful intention, hardly reads like a suicide's last word to those she loved best; and the miserably inadequate reason she gives for putting an end to her life makes the sad document intensely pathetic. "Do not think hardly of me, Will, when I tell you I am going to throw myself over Westminster Bridge. Look after our two poor little children, Pop and George, and tell Bessie I want her to look after them for you. Cheer up, dear Will; you will get on better without me. There will be one trouble less. God bless you!" Such a letter as that, had that been all, would have gone far to prove what some have asserted, that suicides are not of necessity, and from the fact alone, insane. But there was a saving sentence. The poor woman feared she could never meet her household expenses, because a pitiful debt of six shillings had "thrown out her accounts for the week. Moreover," said she, "troubles are coming." There really were no greater troubles than all mothers look forward to with hope, and back upon with pride. Yet Mary Aird was dismayed for the moment at the thought of them, and seeing before her so easy a path to instant and never-ending rest, carried with her to the grave the infant that would soon have owed her the sweet debt of life.

It is impossible, being human, for any to read the brief story without feeling the tenderest pity for the poor sister, wearied all of a sudden of this working world, fainting under the burden, as she supposed it, of exceptional, insurmountable misfortunes. Had any one met her on the way to death, and, knowing her case, offered her six shillings, she might have perhaps turned back, and been now the happy wife and happy mother that she was. She had her secret, however, hidden deep away in her heart — the secret that, by her own death, she would (as she thought) release those she loved best from many of the troubles of life — the secret that her duty to husband and children, the " poor little children Pop and George," called upon her for the instant sacrifice of her life! In other forms the same unhesitating resignation of life presents itself to us as heroism of a grand type; but in the piteously small scale of the surrounding circumstances, and even the familiarity of the nature of the death, the grandeur of such a sacrifice is lost, and we feel only pity for the unhappy creature thus needlessly exchanging her bright home for the grave. False sentiment tempts men often to magnify the bravery of self-inflicted death, forgetting that the insanity which makes suicide so pitiful robs it also of all that commands admiration. In itself the crime is detestable, not only as high treason against the Creator, inasmuch as, to quote the main argument of the Pagan moralists, we betray at the first summons of danger the life it was given us to guard, but also as profaning the nobility of our nature. Man is born with the strong instinct of living, and, as happy, careless childhood is left behind, serious and tender interests grow round the individual life, each of which makes it a more precious possession, and, by admitting others to share in its troubles and joys, robs the owner of all claim to dispose of it as if it were his own, undivided and intact. In death itself there is nothing for hopeful and helpful men and women, the workers of the world, to be afraid of. Men fear death as children fear to go in the dark, and with as much reason. But this manly disregard of superstitious terrors should not degenerate into the holding of life cheap, nor, under the sudden pressure of unusual circumstances, make us lose sight of that bright star of hope which, if we will only look ahead, shines always over to-morrow.

To some races such hopeful prospects seem impossible, and, in the East, especially, the first summons of the enemy finds the garrison ready to yield. This frequency of suicide, however, and the general indifference to the crime as a crime, are among the surest signs of inferiority. All savage tribes, and even some of the nations of the East, though more advanced in civilization, fly to death as the first resource in trouble. They seek the relief of the grave before having sought any other. But the circumstances of their lives, with religion or superstition teaching them that fate predestines everything, and magnifying the most trivial occurrences into calamities from which there is no appeal, often surround their deaths with incidents so picturesque and quaint that they deceive the judgment, and exalt the paltry suicide into an heroic surrender of life.

Such a one is, perhaps, that student's death up in the cloudy wilderness within Blencathara. He had to leave college to go into a trade that was hateful to him; but rather than live apart from his books, he climbed one morning up to the misty heights, taking with him his

Æschylus, Apollonius, and Cæsar, and having read them till daylight failed, made a last pillow for his head of the three volumes, and took a fatal dose of laudanum. Some again, by the terrible blackness of the clouds that had gathered over life, seem almost excused, as the crime of Jocasta against herself, or the death of Nero; while others — like those of Dr. Brown, who had prognosticated the ruin of England, and was so mortified by the brilliant successes of the Pitt administration that he cut his throat; and the Colonel in Dr. Darwin's "Zoönomia," who blew his brains out because he could not eat muffins without suffering from indigestion — tend to the positively ludicrous. We are thus often betrayed, from one cause or another, into forgetting for the moment that the act of suicide is really only one of impatience with the crosses of life, and a confession of defeat. Immeasurably sad it often is, as in the case of Mary Aird; but in spite of the pathos surrounding the unhappy incident I have selected as typically pathetic, it is better to look at it gravely. We would, of course, far rather see in it only a young mother sacrificing her dearest treasures, life and the love of husband and child, under the delusion that her death was for their benefit; but we are compelled to see in it much more than that. Lurking under the delusion lies the faint-hearted apprehension that to-morrow would be, and must be, just the same as to-day, a fear of the future that underlies every wilful suicide, and is at once the most disastrous and deplorable frame of the human mind. If troubles are ahead, the more need for, the more honor in, a resolute hold on life. Our race does not readily yield to despair, and every suicide among us, even though it be a woman's, takes something therefore from our national character; and, in spite of an unavoidable feeling of sincerest pity for those who reckon death among the boons of nature, we ought to condemn with all our hearts the ignoble abandonment of life by those amongst us who have not the courage to wait and see if to-morrow will not cure to-day.

VI.

MY WIFE'S BIRDS.

A REMINISCENCE.

MY wife once made up her mind that she wanted a bird. She had, she told me, many reasons for wanting one. One was that the landlady's son was apprenticed to a bird-cage maker, and had promised to use all his influence with his employer — who, the landlady told my wife, was a very civil man — to get us a cage cheap. Another reason for having a bird was that the old groundsel man at the corner asked her every day if she would not buy a penn'orth of the weed for her dear little birds, and that she felt an impostor (inasmuch as she had no bird) every time she met the groundsel man.

"But, my dear," said I, "you have *not* got a bird; and if you only tell him so, he will give up annoying you."

"He does not annoy me at all," she replied; "he is a very nice, respectable old man indeed, and I am sure no one could have been angry at his way of asking you to buy his groundsel — and then it was so beautifully fresh!"

"But you don't mean to say you bought any?" I asked in surprise.

"Yes, I did," was the answer; "it was so beautifully fresh — and I did so want to have a bird — and so, whenever I refuse to buy any now, he thinks I am too mean to give my birds a pennyworth of groundsel now and then. It is very cruel to birds to keep them without any green food at all."

I felt at the time that there was something wrong about this line of argument, but could not quite see where to fix the error without going very far back to the beginning (though women, it seems to me, always do this), so I let it pass, not thinking it worth while to point out again that, as she had no bird, the grounsel seller's animadversions and suspicions were without foundation, and therefore absurd.

And then my wife went on to give other reasons for wanting to have a bird; but the only one I can remember just now was to the effect that the bird would not give any trouble to anybody but herself, and that it could not possibly matter to me whether she had a bird or not. I am not quite sure that I have given that reason right, but it is about as near as I generally get to some of my wife's reasons for things.

"It will, you see," she repeated, as she cracked an egg, "be no trouble to anybody but myself. I will look after it myself and —"

"The Lord in His pitiful mercy keep an eye upon that bird!" I piously ejaculated.

"Oh, John! — and of course I will feed it and wash it — its cage, I mean; not *feed* the cage, you know, but wash it: and when I go out to do the housekeeping for ourselves," — which, by the way, always seems to me to consist in meeting friends at the gate and then going off with them to look at new music, — "I will do the bird's housekeeping, too."

Now, I really never had any objection to a bird from

the first. On the contrary, I like birds, — little ones. But my wife has, all through, insisted on it that I do not love "God's creatures," as she calls them, and took from the first a certain complacent pride in having made me more Christian-like in this matter. "You won't hurt it, will you, John?" she pleaded, pathetically, when she hung up a linnet.

"*Hurt* it!" I said, in astonishment, for I am a very Buddhist in my tenderness to animals. "On the contrary —"

"Yes, dear, I know how you hate them; and you are a sweet, good old darling to say you love them, just to please me."

"You are quite mistaken," I began, "in supposing —"

"No, I am not, you good old duck, for you always pretended just in the same way that you liked Lucy (my wife's cousin), though I know you don't, for soon after we were married, I remember you called her a gadabout and a gossip."

And the end of it was that I was mean enough to accept the virtues of self-denial and consideration thus thrust upon me. Consequently, I have had ever since to affect a condescension whenever I take notice of the birds, although when my wife is not there I waste a good deal of time over the pretty things.

But "God's creatures," after all, is a term that you can lump most things under. And if my wife had drawn a distinction between the linnet and her great parrot, more like a vulture than a cage-bird, I would have candidly confessed to a difference in my regard for the two fowls. Linnets are very harmless, I fancy. At any rate, ours never does anything more outrageous than splash its water and seed about of a morning. For the rest of the day it is mostly hopping off the floor on to the perch and back again, except when you go to look at it close. It then hops only sideways off the perch on to the wires of the cage, and back again.

But the parrot! It is dead now — and it took as much burying as a horse — was more of a reptile than a bird, I should say. At any rate, it had very few feathers on it after a bit, and the way it worried my wife's Maltese terrier was most unusual, I fancy, in a bird. The first time it pounced down on Tiny, who was only going to eat some of the parrot's pudding, we thought it was going to eat the dog, though I found, on looking it up since, that parrots never eat other animals, as vultures and other birds do sometimes. But it wasn't. It was only pulling fluff off the dog. But Tiny's fluff grows so fast, and he is so light, that we generally pick him up by it. And so, when the parrot began to pull at it, it rolled the dog all about, and as one of the bird's claws got caught in the fluff of the dog and the other in the fluff of the hearth-rug, they got rolled up in the corner of it, — the terrier and the parrot together; and the noises that proceeded from those two, and the confusion there was of hearth-rug and fluff and feathers, defies all description. Getting them unmixed took us ever so long. We had first of all to give the parrot a spoon to hold in its mouth, and then a fork in one claw, while we undid the other. And as soon as it was undone, it got its claw fixed round my thumb, and then, dropping the spoon, it took hold of my cuff with its beak. And when I had got the bird off me, it got fastened on to my wife; for the thing was so frightened at itself, it wanted something, it didn't matter what, to hold on to. But at last we got it on to the curtains, and there it hung half the morning, saying to itself, as it always does when it's put out, "Polly's very sick; poor Polly's going to die." Tiny, in the mean time, had disappeared into the scullery under the sink, and to the last day of the parrot's life, whenever the dog heard the parrot scream, it used to make for the same spot. And as the parrot was mostly screeching all day, the dog pretty well lived under the sink. But the parrot died at last, poor beast.

The few feathers it had on must have had something to do with it, I fancy. If I were a bird, I know, and had so few feathers, I should die too. It does not seem much worth living with so few on. One could hardly call one's self a bird.

So one evening, when I came home, I found Jenny in tears, and there on the hearth-rug, was the poor old parrot, dead, and about as bald as a bird could be — except in a pie. I asked Jenny how it all happened; but she couldn't speak at first for crying, and when she did tell me, it was heart-breaking to hear her sobs between the words.

"You know," she began, "Polly hasn't been eating enough for a long time, and to-day, when I came in from my housekeeping, I saw him looking very sad about something. So I called him, and he came down off his perch. But he couldn't hop; he was too weak, so he walked quite slowly across the floor to me — and so unsteadily! I knew there was something dreadful going to happen. And when he got to my feet he couldn't climb up my dress as he generally does. And I said to him, 'Polly, what's the matter with you?' and he said" — but here she broke down altogether for a bit

—" and he looked up at me and said, '*Polly's very sick.*' And when I picked him up he was as *light* as — oh! *so* light. And he sat on my lap without moving, only breathing very hard. And then after a little, I saw his head drooping, so I touched him to wake him up. And he started up, and shook himself so hard that he rolled over on his side, and then I heard him saying something to himself, so I put down my head to listen. And he opened his eye again quite wide, and looked at me just as if he knew who I was quite well, and whispered to me, '.poor Polly's going to die.' And then he shut his wings up tight, and stretched out one leg after the other — and — and died."

I was very sorry for it, after he was really dead, for Jenny was very fond of him, and the parrot, I think, was very fond of her. So when I looked round and saw Tiny eating the dead bird's pudding, I gave a screech like the parrot used to give, and the little wretch shot off in a flurry of fluff to the sink, where we let him stay until we had buried poor Polly under the laurel-tree. Jenny proposed to have it stuffed; but considering the proposal of stuffing such a naked bird absurd, I evaded the suggestion, nor did she press it.

But all this time I have been anticipating a great deal. It was the first mention of the parrot that set me off on the digression. I have not yet told you how my wife got her birds, or what birds she has got.

Well, I had given my consent, you remember, to a bird being bought; so immediately after breakfast, my wife went out to choose one — " a little one," she said. But before she went out she confided her want to the landlady, who, going out herself soon after, also interested herself in the selection, and told a few bird-fanciers to send up some birds to look at — little ones; moreover, before going out, she told her son that my wife wanted a bird — a little one — so when he went to the cage-maker's he mentioned the fact, and during the day the cage-maker told about twenty bird-fanciers who came in on business that he could put them in the way of a customer — meaning my wife. "She wants a little bird," he said.

Well, I woke next morning a little earlier than usual, and with a vague general feeling that I was somewhere in the country — probably at my uncle's. All the air, outside seemed to be full of twittering, just as I remembered hearing in the early mornings at my uncle's place in the country where sparrows were as thick as the leaves in the ivy on the house, and the robins and wrens, and those kinds of birds, used to swarm in the shrubbery. My wife was awake too, and as soon as she found me stirring she began (as she does on most mornings) to tell me a dream. I always find that other people's dreams haven't, as a rule, much plot in them, and so they don't tell well. Things always seem to come about and end up somehow without much reason.

And what my wife's dream was about I did not exactly understand at the time, but it was about the Tropical Court at the Crystal Palace. She dreamt that it was on fire, and all the parrots had gone mad with fright and were flying about, and so she ran down to the station, with all the creatures after her; but there was no room for her in the train, as all the parrots, and lovebirds, and lories, and paroquets, and cockatoos, and macaws of the Palace were scrambling for places, and there was such a noise and flurrying of feathers she was quite bewildered; and though she told the guard that the birds were travelling without tickets, he only called out "all right," to the engine driver, and the train started off. But this frightened all the birds so that they came streaming out through the windows and lampholes, and flew about the station till it looked as if all the colors out of the advertisements had got loose and were flying around in strips and patches! And so she ran upstairs to the omnibus, but all the cockatoos and things went with her, and it was just the same here, for when she was going to get in, the conductor said it was full inside, though, when she looked at the window she couldn't see a soul, but when she opened the door and looked in she found it was full of parrots and macaws; and though she warned the conductor that none of the birds had got any money, he did not seem to take any notice of her, and only sounded his bell, and so the 'bus started. But this frightened the birds again, so that they all came streaming out through the door, and flew up the street with her to the cab-stand; and there it was just the same — and everywhere all day it was just the same; but though she kept trying to explain to people, in an exasperated and, she felt, unsatisfactory way, that it was absurd and unreasonable for all these birds, which she had nothing to do with, to be following her about so, no one took any adequate interest in the matter, or seemed to think it at all irregular or annoying. Her conversations on the subject with policemen were equally inconclusive and absurd; and so the day went on — and very exhausting it was, she said, with the eternal clamor of the birds, and the smothering feeling of having a cloud of feathery things fluttering round you, and so —

I had been listening all this time after only a very

drowsy fashion, but while she talked there stole over me an impression that there was a strange confusion of bird voices about the premises, and just as she had got to the words "and so," and was taking breath to remember what happened next in her dream, there came from down below a very babel of fowls' languages. In every tongue spoken by birds from China to Peru, we heard screams, squeaks, hootings, and crowings, while behind and through all we were aware of a multitudinous chattering, twittering and chirping, accompanied by a sober obligato of cooing. I stared at my wife and she at me. Was I asleep?

Pinching is a good thing, I remembered, so I pinched my wife. There was no doubt of *her* being awake. I told her apologetically that I had pinched her in order to see if I was awake, and she was beginning to explain to me that I ought to have pinched *myself;* when we heard a knock at the door. "If you please, sir" (it was Mary), "but has a cockytoo gone into your dressing-room? It's got away from the birdman, — which, sir, if you please there's several of them at the door!"

. . . .

All the time I was dressing the vulcrine clamor continued unabated, and when I came downstairs I was not surprised at the sight that awaited me. The passage was filled with bird-cages; and through the front door, which was open, I saw that the front "garden" was filled also, and that round the railings had collected a considerable mob of children, whitewashers' assistants, and errand-boys. I went to the dining-room window and looked out. My appearance was the signal for every bird-man to seize at once two cages and hold them up for inspection. The contents of the cages screamed wildly; all their friends on the ground screamed in sympathy, and the mob outside cheered the birds on to further demonstrations, by ill-naturedly imitating various cries.

I kept away from the window, therefore, and waited till my wife came down. Her delight at the exhibition seemed to me a little misplaced, the more so as she insisted on holding a levee at once. I began my breakfast therefore alone, but I hope I may never have such a meal again. Every other bird, being warranted tame, was allowed to leave its cage, and very soon there was a parrot in the sugar basin, three macaws on the chandeliers, and a cockatoo on the back of each chair. The food on the table attracted a jackdaw, who dragged a rasher of bacon into the jelly-glass before his designs were suspected, and one wretched bird finding me out under the table, climbed up the leg of my trousers by his beak and claws. But my wife got bewildered at last, and appealed to me to settle matters. I did so summarily by explaining that my wife wanted only *one* bird, and that *a little one*,—" a linnet or something of that kind."

The disgust of the bird fanciers was instantly visible, and every man proceeded gloomily to repossess himself of his property. This was not so easy, however, as letting the birds go, and entailed an hour's hunting of parrots from corner to corner. Two cockatoos slipped down behind the sideboard and proceeded to fight there. They were only got out after moving the sideboard (the contents being previously taken out), and when they appeared were dirty beyond recognition and covered with cobwebs and fluff. But we found a long-missing salt spoon. At last, however, all seemed satisfactorily disposed of, when it was discovered that one of the cages was still empty, and a pensive voice from the chandelier drew all eyes upward. It was then discovered that a parrot had got its body inside one of the globes, and I volunteered to release it. So standing up on a chair, I took hold of the protruding tail and lifted the bird out. No sooner, however, did it find itself released than it made one violent effort to escape, and succeeded, leaving the tail in my hands!

I hastened to apologize and to offer the owner the tail, but the man would not accept either the apology or the feathers. On the contrary, he insisted that as I had spoiled the bird for sale I ought now to buy it.

And thus it was that we became possessed of the bird whose death I have already narrated. At first it had a dog's life of it. I was very angry with it for foisting itself upon me; my wife disliked it for its tailless condition; while the parrot itself suspected both of us as having designs upon its remaining feathers. But my wife's heart warmed to it at last, and the bird reciprocated the attachment. And when it died we were really sorry, and so, I think, was the parrot.

Meanwhile my wife was not satisfied with the purchase, and proceeded to select another bird for herself. The result was a canary, as I feared; and lest the canary should be dull with only the parrot, a bullfinch was also bought; and finally, for no better reason that I saw than that "it would be just as easy to attend to three birds as to two," a linnet. Of course the canary proved to be a hen bird, and the linnet, I still believe, is a sparrow. But of the bullfinch there can be no doubt. He looks a bullfinch all over.

The bullfinch had only just been caught. I thought this a point against the bird. But my wife thought it all in its favor. "For now," she said, "we can train it exactly as we like."

Meanwhile the bird, being quite uneducated, was dashing about in its cage, and little feathers came floating down, and all the cage furniture was in a heap in the corner. There was evidently a very clear field for instruction, and my wife was eager to begin at once.

"Bullfinches are very fond of hemp seeds," said she oracularly, and proceeded to offer one to the bird. The result was eminently discouraging, for the terrified creature went into fits. For a time my wife was very patient, and stood there with the slippery little seed between her fingers. The bird, exhausted at last with its frantic efforts at escape, was on the floor of the cage, panting from fear and fatigue.

"I am sure he will get quite tame," said my wife, inspirited by this cessation of the bird's struggles. "Pretty Bully;" and she changed the seed to the left hand, for the other was tired. The motion was sufficient, however, to set the bird off in another paroxysm of fluttering, to which in the same way succeeded another relapse. And so it went on for half an hour, this contest between the wild thing's terror and the woman's patience. And the bird won the day.

"You are a very stupid little bird," said my wife solemnly and emphatically to the open-beaked creature, as she withdrew from the strife to make acquaintance with the canary.

The canary was of another sort altogether, an old hen bird, born and bred in captivity, an artificial person without a scrap of soul.

Nor did its vocal accomplishments recommend it; for being a hen it only chirped, and being very old, it did this drearily. My wife resolved, therefore, to change it. She was offered ninepence for it, and indignantly refused the sum. Finally, she allowed it to go, with seven and sixpence added, in exchange for a young cock bird.

The linnet meanwhile had moulted, and as its new feathers were a long time coming, it came to be looked upon as a shabby creature and the inferior among our pets. It did not resent the invidious comparison nor retaliate for the evident preference shown to the rest, but sitting on its perch at the back window, chuckled good-naturedly to itself all day long, going to sleep early, and growing prodigiously plump.

The bullfinch and canary, however, became soon part of our lives, and every new habit or prettiness was noted and cherished. Both were easily tamed. A friend came in one day, and, going to speak to the bullfinch, was shocked at its wildness.

"Why don't you tame it?" he asked.

"How?" inquired my wife. "I have been trying hard, but I don't think they will ever begin to care for me."

"Oh! starve them," was the reply.

"*Starve* them! never!" said my wife firmly.

But I made a note of the advice, and that very afternoon, as soon as my wife had left the luncheon table, I nearly emptied the seed-boxes into the fire. Next morning my wife noticed, without suspecting anything, how completely the birds had eaten up their allowances. I was of course absorbed in my newspaper. But when my wife went out to do her housekeeping, I took the liberty of turning round the seed-boxes, so that the birds, who meanwhile had been eating voraciously, could get no more. The barbarous fact escaped observation, and, remorse gnawing at my heart, I awaited the morrow with anxiety. Would the birds be tame? But the thought kept recurring to me in the night watches — *would they be dead?* They were not dead, however: on the contrary, they were very much alive. Indeed their extraordinary sprightliness attracted my wife's attention, and all through breakfast she kept drawing my attention to the conversation being kept up by the two birds.

"How happy they are together!" she said. "And how hungry!" I thought.

Breakfast over, she proceeded to attend to her birds, and then the turned boxes were discovered.

"Oh!" she said, "how stupid I have been! Just imagine, these poor birds have had no seed all day! I forgot to turn their seed-boxes round!"

I cut short her self-reproaches and expressions of sympathy.

"Never mind, dear: it has done them no harm apparently. Besides, we can see now whether starving does really tame them. Offer the bullfinch a hemp seed in your fingers."

And the great experiment was tried. I approached to watch. The hungry bird recognized his favorite morsel, but the fingers had still terrors for his untutored mind. "Have a little patience," I said, as I saw my wife's face clouding. The bullfinch mind was grievously agitated. He was very hungry, and there close to him was a hemp seed. But then it was in those dangerous-looking hands. An empty stomach and timid heart fought out the point between them, but the engagement was obstinately contested. The issue trembled a thousand times in the balance. The bullfinch, after sitting for ten minutes with his head very much on one side, would sidle up to the hemp seed and seem on the very point of taking it, when a movement of the dog on the hearth-rug, or the opening of a door, would startle it into its original alarm. My wife held out bravely, and her patience was suddenly and unexpectedly rewarded. The bullfinch had evidently thought the matter out to the end, and had decided that death by starvation was preferable to tempting the terrors of the pretty fingers that offered him food. He was sitting gloomily at the farther end of the perch. But, on a sudden — perhaps it was a twinge inside — he brightened up, pulled himself together, and with a desperate effort pecked at the seed. He did not get it, but the effort had broken the spell, and he soon returned emboldened, and taking more deliberate aim this time, extracted the prize. After this it was plain sailing, and for the rest of the morning, my wife was busy feeding the domesticated bullfinch from her fingers. Meanwhile, the canary had taken its first lesson, and whether it was that hunger was more overpowering, or that (as has since proved the case) it took the bullfinch for its model, it ate from the hand as if to the manner born. The success was complete, and my wife set apart to-morrow for another starvation preparatory to further instruction. But her heart was too soft, and to this day the birds have never been stinted again. Their education, therefore, began and ended together. But I cannot say that I am sorry; for I can think of no accomplishment that would make them more charming company. The cage doors are always open, and the small creatures spend their day as they choose, the bullfinch climbing about among the picture cords, the canary gazing upon his own reflection in the mirror.

Their characters have developed in this freedom, and their individuality is as comic as it is well defined. The bullfinch, sturdy of body, bull-necked, and thick-legged, ranges the room as if all it contained was his own by right of conquest. There is not an article in it which he does not make use of as a perch or plaything. and in every gesture shows himself at home and in possession. As soon as the loaf is put down on the table, he hops on to it, and when my wife replaces the milk-jug, he perches upon that. From there to the nearest tea-cup is only a short hop, and so he makes the round of the breakfast table. When the cloth is removed, he waits, chirping impatiently for his groundsel, and even before it can be arranged for him, he is in the thick of it, his beak stuffed with the flossy flower-heads. The bath, meanwhile, is being prepared, and no sooner is it down on the ground than he perches on the edge, tests its temperature, and pronounces his approval — but does not often bathe. His seed-box has meanwhile been replenished, and in it every morning are put a few hemp seeds. No sooner is it in the cage, than the bullfinch has gone in, and plunging his head down into the seed, is busy picking out the favorite grains. Lest one should be concealed at the bottom, he jerks out as much of the contents as he can, and deliberately empties the remainder by beakfuls. Satisfied that no hemp seed remains, he comes out, and flying to the nearest picture, commences the gymnastics that occupy the greater part of the day. By sunset he is always back in his cage again, and when my wife goes to shut his door, he opens his beak at her threateningly, showing a ridiculous pink throat, and hissing like a miniature goose. This is not the routine of any particular day, but of every day, and so completely has he asserted his position as one of the family, that the ornaments are arranged in reference to his tastes, and when I talked of removing the picture from over the door, the project was at once thrown aside, "for that is Bully's favorite perch."

The canary is a curious contrast. He has as much spirit as the bullfinch, for he resented the first attempt at oppression — it was a question of priority of bathing — with such *élan*, that the bullfinch ceased from troubling, and the two are close friends on the honorable terms of mutual respect. But the canary is conciliatory and retiring. He comes on the breakfast table when it takes his fancy to do so, but he does so unobtrusively, with all the ease of manner that betokens confidence, and yet with all the reserve and modesty of a gentleman. If he wishes for a crumb he takes it, but instead of hopping on the loaf for it, he reaches it off the platter from the table. His day is spent before a looking-glass, in which he studies his own features and gestures, not unhappily, but quietly, as his way is. A jar that holds spills is his usual resort, and, perched on it, he exercises himself in the harmless practice of pulling out the spills. He has never succeeded, but this does not damp his industry. For groundsel he has as great a partiality as the bullfinch, but he waits for his share till it is put in his cage, and then only goes in at his leisure. The bath is a passion with him, and his energy in the water fills the bullfinch — who more often makes believe than really bathes — with such amazement, that while the flurry and splash is going on he watches the canary with all his eyes. The canary sings beautifully, not with the student note that in the trained bird makes a room uninhabitable, but a soft, untutored song that nature whispered to him bar by bar, and so sweet is it that the matter-of-fact bullfinch always listens with attention, until, remembering his own powers, he settles down in a ball of feathers on some favorite vase, and chuckles obstinately through a rustic lay. But my wife ought to have written the account of her own birds herself, for she knows them better than I.

And the little things have found out how gentle and loving she is to God's creatures; and when the room is quiet, and she is sitting working, the bullfinch will leave off his scrambling among the picture cords, and the canary his fruitless tugging at the spills, to sit down on her lap and shoulder, and tell her, as they best can, how fond they are of her.

For me they entertain only a distant regard; but I like them immensely for all that. At any rate, though I speak of them as my wife's birds, I should feel hurt if any one thought that they were not *my* birds too.

VII.

THE LEGEND OF THE BLAMELESS PRIEST.[1]

YEARS upon years ago, when all the world was young, when Atlantis was among the chief islands of it, and the Aryans had not yet descended from their cradle on the roof of the world, there wandered up past the sources of the sleepy Nile the patriarch Kintu and his wife. For many months he travelled, he and his old wife, their one she-goat, and one cow, and carrying with them one banana and one sweet potato. And they were alone in their journey.

From out the leagues of papyrus fen the ibis and the flamingo screamed, and through the matete-canes the startled crocodile plunged under the lily-covered waves. Overhead circled and piped vast flocks of strange waterfowl, puzzled by the sight of human beings, and from the path before them the sulky lion hardly turned away. The hyenas in the rattan brakes snarled to see them pass, and wailing through the forests, that covered the face of the land, came the cry of the lonely lemur. A dreary, desolate country, rich in flowers and fruit, and surpassingly beautiful, but desolate of man.

The elephant was the noblest in the land, and on the water there was none to stand before the river-horse.

---

[1] This legend is founded upon the notes taken in Uganda by Mr. H. M. Stanley for his book "Across the Dark Continent," which it fell to my pleasant lot to edit.—P. R.

And so they plodded on, old Kintu and his wife, until, coming to where the Victoria Nyanza spreads its summer sea through four degrees of latitude, flecked with floating groves, " purple isles of Eden," the patriarch halted, and, the first time for many years, laid down his staff upon the ground. And the mark of the staff may still be seen, eight cubits in length, lying like a deep scar across the basalt boulders piled up on the western shore of the great lake. And then his wife laid down her burden, the one banana and the one potato; and the goat and the cow lay down, for they were all weary with the journey of half a century, during which they had never rested night nor day. And the name they gave the land they stayed at was Uganda, but the name of the land they came from no one knows.

And then Kintu cut the banana and potato into many little pieces, and planted them, each piece twenty miles apart, and they grew so fast that the plant seemed to the eye to be crawling over the ground. And his wife had many sons and daughters, and they were all born adult, and intermarried, so that in a few years all the country was filled with people. The cow and the goat also brought forth adult offspring, and these multiplied so fast that in the second generation every man in the land had a thousand head of cattle. And Kintu was their king, and his people called him the Blameless Priest; for he wronged no one. In his land no blood was ever shed, for he had forbidden his people to eat meat, and when any sinned they were led away by their friends, the man with a woman, for a thousand miles, and left there with cuttings of the banana and the potato; for they never led any one away alone, lest he should die; and once every year, after the gathering of the harvest, Kintu sent messengers to the exiles to know how they did. So the land was at peace from morning to night, and there was plenty in every house. And the patriarch moved about among his people in spotless robes of white, and loved and honored by all as their father.

But after a long time the young men and women grew wicked, for they found out the secret of making wine from the banana and strong drink from the palm fruit and fire-water from the mtama grain; and with this they got drunk together, and when they were drunk they forgot that they were Kintu's children. And first of all they began to dress in bright colors, and then they killed the cattle for food, until at last Kintu was the only man in all his kingdom who was dressed in spotless white, and who had never shed blood. And the wickedness increased; for, having killed animals, they began to fight among themselves, and at last one day a man of Uganda, having got drunk with palm wine, killed one of his tribe with a spear. And the people rose up with a cry, and every man took his spear in his hand, and the whole land of Uganda was in an uproar, the people killing one another. But when it was all over, and the morning came, they saw the dead men lying about among the melon plants, and were frightened, for they had never seen dead men before, and did not know what to do with them; and then they looked about for the patriarch, whom all this while they had forgotten; and lo! he was gone.

And no one would tell them whither.

Till at last a little girl child spoke up: "I saw Kintu and his wife go out of the gate in the early morning, and with them they took a cow and a goat, a banana and a potato; and Kintu said, 'This land is black with blood.' I ran after them, and with me was only my little brother Pokino, and he and I watched Kintu and his wife go away down by the wood to the river that comes from the west."

The children had been the last to see Kintu; for though every one was asked, no one had seen the Blameless Priest go forth except the little ones, Saramba, with the round eyes, and her baby brother Pokino.

Then the people were in great consternation, and ran hither and thither, looking for the patriarch; but he was never found. And when the tumult of the first lamentation was over, Chwa, the eldest son of Kintu, took his shield and spear, and going out into the market-place, shook his spear before the assembled chiefs, and struck his spear upon his shield to show that he was king. And he made all the nation into castes, and to two castes he gave the duty of finding Kintu. Far and near they sought him, crossing strange rivers and subduing many tribes; but the lost patriarch was never seen. And when Chwa was dead, his son shook his spear before the people, and searched for Kintu all his life, and died without finding him. And thirty-eight kings ruled in succession over Uganda, but never again did human eye behold the man they sought.

. . . . . .

Then Ma'anda came to the throne. He was different from all the kings that had preceded him, for he robed himself in white, and no blood might be shed within a mile's distance of his palace, and no man who had killed an animal might come within a spear's throw of his person. He was kind to all, to animals and to men alike, and they called him in Uganda the Good Father. He had given up the search for Kintu, for he knew it was hopeless; but once a year he called all the chiefs together, and warned them that until they gave up fighting among themselves and warring with other tribes, they could never hope to see the Blameless Priest again.

Now one day Ma'anda dreamed strangely, and, rising before dawn, went to his mother and said: "I dreamt in the night that a peasant came to me from the forest and told me something that filled me with joy, but what it was I cannot remember."

She asked, "When did the peasant come?"

He answered, "Just as the hyena was crying for the third time."

She said, "But that is not yet."

And lo! as she spoke, from the mtama crop the hyena cried for the third time, — for the day was breaking, — and Ma'anda's mother said, "Get ready quickly, and take your spear, for I can hear the peasant coming, and he has strange news to tell you, my son." Ma'anda could hear nothing; yet he went away to get ready to receive the messenger. But at the door he met the Katekiro, the chief officer of his household, who said, "There is a madman without, who says he has news for the king. He is only a peasant, but will not go away, for he says that the king must hear his news."

"Let him come in," said the king. And the peasant entered.

"What is it?" asked Ma'anda.

"I may not tell any one but the king and the king's mother: which are they?"

So the king took the peasant into his mother's house, and having carefully seen that no one was listening, the peasant told his tale.

"I went last night to cut wood in the forest, and, being overtaken by the darkness, lay down to sleep by my wood. And in my sleep a person came to me and said, 'Follow me,' and I took up my bill-hook and went with him. And we came to an open space in the forest, and in the open space I saw an old man sitting, and beside him, on either hand, stood a number of old men, all with spears in their hands, and they seemed to have just come from a long march. And though it was dark in the forest, it was quite light where the old men were; and the old man who was sitting said to me, 'Go to Ma'anda, the king, and tell him to come to me with his mother. But let him take care that no one else, not even his dog, follows him. For I have that to tell him which will make him glad, and that to show him that no king of Uganda has yet been able to find.' So I laid down my bill-hook and my head-cloth where I was standing, and I turned and ran swiftly from fear, and I did not stop till I reached the palace. Oh, great king, live forever."

"Show the way," replied Ma'anda, "and we will follow."

So they stole out, those three, — the peasant, the king and his mother, — and, thinking they were unperceived, crept away from the palace through the fence of the matete, before the sun rose and the people were up. But the Katekiro had watched them, and seeing the king go out with only the peasant and his mother, said to himself, "There is some treachery here. I will follow the king, so that no harm may befall him."

And they all went fast through the forest together, and though the king kept turning round to see if any one was following, the Katekiro managed to keep always out of sight, for the king's eyes were dim with age. And at last Ma'anda was satisfied that no one was behind them, and hurried on without looking back. And at evening they came to the spot, and the peasant was afraid to go on. But he pointed before him, and the king, looking, saw a pale light through the trees, and between the trees he thought he saw the figures of men robed in white, moving to and fro. And he advanced slowly towards the light, and as he got nearer it increased in brightness, and then on a sudden he found himself in the glade, and there before him sat the old man surrounded by his aged warriors, and at his feet lay the wood-cutter's bill-hook and head-cloth. Ma'anda stood astonished at the sight, and held his spear fast; but a voice came to his ears, so gentle and so soft that his doubts all vanished, and he came forward boldly.

"Who art thou?" asked the old man.

"I am Ma'anda, the king."

"Who was the first king of Uganda?"

"Kintu."

"Then come nearer, for I have something to tell thee; but why didst thou let any one come with thee except the peasant and thy mother?"

"No one is with me," replied Ma'anda; "I kept looking behind me as I came, and I am sure that no one followed us."

"Well, then, come here and look me in the face. I have something to tell thee from Kintu, and thou shalt thyself see Kintu to-day; but first — why didst thou let any man follow thee?"

And Ma'anda, who was impatient, answered quickly: "No one followed me."

"But a man *did* follow thee," replied the old man, "and there he stands!" pointing with his finger to the Katekiro, whose curiosity had drawn him forth from his hiding. Seeing himself discovered, he stepped forward to the side of the king.

Then Ma'anda's wrath overwhelmed him, and for the first time in his life he raised his hand to strike. And his spear pierced the Katekiro to the heart, who fell with a cry at his feet. At the horror of his deed and his own blood-splashed robe, Ma'anda sprang back, and for an instant covered his face with his hands in an agony of sorrow.

And when he opened his eyes again the forest was all dark, and the old man and his chiefs had vanished!

Nor from that day to this has any one in Uganda seen the Blameless Priest.

OPINIONS OF THE LONDON PRESS

ON THE WRITINGS OF THE

"NEW ENGLISH HUMORIST."

———◆———

"These delightful papers . . . quaint humor and remarkable literary skill and taste. Old Izaac Walton would have enjoyed them immensely; so would White of Selborne, and even Addison would have admired them. . . . A sympathetic power of entering into their life and hitting it off in a happy and humorous manner, with the aid of much literary culture. . . . In reading his loving diatribes against his furred and feathered acquaintances, one cannot help remembering that India has always been the home of the Beast Story. But since the Sanskrit Hito padesa was put together, we question whether any writer has given us such pictures of the floating population of lotus-covered tanks, and the domestic life that goes on in the great Indian trees. To Mr. Robinson, every pipal or mango tree is a many-storied house: each branch is full of vitality and intrigue, as an *étage* of a Parisian mansion. Snakes and toads live in a small way on the ground floor, until the arrival of the mongoose with his writ of ejectment; lizards lead a rackety, bachelor existence in the *entresol;* prosperous parrots occupy suites *en première;* cats and gray squirrels are for ever skipping up or down stairs. The higher stories are the modest abodes of the small artistic world: vocalist bulbuls and dramatic mainas rehearsing their parts. The garrets and topmost perches are peopled with poor predatory kites or vultures; from whom the light-fingered and more deeply criminal crow pilfers, not without a chuckle, their clumsily stolen supper. . . . Mr. Robinson is the Columbus of the banyan-tree. He sails away into its recesses and discovers new worlds. . . . Mr. Robinson has only to do justice to his artistic perceptions, and to his fine vein of humor in order to create for himself a unique place among the essayists of our day." — *The Academy.*

"These charming little word-pictures of Indian life and Indian scenery are, so it appears to us, something more than an unusually bright page in Anglo-Indian literature . . . as much humor as human sympathy. . . . The book abounds in delightful passages; let the reader, who will trust us, find them for himself. . . . Mr. Edwin Arnold, who has introduced this little volume to English readers by a highly-appreciative preface, says truly that from these slight sketches a most vivid impression of every-day Indian life may be gathered. . . . The chief merit of these Indian sketches lies in their truthfulness; their realism is the secret of their vivid poetic life." — *The Examiner.*

"One of the most charming little series of sketches we have ever read. If we could imagine a kind of cross between White of Selborne and the American writer Thoreau, we should be able better to define what manner of author Mr. Phil Robinson is. He is clearly a masterly observer of out-door life in India, and not only records faithfully what he sees, but illuminates the record by flashes of gentle culture such as can only come from a well-stored and scholarly mind, and darts, moreover, sunny rays of humor such as can only proceed from a richly endowed and truly sympathetic nature. All living things he loves, and hence he writes about them reverently and lovingly. What the accomplished author of the preface calls 'the light and laughing science' of this little book will do more to familiarize the English reader with the out-door look of India than anything else, — save, of course, years of residence in the country." — *The Daily Telegraph.*

Press Notices.

"One of the most delightful and fascinating little books with which we have met for a long time. It is a rare pleasure to come across anything so fresh and brilliant. . . . A literary treat is presented in this most clever and striking little volume. We can fancy with what a thorough sense of enjoyment poor Mortimer Collins would have turned over these pages, and how Mr. Robinson's graphic sketches of the ways of birds and the growth of trees would have appealed to Charles Kingsley. It is certainly a striking illustration of the old story, 'Eyes and No Eyes.' His style is particularly happy, and there is a freshness of tone about his whole book which raises it far above the ordinary level. . . . It has been reserved for Mr. Robinson to open this new field of literature to English readers; and we hope that his venture may meet with the success which it deserves, so that the present volume may prove but the first of a long and delightful series. . . ."— *John Bull.*

"This is a charming volume. . . . In his style we are reminded frequently of Charles Lamb. . . . The book has an antique flavor, like the quaint style of Elia; and, like Lamb, Mr. Robinson has evidently made an affectionate acquaintance with some of our early humorists. That he is himself a humorist, and looks at Indian life with a mirthfulness sometimes closely allied to pathos, is the characteristic which is likely first to strike the reader. But he will observe, too, that if Mr. Robinson describes birds, flowers, trees, and insects with the pen of the humorist rather than of the naturalist, it is not because he has failed to note the common objects in his Indian garden with the patient observation of a man of science. The attraction of a book like this will be more easily felt than described; and, just as there are persons unable to enjoy the fragrance of certain flowers or the taste of certain choice wines, it is possible Mr. Robinson's brightly-written pages may not prove universally attractive. Readers who enjoy them at all will enjoy them thoroughly. . . . It would be impossible to convey the full flavor of this distinctly marked volume without extracting freely from its pages. The sketches are so full of freshness and vivacity that the reader, sitting under an English roof, will be able for the moment to see what the writer saw, and to feel what he felt."— *The Pall Mall Gazette.*

"This book is simply charming. . . . A perfect mine of entertaining and unique information. . . . An exquisite literary style, supplementing rare powers of observation; moreover, the resources of a cultivated intellect are brought into play as well as those of a delicate and fertile fancy. The distinguishing characteristic of these charming trifles is perhaps leisureliness, yet something of the quaint grace of our olden writers clings to Mr. Robinson's periods. . . . Mr. Robinson, in short, is one of those few authors who have found their precise *métier*, and can therefore write so as to entrance his readers."— *The Whitehall Review.*

"A delightful little book is 'My Indian Garden,' in which an Anglo-Indian sketches, with a delicacy, grace, and humor that are unflagging and irresistible, some aspects of outdoor life in India which have hitherto, for the most part, escaped the observation of writers on that wonderful land. . . . As an observer of natural history, he is scarcely inferior to Gilbert White, while he has a capacity for recognizing and bringing out the ludicrous aspect of a subject that was denied to the dear old recluse of Selborne, and the literary charm of the book will be apparent to all. Mr. Robinson quaintly mingles shrewd observation of the manners and customs of the creatures he portrays with quizzical and metaphysical speculation. It has been said that Mark Twain's 'New Pilgrim's Progress,' with all its drollery, is about the best and most informatory tourist's hand-book for the Holy Land in existence. Just in the same way Mr. Robinson's 'Noah's Ark' is the best possible companion for a visitor to the London Zoölogical Gardens. Our author has an unerring eye for the ludicrous aspect of things; he pokes fun remorselessly at all animated nature, from the elephant to the mosquito; but amid the play of his humor there are many touches of real pathos, snatches of powerful description, and a great deal of solid information. . . ."— *Edinburgh Scotsman.*

"It is not given to many writers in these days to produce a book, small or large, which shall not in some degree remind the omnivorous reader of many other books, either by reason of its subject-matter, or its mode of treatment, or of both. Mr. Robinson's 'In my Indian Garden,' however, fairly establishes for its author a claim to this rare distinction. A fancy open to all the quaint, humorous, old phil-

Press Notices.

osophical reflections which the objects around him suggest. Underlying this indirect way of looking at things, a genuine love of Indian rural life, and a cultivated taste, are abundantly indicated. Some of the brief descriptive passages are curiously vivid." — *Daily News.*

"Mr. Robinson is a genial naturalist and genuine humorist. A more agreeable pocket-companion we can hardly choose than this volume." — *Illustrated London News.*

"Mr. Robinson's charming essays breathe the true literary spirit in every line. They are not mere machine-made sweetmeats, to be swallowed whole and never again remembered; but they rather resemble the most cunning admixtures of good things, turned out by a skilful craftsman in matters culinary. Whoever once reads this delicious little book will not lay it carelessly aside, but will place it with respectful epicurean tenderness on his favorite shelf, side by side with Oliver Wendell Holmes's 'Kindred Musings,' and not far removed from the fresh country atmosphere of Gilbert White's 'Selborne.' Mr. Robinson plants himself in the verandah of a bungalow, it is true, and surveys nature as it presents itself upon the sweltering banks of the Jumna; but he sees it with an eye trained on the shores of Cam or Isis, and describes it with a hand evidently skilled in the composition of classical lore. Mr. Robinson's humor is too tender not to have a pathetic side; little children come in for no small share of pitiful, kindly notice, and the love for dumb creatures shines out in every page." — *London.*

"Mr. Edwin Arnold's praise is valuable, for it is the praise of one who knows; and Mr. Robinson fully deserves all that is said of him. His style is delightful. He has read much and observed much; and there is a racy flavor of Charles Lamb about him. A book which once begun is sure to be read through, and then read aloud to any to whom the reader wishes to give pleasure." — *The Echo.*

"Bright and fanciful — the author has done for the common objects of India something which Gilbert White did for Selborne — graceful and animated sketches, sometimes full of an intense reality, in other places of a quaint and delicate humor which has a flavor of the 'Essays of Elia.'" — *The Guardian.*

"This dainty volume is one of those rare books that come upon the critic from time to time as a surprise and a refreshment, — a book to be put in the favorite corner of the library, and to be taken up often again with renewed pleasure. Mr. Robinson's brief picturesque vignettes of every-day life in India — always good-natured, often humorous — are real little idylls of exquisite taste and delicacy. Mr. Robinson's style is exuberant with life, overflowing too with reminiscences of Western literature, even the most modern. In his longer and more ambitious descriptions he displays rare graphic power; and his sketches of the three seasons — especially those of the rainy and hot seasons — remind one forcibly of the wonderful realism of Kâlidâsa himself." — *Dublin Review.*

"The author is one of the quaintest and most charming of our modern writers in an almost forgotten kind. Mr. Robinson belongs to that school of pure literary essayists whose types are to be found in Lamb and Christopher North and Oliver Wendell Holmes, but who seem to have died out for the most part with the pre-scientific age. One or two of the pieces remind one not a little of Poe in his mood of pure terror with a tinge of mystery; the story of the 'Man-Eating Tree,' for example, is told with all Poe's minute realism. It is good sterling light literature of a sort that we do not often get in England." — *Pall Mall Gazette.*

"'The Hunting of the Soko' is a traveller's tale of a very exciting kind; and the first of all, 'The Man-Eating Tree,' is quite a master-piece of that kind. But the best and also the longest contribution to the volume is the sketch of an Indian tour called 'Sight-Seeing.' His pictures of India are certainly very vivid." — *St. James's Gazette.*

"Tenderness and pathos; delicate and humorously quaint." — *Pan.*

"In 'The Hunting of the Soko' there is much cleverness in the way in which the human attributes of the quarry are insinuated and worked out, clouding the successful chase with a taint of manslaughter and uncomfortable remorse. The account of the 'Man-Eating Tree,' too, a giant development of our droseras and

Press Notices.

dionæas, is a very good traveller's story. But the best as well as the most considerable of these essays, occupying in fact, two-fifths of the volume, is one entitled 'Sight-Seeing.' Here we have the benefit of the author's familiarity, not merely with the places in India worth seeing, but with the customs and character of the people. With such a 'sight-seer' as guide, the reader sees many things the ordinary traveller would miss, and much information and not a little food for reflection are compressed into a relatively small space in a style which is not only pleasant but eloquent." — *The Athenæum.*

"A deftly-mixed olla-podrida of essays, travel, and stories. 'Sight-Seeing' is one of those happy efforts which hit off the real points of interest in a journey. 'My Wife's Birds' is an essay, genial and humorous; the 'Daughter of Mercy,' an allegory, tender and suggestive. But the tales of adventure carry off the palm. These stories are marvellous and fanciful, yet imaginative in the highest sense. 'The Man-Eating Tree' and the 'Hunting of the Soko,' blend thrilling horror and weird superstition with a close imitation of popular stories of actual adventure." — *The World.*

"In a series of powerfully drawn sketches, Mr. Robinson shows that he belongs to the happy few in whom intimate acquaintance with Indian objects has created no indifference. The vignettes which he paints are by turns bumorous and pathetic, serious and powerful, charming and artistic. From them we gain a vivid impression of the every-day world of India. They show us in really admirable descriptions, bright and quaint, what a wealth of material for Art, Literature, and Descriptive Painting lies latent even in the daily experiences of an Englishman in India The author writes about butterflies and insects, things furred and feathered, flowers and trees, with a keen eye for the life and instincts of Indian scenery, and with a delightful sympathy for the East. . . . His exquisite sketches remind one of the classical work — 'White's Natural History of Selborne.' In Mr. Robinson's book there is to be found the same patience in observation united to the charm of a highly-cultured mind. . . . Where everything is so good it would be idle to show a preference by quotation." — 𝔐𝔞𝔤𝔞𝔷𝔦𝔫 𝔣ü𝔯 𝔡𝔦𝔢 𝔏𝔦𝔱𝔢𝔯𝔞𝔱𝔲𝔯 𝔡𝔢𝔰 𝔄𝔲𝔰𝔩𝔞𝔫𝔡𝔢𝔰.

"Mr. Phil. Robinson has his own way of looking at Nature, and a very pleasant way it is. His love of his subject is as genuine, perhaps more so, than that of the solemn naturalist who writes with a pen of lead: he can be at once lively and serious; and his knowledge, which resembles in variety the contents of an ostrich's stomach, is exhibited without effort. Indeed, it would be incorrect to say that it is exhibited at all. His style is, no doubt, achieved with art, but the art is not seen, and his easy method of expressing what he knows may deceive the unwary reader. . . . This delightful volume! A book which deserves the attention both of old and young readers." — *The Spectator.*

"When Mr. Robinson sent out those delightful chapters entitled 'In My Indian Garden,' it was evident that a new genius had appeared on the horizon of English literature. In that exquisite little book, the original and accurate observations of animal life which charmed the naturalist were conveyed with a humor so entirely new and clothed with a grace so perfect as to give a very high literary value to the work as well as a signal promise of further performance on a yet larger scale. . . . His purely literary quality reminds us of the old masters of humor; but it has the unique advantage of alliance with a range of exact knowledge of the animal world of which none of Mr. Robinson's predecessors can boast. And yet our author, with all his knowledge and love of animals, is preeminently a classic humorist. His rare and distinctive faculty is seen in his way of inverting our method of studying animals. In his scheme of investigating nature, man does not play his usually proud part of discoverer and exponent of his fellow animals in fur and feathers; rather he is discovered and expounded by them. When the Unicorn in Mr. Lewis Carroll's *Through the Looking-glass* first saw Alice, he remarked that he had always thought little girls were fabulous creatures. Mr. Robinson possesses in perfection this power of presenting man from what may be supposed to be an animal's point of view. And the view that every animal exists for itself and that all barriers to its self-interest are so many accidents and interferences with the scheme of nature, finds in our author's hands the most startling and amusing expression. . . . Mr. Robinson possesses grace, felicity, and literary wealth which no mere culture could ever attain; he is a genius of a rare and classic kind. A 'Morning in the Zoo' with such a companion will be found to have the charm of Thoreau without his vanity; the humor of Lamb, never labored or attenuated into wire-drawn conceits." — *London Standard.*

"Mr. Phil. Robinson is an entertaining writer: he is genial and humorous, with a knack of saying things in the manner of Charles Lamb. . . . He has undoubtedly a great liking for animals, a special knowledge of their works and ways, of their homes and haunts, and writes about them not in the style of a natural history, but with the freedom and gracefulness of a novelist or humorist. This book is well fitted to wile away the hours which can be stolen from absorbing work. The author chats pleasantly and charmingly about animals, with frequent digressions, which sometimes are almost startling enough to suggest an inquiry as to what possible relation the digression has with the book; and yet, after all, the digression is as entertaining as the book proper. . . . We have but dipped into this thoroughly interesting and very admirable book, which tells us a very great deal about all kinds of animals from all parts of the world, and from its seas and rivers. It is full of real poetry of feeling, and contains much that philosophers and divines may ponder with exceeding advantage, and all sorts of readers will peruse with intense interest. We can scarcely give the book higher praise than this, and all this it richly deserves." — *The London Literary World.*

"Even so admirable and delightful a writer as Mr. Phil. Robinson cannot afford to despise that incalculable element in human affairs which goes by the name of luck; and he may be congratulated upon the fact that his latest volume comes under the notice of the reading world at a moment when that world has been brought into a condition of peculiar and beautiful preparedness for its reception. When Jumbo is the hero of the hour, and when, in body or in mind, millions of our countrymen, countrywomen, and country children, have been making pilgrimages to his shrine in Regent's Park, the record of 'Mornings at the Zoo,' can hardly fail to exercise a powerful if melancholy fascination; and when the recorder is a man like Mr Phil. Robinson the fascination is one that can amply justify itself to itself or to the world, and is not to be regarded as a mere spring frenzy or midsummer madness. . . . He is not a joke manufacturer. When the joke comes it is welcome, all the more welcome for coming spontaneously: and when it stays away, its place can easily be filled by some little tit-bit of recent scientific speculation or result of personal observation of the manners and customs of Mr. Robinson's brute friends. For 'Noah's Ark' has something more than mere humor to recommend it. The humor is, in fact, but the mere decoration of a body of knowledge; and the man with no more sense of fun than a hippopotamus might read it with edification as a contribution to 'natural' as well as to 'unnatural' history. Artemus Ward proudly remarked of himself that he had 'a very animal mind,' and Mr. Phil. Robinson might with even better reason indulge in the same boast. He is a true lover of beasts, birds, and fishes; and because he is a true lover he is a keen observer, and because he is a keen observer he is a pleasant writer concerning the ways and the works — one might almost say the words — of the denizens of field and forest, of air and water. 'If you would be generous,' he says, in his brief postscript, 'do not think me too much in earnest when I am serious, or altogether in fun because I jest;' and one of the pleasantest features of this pleasant work is that it does not tire us by subjecting the mind to the fatigue of maintaining one attitude too long, but, like a cunningly constructed arm-chair, enables us to be comfortable in a dozen consecutive positions. Some good books can be recommended to this person or to that; they resemble the square or the round peg which adapts itself admirably to the square or round hole. But 'Noah's Ark,' if the metaphor be not too undignified, is like the 'self-fitting candle' which is at home in any receptacle. It is — to drop metaphor — a book for everybody." — *The Overland Mail.*

Press Notices.

THE INDIAN PRESS.

"Mr. Phil. Robinson has struck out a new path in Anglo-Indian literature. . . . His essays are singularly fresh and charming. They come nearer to the tender wisdom of Elia than anything which has hitherto issued from an Anglo-Indian pen. . . . Every one of the thirty or forty essays has some special vein of humor of its own." — *Englishman.*

"Distinguished by all the graces of a style which ought some day to give Mr. Phil. Robinson a high place among our popular writers." — *India Daily News.*

"Not only clever and interesting, but instructive; . . . altogether the best thing of its kind we have come across in print." — *The Examiner.*

"To say that this is a charming book is merely to repeat what almost every reader of the *Calcutta Review* must have often heard said. It is altogether the very pleasantest reading of its kind that has ever appeared in India, and we would that it oftener fell to our lot to have such books to criticise." — *The Calcutta Review.*

"It is given to few to describe with such appreciative grace and delicately phrased humor as Mr. Robinson. . . . Marked by keen observation, felicitous touches of description, and half-quaint, half-graceful bits of reflection and comment, . . . containing some most exquisite sketches of natural history." — *Times of India.*

"A delightful little book. There is a similarity between the author's book and his subject which may escape the notice of the ordinary reader. Where is the casual observer who, having walked through an Indian garden, has not noticed the almost total absence of flowers? Yet send a Malee into that identical Indian garden, and he will cull you a bouquet which for brightness and beauty can hard'y be surpassed by anything in Covent Garden; and it is precisely the same with this little volume of Phil. Robinson's. A little book brimful of interest, written with much grace, and a considerable amount of quaint humor which is very refreshing. We sincerely trust he will give the public his Indian experiences in other fields which, cultivated by him, we doubt not will prove equally rich in production." — *Times of India* (Second Notice).

"These most charming essays." — *The Delhi Gazette.*

"Very charming; dealing with familiar things with an appreciative grace that idealizes whatever it touches. Again and again we are reminded by the dainty embodiment of some quaint fancy of the essays of Charles Lamb; . . . quite delicious and abounding in little descriptive touches that are almost perfect; cabinet word-pictures painted in a sentence." — *Bombay Gazette.*

"Admirable little work." — *Friend of India.*

"A notable little book: within a small compass a wealth of fresh thoughts" — *Madras Mail.*

www.ingramcontent.com/pod-product-compliance
Lightning Source LLC
Chambersburg PA
CBHW032019220426
43664CB00006B/301